MATLAB Mathematical Analysis

███

César Pérez López

apress®

MATLAB Mathematical Analysis

ISBN-13 (pbk): 978-1-4842-0350-7

ISBN-13 (electronic): 978-1-4842-0349-1

Managing Director: Welmoed Spahr
Lead Editor: Jeffrey Pepper
Technical Reviewer: Jonah Lissner
Editorial Board: Steve Anglin, Louise Corrigan, Jonathan Gennick, Robert Hutchinson, Michelle Lowman, James Markham, Matthew Moodie, Jeff Olson, Jeffrey Pepper, Douglas Pundick, Ben Renow-Clarke, Gwenan Spearing, Steve Weiss
Coordinating Editor: Mark Powers
Copy Editor: Barnaby Sheppard
Compositor: SPi Global
Indexer: SPi Global
Artist: SPi Global
Cover Designer: Anna Ishchenko

Distributed to the book trade worldwide by Springer Science+Business Media New York, 233 Spring Street, 6th Floor, New York, NY 10013. Phone 1-800-SPRINGER, fax (201) 348-4505, e-mail orders-ny@springer-sbm.com, or visit www.springeronline.com. Apress Media, LLC is a California LLC and the sole member (owner) is Springer Science + Business Media Finance Inc (SSBM Finance Inc). SSBM Finance Inc is a Delaware corporation.

For information on translations, please e-mail rights@apress.com, or visit www.apress.com.

Apress and friends of ED books may be purchased in bulk for academic, corporate, or promotional use. eBook versions and licenses are also available for most titles. For more information, reference our Special Bulk Sales–eBook Licensing web page at www.apress.com/bulk-sales.

Any source code or other supplementary material referenced by the author in this text is available to readers at www.apress.com/9781484203507. For detailed information about how to locate your book's source code, go to www.apress.com/source-code/.

Contents at a Glance

About the Author xi

About the Technical Reviewer xiii

Introduction xv

■Chapter 1: MATLAB Introduction and Working Environment 1

■Chapter 2: Numbers, Operators, Variables and Functions 13

■Chapter 3: Complex Numbers and Functions of Complex Variables 71

■Chapter 4: Graphics in MATLAB. Curves, Surfaces and Volumes 125

■Chapter 5: Limits of Sequences and Functions. Continuity in One
and Several Variables 183

■Chapter 6: Numerical Series and Power Series 203

■Chapter 7: Derivatives. One and Several Variables 225

■Chapter 8: Integration in One and Several Variables. Applications 279

■Chapter 9: Differential Equations 325

Contents

About the Author xi

About the Technical Reviewer xiii

Introduction xv

■Chapter 1: MATLAB Introduction and Working Environment 1

Introduction to Working with MATLAB 1

Numerical Calculations with MATLAB 4

Symbolic Calculations with MATLAB 6

Graphics with MATLAB 8

MATLAB and Programming..11

■Chapter 2: Numbers, Operators, Variables and Functions..13

Numbers...13

Integers and Integer Variable Functions...16

Real Numbers and Functions of Real Variables..18

Trigonometric Functions..20

Hyperbolic Functions...21

Exponential and Logarithmic Functions 22

Numeric Variable-Specific Functions 23

One-Dimensional, Vector and Matrix Variables 24

Elements of Vector Variables 26

Elements of Matrix Variables 27

Specific Matrix Functions..30

Random Numbers...34

Operators...36

    Arithmetic Operators 36

    Logical Operators 39

    Relational Operators 40

Symbolic Variables 42

Symbolic Functions and Functional Operations: Composite and Inverse Functions 44

Commands that Handle Variables in the Workspace and Store them in Files...........................47

Chapter 3: Complex Numbers and Functions of Complex Variables.............71

Complex Numbers 71

General Functions of Complex Variables 72

    Trigonometric Functions of a Complex Variable 72

    Hyperbolic Functions of a Complex Variable 74

    Exponential and Logarithmic Functions of a Complex Variable 75

    Specific Functions of a Complex Variable...76

Basic Functions with a Complex Vector Argument...77

Basic Functions with a Complex Matrix Argument..84

General Functions with a Complex Matrix Argument 89

    Trigonometric Functions of a Complex Matrix Variable 89

    Hyperbolic Functions of a Complex Matrix Variable 94

    Exponential and Logarithmic Functions of a Complex Matrix Variable....................99

    Specific Functions of Complex Matrix Variables..101

Operations with Real and Complex Matrix Variables..104

Chapter 4: Graphics in MATLAB. Curves, Surfaces and Volumes..............125

Introduction 125

Exploratory Graphics 125

Curves in Explicit, Implicit, Parametric and Polar Coordinates............................133

Three-Dimensional (3D) Curves 144

Explicit and Parametric Surfaces: Contour Plots..146

Three-Dimensional Geometric Forms...152

Specialized Graphics 156

2D and 3D Graphics Options...164

■Chapter 5: Limits of Sequences and Functions. Continuity in One
and Several Variables...183

Limits...183

Sequences of Functions 186

Continuity 187

Limits in Several Variables. Iterated and Directional Limits.............................190

Continuity in Several Variables..194

■Chapter 6: Numerical Series and Power Series...203

Numerical Series of Non-negative Terms...203

Convergence Criteria: The Ratio Test..204

Raabe's Criterion 205

The Root Test...206

Other Convergence Criteria 208

Alternating Numerical Series. Dirichlet and Abel's Criteria..............................209

Power Series 210

Power Series Expansions..212

■Chapter 7: Derivatives. One and Several Variables.......................................225

Derivatives...225

Partial Derivatives 228

Applications of Differentiation. Tangents, Asymptotes,
Extreme Points and Points of Inflection 229

Differentiation in Several Variables 233

Extreme Points in Several Variables..238

Conditional minima and maxima. The method of "Lagrange multipliers"..........246

Vector Differential Calculus...249

The Composite Function Theorem 250

The Implicit Function Theorem 251

The Inverse Function Theorem 252

The Change of Variables Theorem 253

Series Expansions in Several Variables.. 254

Curl, Divergence and the Laplacian 255

Rectangular, Spherical and Cylindrical Coordinates.. 257

■**Chapter 8: Integration in One and Several Variables. Applications** **279**

Integrals 279

Indefinite Integrals, Change of Variables and Integration by Parts.............................. 281

Integration by Reduction and Cyclic Integration 283

Rational and Irrational Integrals. Binomial Integrals... 283

Definite Integrals and Applications 284

Curve Arc Length... 284

The Area between Two Curves 287

Surfaces of Revolution 291

Volumes of Revolution... 292

Curvilinear Integrals 293

Improper Integrals... 295

Parameter Dependent Integrals 295

Approximate Numerical Integration 297

Special Integrals.. 300

Definite Integrals and Applications. Several Variables 302

Planar Areas and Double Integration... 302

Calculation of Surface Area by Double Integration.. 304

Calculation of Volumes by Double Integration... 305

Calculation of Volumes and Triple Integrals.. 306

Green's Theorem 308

The Divergence Theorem 309

Stokes' Theorem 310

■Chapter 9: Differential Equations...325

First Order Differential Equations..325

Numerical Solutions of Differential Equations...328

Ordinary Differential Equations with Initial Values 328

Ordinary Differential Equations with Boundary Values 331

Partial Differential Equations...333

About the Author

César Pérez López is a Professor at the Department of Statistics and Operations Research at the University of Madrid. César Pérez López is also a Mathematician and Economist at the National Statistics Institute (INE) in Madrid, a body which belongs to the Superior Systems and Information Technology Department of the Spanish Government. César also currently works at the Institute for Fiscal Studies in Madrid.

About the Technical Reviewer

Jonah Lissner is a research scientist and PhD candidate in theoretical physics, power engineering, complex systems, metamaterials, geophysics, and computational theory. He has strong cognitive ability in empiricism and scientific reason for the purpose of hypothesis building, theory learning, mathematical and axiomatic modeling and testing for abstract problem-solving. His dissertations, research publications and projects, curriculum vitae, journal contributions, blogs, science fiction novels and systems are listed at http://Lissnerresearch.weebly.com.

About the Technical Reviewer

Introduction

MATLAB is a platform for scientific computing that can work in almost all areas of the experimental sciences, engineering, mathematics and financial solutions. Logically, this software allows you to work in the field of mathematical analysis through a wide variety of commands and functions. *MATLAB Mathematical Analysis* is a reference to these commands and brief discussions of how to solve a very wide array of problems. It is not meant to be a tutorial on MATLAB, but a user of MATLAB should be able to follow the book easily and look up various types of problems or commands and see quick examples of how they work. This book covers a wide array of content and so it is a great place to find new features, topics or commands that you might not have known existed.

The book begins by introducing the reader to the use of numbers of all types and bases, operators, variables and functions in the MATLAB environment. Then it delves into working with complex variables. A large section is devoted to working with developing graphical representations of curves, volumes, and surfaces. MATLAB functions allow working with two-dimensional and three-dimensional graphics, statistical graphs, curves and surfaces in explicit, implicit, parametric and polar coordinates. Additional work implements twisted curves, surfaces, meshes, contours, volumes and graphical interpolation.

Vectors and matrices are a major feature of MATLAB and so they are treated throughout the book as the topics come up and include applications in many of the areas.

The following content block develops computation of limits and functions, continuity and numerical and power series. Then differentiability is addressed in one and several variables including differential theorems for vector fields. It continues to address integration in one or more variable, and multiple integrals and their applications. Finally differential equations are treated and some of their applications.

MATLAB Mathematical Analysis offers a broad resource for looking up commands. Unlike most references, it can be read from start to finish and jumping into chapters to look up is not an issue. So one of the aspects of the book is its flexibility and the other main benefit is the breadth of coverage.

Also Available

- MATLAB Programming for Numerical Analysis, 978-1-4842-0296-8
- MATLAB Differential Equations, 978-1-4842-0311-8
- MATLAB Control Systems Engineering, 978-1-4842-0290-6
- MATLAB Linear Algebra, 978-1-4842-0323-1
- MATLAB Differential and Integral Calculus, 978-1-4842-0305-7
- MATLAB Graphical Programming, 978-1-4842-0317-0

CHAPTER 1

■ ■ ■

MATLAB Introduction and Working Environment

Introduction to Working with MATLAB

Whenever you use a program of this type, it is necessary to know the general characteristics of how the program interprets notation. This chapter will introduce you to some of the practices used in the MATLAB environment. If you are familiar with using MATLAB, you may wish to skip over this chapter.

The best way to learn MATLAB is to use the program. Each example in the book consists of the header with the prompt for user input ">>" and the response from MATLAB appears on the next line. See Figure 1-1.

```
MATLAB Command Window
File  Edit  Options  Windows  Help
Commands to get started: intro, demo, help help
Commands for more information: help, whatsnew, info, subscribe
» A=[1 2 3; 4 5 6; 7 8 9]

A =

     1     2     3
     4     5     6
     7     8     9

» B=inv(A)

Warning: Matrix is close to singular or badly scaled.
         Results may be inaccurate. RCOND = 2.937385e-018


B =

  1.0e+016 *

    0.3152   -0.6304    0.3152
   -0.6304    1.2609   -0.6304
    0.3152   -0.6304    0.3152

»

Inicio    MATLAB Command W...                              20:31
```

Figure 1-1.

1

At other times, depending on the type of user input used, MATLAB returns the response using the expression "**ans =**". See Figure 1-2.

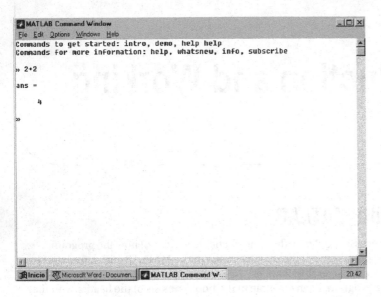

Figure 1-2.

In a program like MATLAB it is always necessary to pay attention to the difference between uppercase and lowercase letters, types of parentheses or square brackets, the amount of spaces used in your input and your choice of punctuation (e.g., commas, semicolons). Different uses will produce different results. We will go over the general rules now.

Any input to run MATLAB should be written to the right of the header (the prompt for user *input* ">>"). You then obtain the response in the lines immediately below the input.

When an input is proposed to MATLAB in the command window that does not cite a variable to collect the result, MATLAB returns the response using the expression ***ans*=**.

If at the end of the input we put a semicolon, the program runs the calculation(s) and keeps them in memory (*Workspace*), but does not display the result on the screen (see the first input in Figure 1-3 as an example).

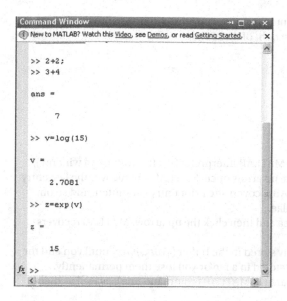

Figure 1-3.

The *input* prompt appears ">> " to indicate that you can enter a new entry.

If you enter and define a variable that can be calculated, you can then use that variable as the argument for subsequent entries. This is the case for the variable v in Figure 1-3, which is subsequently used as an input in the exponential function.

Like the C programming language, MATLAB is sensitive to the difference between uppercase and lowercase letters; for example, "*Sin (x)*" is different from "*sin (x)*". The names of all built-in functions begin with lowercase. There should be no spaces in the names of symbols of more than one letter or in the names of functions. In other cases, spaces are simply ignored. They can be used in some cases to make *input* more readable. Multiple entries in the same line of command, separated by commas, can also be used. In this case, press *Enter* at the end of the last entry (see Figure 1-4). If you use a semicolon at the end of one of the entries of the line, as we stated before, its corresponding output is ignored.

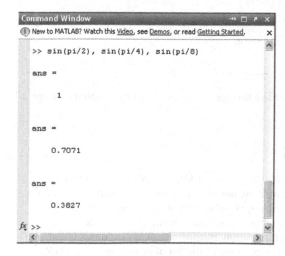

Figure 1-4.

It is possible to enter descriptive comments in a command input line by starting the comment with the "%" sign. When you run the input, MATLAB ignores the rest of the line to the right of the % sign:

```
>> L = log (123) % L is a natural logarithm

L =

     4.8122
>>
```

To simplify the introduction of a script to be evaluated by the MATLAB interpreter (via the command window), you can use the arrow computer keys. For example, if you press the up arrow once, MATLAB will recover the last entry submitted in MATLAB. If you press the up arrow key twice, MATLAB recovers the prior entry submitted, and so on. This can save you the headache of re-entering complicated formulae.

Similarly, if you type a sequence of characters in the *input* area and then click the up arrow, MATLAB recovers the last entry that begins with the specified string.

Commands entered during a MATLAB session are temporarily stored in the buffer (*Workspace*) until you end the session with the program, at which time they can be permanently stored in a file or you lose them permanently.

Below is a summary of the keys that can be used in the *input* area of MATLAB (command line), as well as their functions:

Up arrow (Ctrl-P)	Retrieves the previous line.
Arrow down (Ctrl-N)	Retrieves the following entry.
Arrow to the left (Ctrl-B)	Takes the cursor to the left, a character.
Arrow to the right (Ctrl-F)	Takes the cursor to the right, a character.
CTRL-arrow to the left	Takes the cursor to the left, a word.
CTRL-arrow to the right	Takes the cursor to the right, a word.
Home (Ctrl-A)	Takes the cursor to the beginning of the line.
End (Ctrl-E)	Takes the cursor at the end of the current line.
Exhaust	Clears the command line.
Delete (Ctrl-D)	Deletes the character indicated by the cursor.
BACKSPACE	Deletes the character to the left of the cursor.
CTRL-K	Deletes all of the current line.

The command *clc* clears the command window, but does not delete the content of the Workspace (that content remains in memory).

Numerical Calculations with MATLAB

You can use MATLAB as a powerful numerical calculator. Most calculators handle numbers only with a preset degree of precision, however MATLAB performs exact calculations with the necessary precision. In addition, unlike calculators, we can perform operations not only with individual numbers, but also with objects such as arrays.

Most of the themes in classical numerical calculations, are treated in this software. It supports matrix calculations, statistics, interpolation, fit by least squares, numerical integration, minimization of functions, linear programming, numerical algebraic and resolution of differential equations and a long list of processes of numerical analysis that we'll see later in this book.

Here are some examples of numerical calculations with MATLAB. (As we all know, for results it is necessary to press Enter once you have written the corresponding expressions next to the prompt ">>")

We can simply calculate 4 + 3 and get as a result 7. To do this, just type 4 + 3, and then Enter.

>> **4 + 3**

Ans =

7

Also we can get the value of 3 to the 100th power, without having previously set the level of precision. For this purpose press 3 ^ 100.

>> **3 ^ 100**

Ans =

5. 1538e + 047

You can use the command "format long e" to pass the result of the operation with 16 digits before the exponent (scientific notation).

>> **format long e**

>> **3 ^ 100**

ans =

5.153775207320115e+047

We can also work with complex numbers. We will get the result of the operation (2 + 3i) raised to the 10th power, by typing the expression (2 + 3i) ^ 10.

>> **(2 + 3i) ^ 10**

Ans =

-1. 415249999999998e + 005 - 1. 456680000000000e + 005i

The previous result is also available in short format, using the "format short" command.

>> **format short**
>> **(2 + 3i) ^ 10**

ans =

-1.4152e+005- 1.4567e+005i

Also we can calculate the value of the Bessel function found for 11.5. To do this type Besselj (0,11.5).

```
>> besselj(0, 11.5)
```

ans =

  -0.0677

Symbolic Calculations with MATLAB

MATLAB handles symbolic mathematical computation, manipulating formulae and algebraic expressions easily and quickly and can perform most operations with them. You can expand, factor and simplify polynomials, rational and trigonometric expressions, you can find algebraic solutions of polynomial equations and systems of equations, can evaluate derivatives and integrals symbolically, and find function solutions for differential equations, you can manipulate powers, limits and many other facets of algebraic mathematical series.

To perform this task, MATLAB requires all the variables (or algebraic expressions) to be written between single quotes to distinguish them from numerical solutions. When MATLAB receives a variable or expression in quotes, it is considered symbolic.

Here are some examples of symbolic computation with MATLAB.

1. Raise the following algebraic expression to the third power: $(x + 1) (x+2)-(x+2)^2$. This is done by typing the following expression: expand ('$((x + 1) (x+2) - (x+2)^2)^3$'). The result will be another algebraic expression:

   ```
   >> syms x; expand (((x + 1) *(x + 2)-(x + 2) ^ 2) ^ 3)
   ```

   Ans =

   *-x ^ 3-6 * x ^ 2-12 * x-8*

   Note in this example, the *syms x* which is needed to initiate the variable *x*.
   You can then factor the result of the calculation in the example above by typing: factor ('$((x+1)*(x+2)-(x+2)^2)^3$')

   ```
   >> syms x; factor(((x + 1)*(x + 2)-(x + 2)^2)^3)
   ```

   ans =

   -(x+2)^3

2. You can resolve the indefinite integral of the function $(x^2) sine (x)^2$ by typing: int ('$x^2 * sin (x)^2$', 'x')

   ```
   >> int('x^2*sin(x)^2', 'x')
   ```

   ans =

   *x ^ 2 * (-1/2 * cos (x) * sin (x) + 1/2 * x)-1/2 * x * cos (x) ^ 2 + 1/4 **
   *cos (x) * sin (x) + 1/4 * 1/x-3 * x ^ 3*

You can simplify the previous result:

```
>> syms x; simplify(int(x^2*sin(x)^2, x))
```

ans =

sin(2*x)/8 - (x*cos(2*x))/4 - (x^2*sin(2*x))/4 + x^3/6

You can express the previous result with more elegant mathematical notation:

```
>> syms x; pretty(simplify(int(x^2*sin(x)^2, x)))
```

```
                     2               3
  sin(2 x)   x cos(2 x)   x  sin(2 x)   x
  -------- - ---------- - ----------- + --
     8           4             4         6
```

3. We can solve the equation 3ax-7 x ^ 2 + x ^ 3 = 0 (where a, is a parameter):

```
>> solve('3*a*x-7*x^2 + x^3 = 0', 'x')
```

ans =

```
[                    0]
[7/2+1/2 *(49-12*a)^(1/2)]
[7/2-1/2 *(49-12*a)^(1/2)]
```

4. We can find the five solutions of the equation x ^ 5 + 2 x + 1 = 0:

ans =

```
                     -0.48638903593454300001655725369801
    0.94506808682313338631496614476119 + 0.85451751443904587692179191887616*i
    0.94506808682313338631496614476119 - 0.85451751443904587692179191887616*i
  - 0.70187356885586188630668751791218 - 0.87969719792982402287026727381769*i
  - 0.70187356885586188630668751791218 + 0.87969719792982402287026727381769*i
```

On the other hand, MATLAB may use the libraries of the Maple V program to work with symbolic math and can thus extend its field of application. In this way, you can use MATLAB to work on problems in areas including differential forms, Euclidean geometry, projective geometry, statistics, etc.

At the same time, you also can expand your options for numerical calculations using the libraries from MATLAB and libraries of Maple (combinatorics, optimization, theory of numbers, etc.).

Graphics with MATLAB

MATLAB produces graphs of two and three dimensions, as well as outlines and graphs of density. You can represent both the graphics and list the data in MATLAB. MATLAB allows you to control colors, shading and other graphics features, and also supports animated graphics. Graphics produced by MATLAB are portable to other programs.

Here are some examples of MATLAB graphics:

1. You can represent the function xsine (x) for x ranging between -π/4 and π/4, using 300 equidistant points for the intervals. See Figure 1-5.

```
>> x = linspace(-pi/4,pi/4,300);
>> y = x.*sin(1./x);
>> plot(x,y)
```

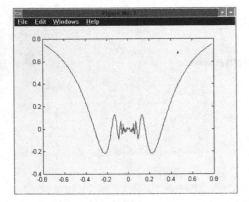

Figure 1-5.

Note the dots (periods) in this example in the second line. These are not decimal points and should not be confused as such. These indicate that if you are working with vectors or matrices that the following operator needs to be applied to every element of the vector or matrix. For an easy example, let's use $x.*3$. If x is a matrix, then all elements of x should be multiplied by 3. Again, be careful to avoid confusion with decimal points. It is sometimes wise to represent .6 as 0.6, for instance.

2. You can add the options frame and grille to the graph above, as well as create your own chart title and labels for axes. See Figure 1-6.

```
>> x = linspace(-pi/4,pi/4,300);
>> y = x.*sin(1./x);
>> plot(x,y);
>> grid;
>> xlabel('Independent variable X');
>> ylabel ('Independent variable Y');
>> title ('The functions y=sin(1/x)')
```

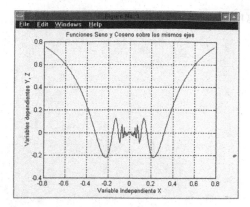

Figure 1-6.

3. You can generate a graph of the surface for the function z = sine (sqrt(x^2+y^2)) / sqrt(x^2+y^2), where x and y vary over the interval (- 7.5, 7.5), taking equally spaced points in 5 tenths. See Figure 1-7.

```
>> x =-7.5: .5:7.5;
>> y = x;
>> [X, Y] = meshgrid(x,y);
>> Z = sin(sqrt(X.^2+Y.^2))./sqrt(X.^2+Y.^2);
>> surf (X, Y, Z)
```

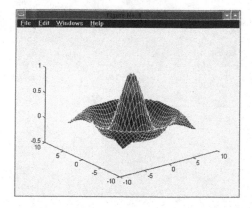

Figure 1-7.

In the first line of this example, note that the range is specified using colons. We did not use 0.5 and you can see that it can make the input somewhat confusing to a reader.

These 3D graphics allow you to get an idea of the figures in space, and are very helpful in visually identifying intersections between different bodies, generation of developments of all kinds and volumes of revolution.

4. You can generate a three dimensional graphic corresponding to the helix in parametric coordinates: x = sine (t), y = cosine (t), z = t. See Figure 1-8.

```
>> t = 0:pi/50:10*pi;
>> plot3(sin(t),cos(t),t)
```

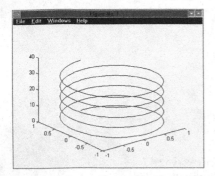

Figure 1-8.

We can represent a planar curve given by its polar coordinates r = cosine (2t) * sine (2t) for t varying between 0 and 2π, taking equally spaced points in one-hundredths of the considered range. See Figure 1-9.

```
>> t = 0:.01:2 * pi;
>> r = sin(2*t).* cos(2*t);
>> polar(t,r)
```

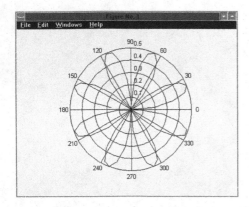

Figure 1-9.

5. We can also make a graph of a function considered as symbolic, using the command "ezplot". See Figure 1-10.

```
>> y ='x ^ 3 /(x^2-1)';
>> ezplot(y,[-5,5])
```

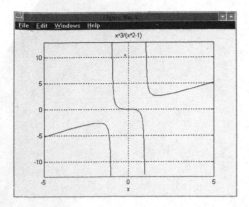

Figure 1-10.

In the corresponding chapter on graphics we will extend these concepts.

MATLAB and Programming

By properly combining all the objects defined in MATLAB appropriate to the work rules defined in the pro,
can build useful mathematical research programming code. Programs usually consist of a series of instructi
which values are calculated, assigned a name and are reused in further calculations.

As in programming languages like C or Fortran, in MATLAB you can write programs with loops, control flo
conditionals. In MATLAB you can write procedural programs, (i.e., to define a sequence of standard steps to run)
As in C or Pascal, a Do, For, or While loop may be used for repetitive calculations. The language of MATLAB also
includes conditional constructs such as If Then Else. MATLAB also supports logic functions, such as And, Or,
Not and Xor.

MATLAB supports procedural programming (iterative, recursive, loops...), functional programming and
object-oriented programming. Here are two simple examples of programs. The first generates the order n Hilbert
matrix, and the second calculates the Fibonacci numbers.

```
% Generating the order n Hilbert matrix
t = '1/(i+j-1)';
for i = 1:n
for j = 1:n
a(i,j) = eval(t);
end
end


% Calculating Fibonacci numbers
f = [1 1]; i = 1;
while f(i) + f(i-1) < 1000
f(i+2) = f(i) + f(i+1);
i = i+1
end
```

CHAPTER 2

■ ■ ■

Numbers, Operators, Variables and Functions

Numbers

The numerical scope of MATLAB is very wide. Integer, rational, real and complex numbers, which in turn can be arguments of functions giving rise to whole, rational, real and complex functions. Therefore, the complex variable is a treatable field in MATLAB. This chapter will look at the basic functionality of MATLAB.

Arithmetic operations in MATLAB are defined according to the standard mathematical conventions. The following table presents the syntax of basic arithmetic operations:

x + y	*Sum*
	>> 4 + 8
	Ans =
	12
x - y	*Difference*
	>> 4 - 8
	Ans =
	-4
x * y or x y	*Product*
	>> 4 * 8
	Ans =
	32

(*continued*)

x/y	*Division*
	`>> 4/8`
	`Ans =`
	`0.5000`
x ^ y	*Power*
	`>> 4 ^ 8`
	`Ans =`
	`65536`

MATLAB performs arithmetic operations as if it were a conventional calculator, but with total precision in the calculation. The results of operations presented are accurate for the default or for the degree of precision that the user prescribes. But this only affects the presentation. The feature that differentiates MATLAB from other numerical calculation programs in which the word length of the computer determines the accuracy, is that the calculation accuracy is unlimited in the case of MATLAB. MATLAB can represent the results with the accuracy that is required, although internally it always works with exact calculations to avoid rounding errors. MATLAB offers different approximate representation formats, which sometimes facilitate the interpretation of the results.

The following are the commands relating to the presentation of the results:

short format	*It offers results with 4 decimal. It's the format default of MATLAB*
	`>> sqrt(23)`
	`ans =`
	`4.7958`
long format	*It delivers results with 16 decimal places*
	`>> format long; sqrt(23)`
	`Ans =`
	`4.795831523312719`
format long e	*Provides the results to 16 decimal places using the power of 10*
	`>> format long e; SQRT (23)`
	`Ans =`
	`4.795831523312719e + 000`
format short e	*Provides the results to four decimal places with the power of 10*
	`>> format short e; SQRT (23)`
	`Ans =`
	`4.7958e + 000`

(continued)

format long g	*It offers results in optimal long format*
	`>> format long g; SQRT (23)`
	`Ans =`
	`    4.79583152331272`
format short g	*It offers results in optimum short format*
	`>> format short g; SQRT (23)`
	`Ans =`
	`    4.7958`
bank format	*It delivers results with 2 decimal places*
	`>> bank format; SQRT (23)`
	`Ans =`
	`    4.80`
format rat	*It offers the results in the form of a rational number approximation*
	`>> format rat; SQRT (23)`
	`Ans =`
	`    1151/240`
format +	*Offers a binary result using the sign (+, -) and ignores the imaginary part of the complex numbers*
	`>> format +; sqrt(23)`
	`Ans =`
	`    +`
format hex	*It offers results in hexadecimal system*
	`>> format hex; sqrt(23)`
	`ans =`
	`    40132eee75770416`
VPA 'operations' n	*It provides the result of operations with n exact decimal digits*
	`>> vpa 'sqrt(23)' 20`
	`ans =`
	`    4.7958315233127195416`

Integers and Integer Variable Functions

MATLAB works with integers and exact integer variable functions. Regardless of the format of presentation of the results, calculations are exact. Anyway, the command *vpa* allows exact outputs with the precision required.

In terms of functions with integer variables, the most important thing that MATLAB includes are as follows (the expressions between quotation marks have format string):

rem (n, m)	*Remainder of the division of n by m (valid function for n and m-real)*
	`>> rem(15,2)`
	`ans =`
	`1`
sign (n)	*Sign of n (1 if n > 0; -1 if n < 0)*
	`>> sign(-8)`
	`ans =`
	`-1`
max (n1, n2)	*Maximum of the numbers n1 and n2*
	`>> max(17,12)`
	`ans =`
	`17`
min (n1, n2)	*Minimum of the numbers n1 and n2*
	`>> min(17,12)`
	`ans =`
	`12`
gcd (n1, n2)	*Greatest common divisor of n1 and n2*
	`>> gcd(17,12)`
	`ans =`
	`1`
lcm (n1, n2)	*Least common multiple of n1 and n2*
	`>> lcm(17,12)`
	`ans =`
	`204`

(continued)

factorial (n)	*N factorial (n(n-1) (n-2)...)1)*
	`>> factorial(9)`
	`ans =`
	362880
factor (n)	*It decomposes the factorization of n*
	`>> factor(51)`
	`ans =`
	3 17
dec2base (decimal, n_base)	*Converts a specified decimal (base-10) number to the new base given by n_base*
	`>> dec2base(2345,7)`
	`ans =`
	6560
base2dec(numero,b)	*Converts the given base b number to a decimal number*
	`>> base2dec('ab12579',12)`
	`ans =`
	32621997
dec2bin (decimal)	*Converts a specified decimal number to base 2 (binary)*
	`>> dec2bin(213)`
	`ans =`
	11010101
dec2hex (decimal)	*Converts the specified decimal number to a base 16 (hexadecimal) number*
	`>> dec2hex(213)`
	`ans =`
	D5
bin2dec (binary)	*Converts the binary number to a decimal based number*
	`>> bin2dec('1110001')`
	`ans =`
	113
hex2dec (hexadecimal)	*It converts the specified base 16 number to decimal*
	`>> hex2dec('FFAA23')`
	`ans =`
	16755235

Real Numbers and Functions of Real Variables

A rational number is of the form p/q, where p is an integer and q another integer. The way in which MATLAB processes rationals is different from that of the majority of calculators. The rational numbers are ratios of integers, and MATLAB also can work with them so that the result of expressions involving rational numbers is always another rational or whole number. So, it is necessary to activate this format with the command *format rat*. But MATLAB also returns solutions with decimals as the result if the user so wishes by activating any other type of format (e.g. *format short* or *long format*). We consider the following example:

```
>> format rat;
>> 1/6 + 1/5-2/10

Ans =

        1/6
```

MATLAB deals with rationals as ratios of integers and keeps them in this form during the calculations. In this way, rounding errors are not dragged into calculations with fractions, which can become very serious, as evidenced by the theory of errors. Once enabled in the rational format, operations with rationals will be exact until another different format is enabled. When the rational format is enabled, a number in floating point, or a number with a decimal point is interpreted as exact and MATLAB is exact in how the rational expression is represented with the result in rational numbers. At the same time, if there is an irrational number in a rational expression, MATLAB retains the number in the rational form so that it presents the solution in the rational form. We consider the following examples:

```
>> format rat;
>> 2.64/25+4/100

Ans =

      91/625

<Note that this is the result of 66/625 + 25/625.>

>> 2.64/sqrt(25)+4/100

Ans =

      71/125

>> sqrt(2.64)/25+4/100

Ans =

      204/1943
```

MATLAB also works with the irrational numbers representing the results with greater accuracy or with the accuracy required by the user, bearing in mind that the irrational cannot be represented as exactly as the ratio of two integers. Below is an example.

```
>> sqrt (235)

Ans =

    15.3297
```

There are very typical real constants represented in MATLAB as follows:

pi	*Number π = 3.1415926*
	`>> 2 * pi`
	`Ans =`
	`    6.2832`
exp (1)	*Number e = 2.7182818*
	`>> exp (1)`
	`Ans =`
	`    2.7183`
inf	*Infinity (for example 1/0)*
	`>> 1/0`
	`Ans =`
	`    INF`
nan	*Uncertainty (for example 0/0)*
	`>> 0/0`
	`Ans =`
	`    NaN`
realmin	*Least usable positive real number*
	`>> realmin`
	`Ans =`
	`    2.2251e-308`
realmax	*Largest usable positive real number*
	`>> realmax`
	`Ans =`
	`    1.7977e + 308`

MATLAB has a range of predefined functions of real variables. The following sectionss present the most important.

Trigonometric Functions

Below is a table with the trigonometric functions and their inverses that are incorporated in MATLAB illustrated with examples.

Function	Inverse
sin (x) *sine*	**asin (x)** *arcsine*
>> sin(pi/2)	>> asin (1)
ans =	ans =
1	1.5708
cos (x) *cosine*	**acos (x)** *arccosine*
>> cos (pi)	>> acos (- 1)
ans =	ans =
-1	3.1416
tan(x) *tangent*	**atan(x) atan2 (x) and** *arctangent*
>> tan(pi/4)	>> atan (1)
ans =	ans =
1.0000	0.7854
csc(x) *cosecant*	**acsc (x)** *arccosecant*
>> csc(pi/2)	>> acsc (1)
ans =	ans =
1	1.5708
sec (x) *secant*	**asec (x)** *arcsecant*
>> sec (pi)	>> asec (- 1)
ans =	ans =
-1	3.1416
cot (x) *cotangent*	**acot (x)** *arccotangent*
>> cot(pi/4)	>> acot (1)
ans =	ans =
1.0000	0.7854

Hyperbolic Functions

Below is a table with the hyperbolic functions and their inverses that are incorporated in MATLAB illustrated with examples.

Function	Reverse
sinh (x) *hyperbolic sine*	**asinh (x)** *hyperbolic arcsine*
>> sinh (2)	>> asinh (3.6269)
ans =	ans =
3.6269	2.0000
cosh(x) *hyperbolic cosine*	**acosh(x)** *hyperbolic arccosine*
>> cosh (3)	>> acosh (10.0677)
ans =	ans =
10.0677	3.0000
tanh(x) *hyperbolic tangent*	**atanh (x)** *hyperbolic arctangent*
>> tanh (1)	>> atanh (0.7616)
ans =	ans =
0.7616	1.0000
csch (x) *hyperbolic cosecant*	**acsch (x)** *hyperbolic arccosecant*
>> csch (3.14159)	>> acsch (0.0866)
ans =	ans =
0.0866	3.1415
sech (x) *hyperbolic secant*	**asech (x)** *hyperbolic arcsecant*
>> sech (2.7182818)	>> asech (0.1314)
ans =	ans =
0.1314	2.7183
coth (x) *hyperbolic cotangent*	**acoth (x)** *hyperbolic arccotangent*
>> coth (9)	>> acoth (0.9999)
ans =	ans =
1.0000	4.9517 + 1.5708i

Exponential and Logarithmic Functions

Below is a table with the exponential and logarithmic functions that are incorporated in MATLAB illustrated with examples.

Function	Meaning

exp (x)	*Exponential function in base e (e ^ x)*
	
	 ```>> exp (log (7))```
	
	 ```Ans =```
	
	 7

log (x)	*Logarithmic function base e of x*
	
	 ```>> log (exp (7))```
	
	 ```Ans =```
	
	 7

log10 (x)	*Base 10 logarithmic function*
	
	 ```>> log10 (1000)```
	
	 ```Ans =```
	
	 3

log2 (x)	*Logarithmic function of base 2*
	
	 ```>> log2(2^8)```
	
	 ```Ans =```
	
	 8

pow2 (x)	*Power function base 2*
	
	 ```>> pow2 (log2 (8))```
	
	 ```Ans =```
	
	 8

sqrt (x)	*Function for the square root of x*
	
	 ```>> sqrt(2^8)```
	
	 ```Ans =```
	
	 16

Numeric Variable-Specific Functions

MATLAB incorporates a group of functions of numerical variable. Among these features are the following:

Function	Meaning
abs (x)	*Absolute value of the real x*
	`>> abs (- 8)`
	`Ans =`
	`    8`
floor (x)	*The largest integer less than or equal to the real x*
	`>> floor (- 23.557)`
	`Ans =`
	`    -24`
ceil (x)	*The smallest integer greater than or equal to the real x*
	`>> ceil (- 23.557)`
	`Ans =`
	`    -23`
round (x)	*The closest integer to the real x*
	`>> round (- 23.557)`
	`Ans =`
	`    -24`
fix (x)	*Eliminates the decimal part of the real x*
	`>> fix (- 23.557)`
	`Ans =`
	`    -23`
rem (a, b)	*It gives the remainder of the division between the real a and b*
	`>> rem (7.3)`
	`Ans =`
	`    1`
sign (x)	*The sign of the real x (1 if x > 0; - 1 if x < 0)*
	`>> sign (- 23.557)`
	`Ans =`
	`    -1`

One-Dimensional, Vector and Matrix Variables

MATLAB is software based on matrix language, and therefore focuses especially on tasks for working with arrays.

The initial way of defining a variable is very simple. Simply use the following syntax:

Variable = object

where the object can be a scalar, a vector or a matrix.

If the variable is an array, its syntax depends on its components and can be written in one of the following ways:

Variable = [v1 v2 v3... vn]
Variable = [v1, v2, v3,..., vn]

If the variable is an array, its syntax depends on its components and can be written in one of the following ways:

Variable = [v11 v12 v13... v1n; v21 v22 v23... v2n;...]
Variable = [v11, v12, v13,..., v1n; v21, v22, v23,..., v2n;...]

Script variables are defined in the command window from MATLAB in a natural way as shown in Figure 2-1.

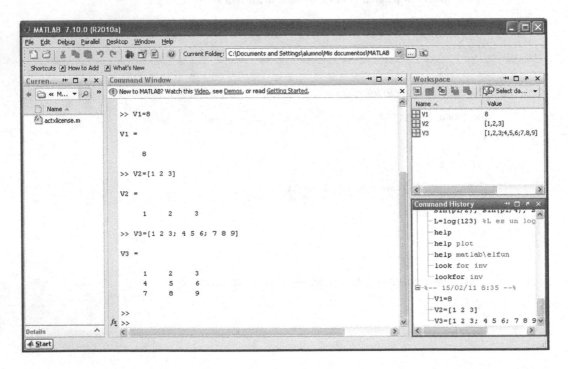

Figure 2-1.

The workspace (*Workspace*) window contains all variables that we will define in the session. The value of any of these variables is recoverable by typing their names on the command window (Figure 2-2).

Figure 2-2.

Also, in the command history window (*Command History*) we can find all the syntax we execute from the command window.

Once a variable is defined, we can operate on it using it as a regular variable in mathematics, bearing in mind that the names of the variables are sensitive to upper and lower case. Figure 2-3 shows some operations with one-dimensional, vector and matrix variables. It is important to note the error that occurred when calculating the logarithm of V2. The mistake was changing the variable to lowercase so that it was not recognized.

Figure 2-3.

MATLAB variables names begin with a letter followed by any number of letters, digits or underscores with a 31 character maximum.

There are also specific forms for the definition of vector variables, among which are the following:

variable = [a: b]	*Defines the vector whose first and last elements are a and b, respectively, and the intermediate elements differ by one unit*
	`>> vector1 = [2:6]`
	`vector1 =`
	2 3 4 5 6
variable = [a: s:b]	*Defines the vector whose first and last elements are a and b, and the intermediate elements differ in the amount specified by the increase in s*
	`>> vector2 = [2:2:8]`
	`Vector2 =`
	2 4 6 8
Nvariable = linespace [a, b, n]	*Defines the vector whose first and last elements are a and b, and has in total n evenly spaced elements*
	`>> vector3 = linespace (10,30,6)`
	`Vector3 =`
	10 14 18 22 26 30

Elements of Vector Variables

MATLAB allows the selection of elements of vector variables using the following commands:

x (n)	*Returns the nth element of the vector x*
	`>> X =(2:8)`
	`X =`
	2 3 4 5 6 7 8
	`>> X (3)`
	`Ans =`
	4
x(a:b)	*Returns the elements of the vector x between the a-th and the b-th elements, both inclusive*
	`>> X (3:5)`
	`Ans =`
	4 5 6

(continued)

x(a:p:b)	*Returns the elements of the vector x located between the a-th and the b-th elements, both inclusive, but separated by units where a < b.*

```
>> X (1:2:6)
Ans =
     2-4-6
```

x(b:-p:a)	*Returns the elements of the vector x located between the b- and a-th, both inclusive, but separates by p units and starting with the b-th element (b > a)*

```
>> X(6:-2:1)
Ans =
     7-5-3
```

Elements of Matrix Variables

The same as in the case of vectors, MATLAB allows the selection of elements of array variables using the following commands:

A(m,n)	*Defines the (m, n) element of the matrix A (row m and column n)*

```
>> A = [3 5 7 4; 1 6 8 9; 2 6 8 1]
A =
     3 5 7 4
     1 6 8 9
     2 6 8 1
>> A (2,4)
Ans =
     9
```

A(a:b,c:d)	*Defines the subarray of A formed by the intersection of the a-th and the b-th rows and the the c-th and the d-th columns*

```
>> A(1:2,2:3)
Ans =
     5 7
     6 8
```

(continued)

A(a:p:b,c:q:d)	*Defines the subarray of A formed by rows between the a-th and the b-th spaced by using p in p, and the columns between the c-th and the d-th spaced by using q in q*

```
>> A(1:2:3,1:2:4)

Ans =

    3 7
    2 8
```

A([a b],[c d])	*Defines the subarray of A formed by the intersection of the a-th and b-th rows and c-th and d-th columns*

```
>> A([2 3],[2 4])

Ans =

    6 9
    6 1
```

A([a b c...],) **([e f g...])**	*Defines the subarray of A formed by the intersection of rows a, b, c,... and columns e, f, g,...*

```
>> A([2 3],[1 2 4])

Ans =

    1-6-9
    2-6-1
```

A(:,c:d)	*Defines the subarray of A formed by all the rows from A and columns between the c-th and the d-th*

```
>> A(:,2:4)

Ans =

    5 7 4
    6 8 9
    6 8 1
```

A(:,[c d e...])	*Defines the subarray of A formed by all the rows from A and columns c, d, e,...*

```
>> A(:,[2,3])

Ans =

    5 7
    6 8
    6 8
```

A(a:b,:)	*Defines the subarray of A formed by all the columns in A and rows between the a-th and the b-th*

```
>> A(2:3,:)

Ans =

    1 6 8 9
    2 6 8 1
```

(continued)

A([a b c...],:)   *Defines the subarray of A formed by all the columns in A and rows a, b, c,...*

```
>> A([1,3],:)

Ans =

   3 5 7 4
   2 6 8 1
```

A(a,:)   *Defines the a-th row of the matrix A*

```
>> A(3,:)

Ans =

   2 6 8 1
```

A(:,b)   *Defines the b-th column of the matrix A*

```
>> A(:,3)

Ans =

   7
   8
   8
```

A (:)   *Defines a vector column whose elements are the columns of A placed order one below another*

```
>> A (:)

Ans =

   3
   1
   2
   5
   6
   6
   7
   8
   8
   4
   9
   1
```

A(:,:)   *It is equivalent to the matrix A*

```
>> A(:,:)

Ans =

   3 5 7 4
   1 6 8 9
   2 6 8 1
```

(continued)

[A, B, C,...]	*Defines the matrix formed by the subarrays A, B, C,...*

```
>> A1 = [2 6; 4 1], A2 = [3 8; 6 9]

A1 =

    2 6
    4 1

A2 =

    3 8
    6 9

>> [A1, A2]

Ans =

    2 6 3 8
    4 1 6 9
```

Specific Matrix Functions

MATLAB uses a group of predefined matrix functions that facilitate the work in the matrix field. The most important are the following:

diag (v)	*Create a diagonal matrix with the vector v in the diagonal*

```
>> diag([2 0 9 8 7])

Ans =

    2   0   0   0   0
    0   0   0   0   0
    0   0   9   0   0
    0   0   0   8   0
    0   0   0   0   7
```

diag (A)	*Extract the diagonal of the matrix as a vector column*

```
>> A = [1, 3, 5; 2 0 8; -1-3 2]

A =

    1 3 5
    2 0 8
    -1-3 2

>> diag (A)

Ans =

    1
    0
    2
```

(continued)

eye (n)	*It creates the identity matrix of order n*

```
>> eye (4)

Ans =

    1 0 0 0
    0 1 0 0
    0 0 1 0
    0 0 0 1
```

eye (m, n)	*Create order mxn matrix with ones on the main diagonal and zeros elsewhere*

```
>> eye (3.5)

Ans =

    1    0    0    0    0
    0    1    0    0    0
    0    0    1    0    0
```

zeros (m, n)	*Create the zero matrix of order m x n*

```
>> zeros (2,3)

Ans =

    0 0 0
    0 0 0
```

ones (m, n)	*Create the matrix of order with all its elements 1 m x n*

```
>> ones (2,3)

Ans =

    1 1 1
    1 1 1
```

rand (m, n)	*It creates a uniform random matrix of order m x n*

```
>> rand (4.5)

Ans =

    0.8147   0.6324   0.9575   0.9572   0.4218
    0.9058   0.0975   0.9649   0.4854   0.9157
    0.1270   0.2785   0.1576   0.8003   0.7922
    0.9134   0.5469   0.9706   0.1419   0.9595
```

(continued)

randn (m, n)	*Create a normal random matrix of order m x n*

```
>> randn (4.5)

Ans =

      0.6715    0.4889    0.2939 - 1.0689    0.3252
     -1.2075    1.0347 - 0.7873 - 0.8095 - 0.7549
      0.7172    0.7269    0.8884 - 2.9443    1.3703
      1.6302 - 0.3034 - 1.1471    1.4384 - 1.7115
```

flipud (A)	*Returns the matrix whose rows are placed in reverse order (from top to bottom) to the rows of matrix A*

```
>> flipud (A)

Ans =

    -1-3 2
     2 0 8
     1 3 5
```

fliplr (A)	*Returns the matrix whose columns are placed in reverse (from left to right) of A*

```
>> fliplr (A)

Ans =

     5 3 1
     8 0 2
     2-3-1
```

rot90 (A)	*Rotates 90 degrees the matrix A*

```
>> rot90 (A)

Ans =

     5 8 2
     3 0-3
     1 2-1
```

reshape(A,m,n)	*Returns the array of order extracted from matrix m x n taking consecutive items by columns*

```
>> reshape(A,3,3)

Ans =

     1 3 5
     2 0 8
    -1-3 2
```

(continued)

size (A)	*Returns the order (size) of the matrix A*

```
>> size (A)

Ans =

      3 3
```

length (v)	*Returns the length of the vector v*

```
>> length([1 3 4 5-1])

Ans =

      5
```

tril (A)	*Returns the lower triangular part of matrix A*

```
>> tril (A)

Ans =

      1 0 0
      2 0 0
     -1-3 2
```

triu (A)	*Returns the upper triangular part of matrix A*

```
>> (A) triu

Ans =

      1 3 5
      0 0 8
      0 0 2
```

A'	*Returns the transposed matrix from A*

```
>> A'

Ans =

      1 2-1
      3 0-3
      5 8 2
```

Inv (A)	*Returns the inverse matrix of matrix A*

```
>> inv(A)

Ans =

     -0.5714    0.5000 - 0.5714
      0.2857 - 0.1667 - 0.0476
      0.1429    0.1429         0
```

Random Numbers

MATLAB incorporates features that make it possible to work with randomised numbers. The functions *rand* and *randn* are basic functions that generate random numbers distributed uniformly and normally respectively. Below are the most common functions for working with random numbers.

---

rand	*Returns a random decimal number uniformly distributed in the interval [0,1]*

```
>> rand

Ans =

      0.8147
```

rand (n)	*Returns an array of size n x n whose elements are uniformly distributed random decimal numbers in the interval [0,1]*

```
>> rand (3)

Ans =

      0.9058 0.6324 0.5469
      0.1270 0.0975 0.9575
      0.9134 0.2785 0.9649
```

rand (m, n)	*Returns an array of dimension m x n whose elements are uniformly distributed random decimal numbers in the interval [0,1]*

```
>> rand (2,3)

Ans =

      0.1576 0.9572 0.8003
      0.9706 0.4854 0.1419
```

rand (size (a))	*Returns an array of the same size as the matrix A and whose elements are uniformly distributed random decimal numbers in the interval [0,1]*

```
>> rand (size (eye (3)))

Ans =

      0.4218 0.9595 0.8491
      0.9157 0.6557 0.9340
      0.7922 0.0357 0.6787
```

rand ('seed')	*Returns the current value of the uniform random number generator seed*

```
>> rand('seed')

Ans =

      931316785
```

(continued)

rand('seed',n)	*Placed in the number n, the current value of the uniform random number generator seed*

```
>> rand ('seed')

Ans =

    931316785

>> rand ('seed', 1000)
>> rand ('seed')

Ans =

    1000
```

randn	*Returns a random decimal distributed number according to a normal distribution of mean 0 and variance 1*

```
>> randn

Ans =

    -0.4326
```

randn (n)	*Returns an array of size n x n whose elements are distributed random decimal numbers according to a normal distribution of mean 0 and variance 1*

```
>> randn (3)

Ans =

    -1.6656 - 1.1465 - 0.0376
     0.1253   1.1909   0.3273
     0.2877   1.1892   0.1746
```

randn (m, n)	*Returns an array of dimension m x n whose elements are distributed random decimal numbers according to a normal distribution of mean 0 and variance 1*

```
>> randn (2,3)

Ans =

    -0.1867 - 0.5883 - 0.1364
     0.7258   2.1832   0.1139
```

randn (size (A))	*Returns an array of the same size as the matrix A and whose elements are distributed according to a normal distribution of mean 0 and variance 1 as random decimal numbers*

```
>> randn (size (eye (3)))

Ans =

     1.0668 - 0.8323   0.7143
     0.0593   0.2944   1.6236
    -0.0956 - 1.3362 - 0.6918
```

(continued)

randn ('seed')	*Returns the current value of the normal random number generator seed*

```
>> randn ('seed')

Ans =

    931316785
```

randn('seed',n)	*Placed in the n number the current value of the uniform random number generator seed*

```
>> randn ('seed', 1000)
>> randn ('seed')

Ans =

    1000
```

Operators

MATLAB is a language that incorporates arithmetic, logical and relational operators in the same way as any other language. The following are the types of operators referred to in the scope of the MATLAB language.

Arithmetic Operators

MATLAB incorporates the usual arithmetic operators (addition, subtraction, multiplication and division) to work with numbers. MATLAB extends the meaning of these operators to work with scalars, vectors and matrices, as shown in the following table:

Operator	Role Played
+	*Sum of scalar, vector, or matrix*

```
>> A = [1 3 -2 6]; B = [4 -5 8 2]; c = 3;
>> V1 = A + c

V1 =

    4 6 1 9

>> V2 = A + B

V2 =

    5 -2 6 8
```

(*continued*)

Operator	Role Played
-	*Subtraction of scalar, vector, or matrix*

```
>> V3 = A-c

V3 =

    -2    0   -5    3

>> V4 = A - B

V4 =

    -3  8 -10 4
```

*	*Product of scalars or arrays or scalars vectors or matrices* *Defines the subarray of A formed by the intersection of the a-th* *and the b-th rows and the the c-th and the d-th columns*

```
>> V3 = A * c

V3 =

    3 9 -6 18
```

.*	*Product of scalar or vector element to element*

```
>> V4 = A * B

V4 =

    4 -15 -16 12
```

.^	*Power of vectors (A. ^ B = [A(i,j)B (i, j)], vectors A and B)*

```
>> V6 = a ^ B

V6 =

    1.0000 0.0041 256.0000 36.0000

>> A ^ c

Ans =

    1 27 -8 216

>> c. ^ A

Ans =

    3.0000 27.0000 0.1111 729.0000
```

(continued)

Operator	Role Played
./	$A / B = [A(i,j)/b(i,j)]$, being A and B vectors where $[dim(A) = dim(B)]$
	>> V7 = A. / B
	V7 =
	0.2500 - 0.6000 - 0.2500 3.0000
.\	$A.\backslash B = [B(i,j)/A(i,j)]$, being A and B vectors where $[dim(A) = dim(B)]$
	>> V8 = A. \B
	V8 =
	4.0000 - 1.6667 - 4.0000 0.3333
\	$A\backslash B = inv(A) * B$, with A and B being matrices
	>> A = rand (4)
	A =
	0.6868 0.5269 0.7012 0.0475 0.5890 0.0920 0.9103 0.7361 0.9304 0.6539 0.7622 0.3282 0.8462 0.4160 0.2625 0.6326
	>> B = randn (4)
	B =
	-0.1356 - 0.0449 - 0.0562 0.4005 -1.3493 - 0.7989 0.5135 - 1.3414 -1.2704 - 0.7652 0.3967 0.3750 0.9846 0.8617 0.7562 1.1252
	>> A\B
	Ans =
	25.0843 17.5201 - 1.8497 7.1332 -25.8285 - 17.9297 2.4290 - 4.6114 -4.4616 - 3.1424 - 0.2409 - 2.7058 -13.1598 - 8.9778 2.1720 - 3.6075

(continued)

Operator	Role Played
/	*Ratio scale of b/a = B * inv (A), with A and B being matrices*

```
>> B/A

Ans =

    -4.8909    0.0743    4.8972 - 1.6273
     4.6226    0.9230 - 4.2151 - 1.3541
   -10.2745    1.2107   10.4001 - 5.4409
    -9.6925 - 0.1247   11.1342 - 3.1260
```

| ^ | *Power of scalar or power scale matrix (M p)* |

```
>> A ^ 3

Ans =

    3.5152 2.1281 3.1710 1.6497
    4.0584 2.3911 3.7435 1.9881
    4.6929 2.8299 4.2067 2.2186
    3.5936 2.1520 3.2008 1.7187
```

Logical Operators

MATLAB also includes the usual logical operators using the most common notation for them. The results of the logical operators usually are 1 if true and or if false. These operators are shown in the following table.

~ A	*Logical negation (NOT) or A supplementary*

```
>> not(2 > 3)

Ans =

    1
```

| A & B | *Logical conjunction (AND) or the intersection of A and B* |

```
>> (2 > 3) & (5 > 1)

Ans =

    0
```

(continued)

A | B	Logical disjunction (OR) or the union of A and B

	`>> (2 > 3) |(5 > 1)`
	
	`Ans =`
	
	`1`

XOR (A, B)	OR exclusive (XOR) or symmetric difference of A and B (it's true [1] if A or B is true, but not both)

	`>> xor ((2 > 3),(5 > 1))`
	
	`Ans =`
	
	`1`

Relational Operators

MATLAB also deals with relational operations that run comparisons element by element between two matrices, and returns an array of the same size whose elements are zero if the corresponding relationship is true, or one if the corresponding relation is false. The relational operators can also compare scalar vectors or matrices, in which case it is compared to climbing with all the elements of the array. The following table shows the relational operators in MATLAB.

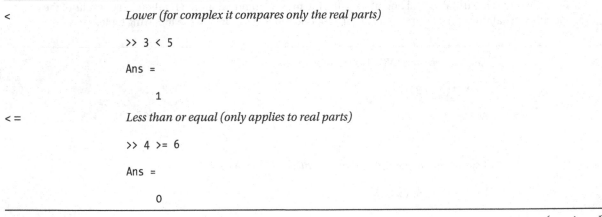

<	Lower (for complex it compares only the real parts)

	`>> 3 < 5`
	
	`Ans =`
	
	`1`

< =	Less than or equal (only applies to real parts)

	`>> 4 >= 6`
	
	`Ans =`
	
	`0`

(continued)

>	*Wholesale (only applies to real parts)*

```
>> X = 3 * ones (3.3)

X =

    3 3 3
    3 3 3
    3 3 3

>> X > [1 2 3; 4 5 6; 1 2 3]

Ans =

    1 1 0
    0 0 0
    1 1 0
```

> =	*Greater than or equal (only applies to real parts)*

```
>> X >= [1 2 3; 4 5 6; 1 2 3]

Ans =

    1 1 1
    0 0 0
    1 1 1
```

x == y	*Equality (affects complex numbers)*

```
>> X == ones (3,3)

Ans =

    0 0 0
    0 0 0
    0 0 0
```

x ~ = y	*Inequality (affects complex numbers)*

```
>> X ~= ones (3,3)

Ans =

    1 1 1
    1 1 1
    1 1 1
```

Symbolic Variables

So far we have always handled numerical variables. However, MATLAB allows you to manage symbolic mathematical computation, manipulating formulae and algebraic expressions easily and quickly and perform operations with them.

However, to accomplish these tasks it is necessary to have the MATLAB *Symbolic Math Toolbox* module.
Algebraic expressions or variables to be symbolic have to be declared as such with the command *syms*, before they are used. The following table shows the command syntax of conversion variables and symbolic expressions.

syms x y z... t	*Converts the variables x, y and z,..., t into symbolic*

	```>> syms x y```
	```>> x+x+y-6*y```
	
	```Ans =```
	
	``` 2 * x - 5 * y```

syms x y z... t real	*Converts the variables x, y and z,..., t into symbolic with actual values*

	```>> syms a b c real;```
	```>> A = [a b c; c a b; b c a]```
	
	```A =```
	
	``` [a, b, c]```
	``` [c, a, b]```
	``` [b, c, a]```

syms x and z... t unreal	*Converts the variables x, y and z,..., t into symbolic with no actual values*
syms	*Symbolic workspace variables list*

	```>> syms```
	
	```'A' 'a' 'ans' 'b' 'c' 'x' 'y'```

y = sym ('x')	*Converts the variable or number x in symbolic (equivalent to syms x)*

	```>> rho = sym ('(1 + sqrt (5)) / 2')```
	
	```Rho =```
	
	``` 5 ^(1/2)/2 + 1/2```

y = sym ('x', real)	*It becomes a real symbolic variable x*
y = sym('x', unreal)	*It becomes a non-real symbolic variable x*

(continued)

S = sym (A)	*Creates a symbolic object starting with A, where A may be a string, a scalar, an array, a numeric expression, etc.*

```
>> S = sym([0.5 0.75 1; 0 0.5 0.1; 0.2 0.3 0.4])

S =

    [1/2,  3/4,    1]
    [  0,  1/2, 1/10]
    [1/5, 3/10,  2/5]
```

S = sym (at, 'option')	*Converts the array, scalar or a numeric expression to symbolic according to the specified option. The option can be 'f' for floating point, 'r' for rational, 'e' for error format and 'd' for decimal*
numeric(x) or double(x)	*It becomes the variable or expression x to numeric double-precision*
pretty (expr)	*Converts the symbolic expression to written mathematics*

```
>> pretty (rho)

1/2
5       1
---- + -
2       2
```

Digits	*The current accuracy for symbolic variables*

```
>> digits

Digits = 32
```

digits (d)	*The precision of symbolic variables in d exact decimal digits*

```
>> digits (25)
>> digits

Digits = 25
```

vpa ('expr')	*Numerical result of the expression with decimals of precision in digits*

```
>> phi = vpa ('(1 + sqrt (5)) / 2')

Phi =

      1.6180339887498948482045587
```

(continued)

vpa('expr', n)	*Numerical results of the expression with n decimal digits*

```
>> phi = vpa ('(1 + sqrt (5)) / 2', 10)

Phi =

      1.618033989
```

vpa (expr, n)	*Numerical result of the expression with n decimal digits*

```
>> phi = vpa ((1 + sqrt (5)) / 2.20)

Phi =

      1.6180339887498949025
```

Symbolic Functions and Functional Operations: Composite and Inverse Functions

In MATLAB, it is possible to define functions to measure of one and several variables using the syntax $f = $ *'function'*.

Also you can use the syntax $f = function$ if all variables have been defined previously as symbolic with *syms*. Subsequently it is possible to make substitutions to your arguments according to the notation which is presented in the following table.

The results tend to simplify the commands *simple* and *simplify*.

f = 'function'	*It defines the function f as symbolic*

```
>> f1 ='x ^ 3'

F1 =

    x ^ 3

>> f2 ='z ^ 2 + 2 * t'

F2 =

    z ^ 2 + 2 * t

>> syms x t z
>> g1 = x ^ 2

G1 =

    x ^ 2

>> g2 = sqrt (x+2 * z + exp (t))

G2 =

    (x + 2 * z + exp (t)) ^(1/2)
```

(*continued*)

subs(f, a)	*Applies the function f at the point a*
	`>> subs(f1,2)`
	`Ans =`
	8
subs (f, variable, value)	*Replaces the variable by a value*
	`>> subs(f1,x,3)`
	`Ans =`
	27
subs(f, {x,y,...}, {a,b,...})	*Replaces the variables in the equation f {x, y,..} with the values {a, b,...}*
	`>> subs(f2, {z,t}, {1,2})`
	`Ans =`
	5

MATLAB additionally implements various functional operations which are summarized in the following table:

f + g	*Adds the functions f and g (f + g)*
	`>> syms x` `>> f = x ^ 2 + x + 1; g = 2 * x ^ 2-x ^ 3 + cos (x); h =-x+log (x);`
	`>> f + g`
	`Ans =`
	`x + cos (x) + 3 * x ^ 2 - x ^ 3 + 1`
f+g+h+...	*Performs the sum f+g+h +...*
	`>> f+g+h`
	`Ans =`
	`cos (x) + log (x) + 3 * x ^ 2 - x ^ 3 + 1`
f-g	*Find the difference of f and g (f-g)*
	`>> f-g`
	`Ans =`
	`x cos (x) - x ^ 2 + x ^ 3 + 1`

(continued)

f-g-h-...	*Performs the difference f-g-h-...*

>> f-g-h

Ans =

    2 * x - cos (x) - log (x) - x ^ 2 + x ^ 3 + 1

f*g	*Creates the product of f and g (f*g)*

>> f * g

Ans =

    (cos (x) + 2 * x ^ 2 - x ^ 3) * (x^2 + x + 1)

f*g*h*...	*Creates the product f*g*h*...*

>> f * g * h

Ans =

-(x - log (x)) * (cos (x) + 2 * x ^ 2 - x ^ 3) * (x^2 + x + 1)

f/g	*Performs the ratio between f and g (f/g)*

>> f/g

Ans =

    (x ^ 2 + x + 1) / (cos (x) + 2 * x ^ 2 - x ^ 3).

f/g/h/...	*Performs the ratio f/g/h...*

>> f

Ans =

-(x^2 + x + 1) / ((x - log (x)) * (cos (x) + 2 * x ^ 2 - x ^ 3))

f^k	*Raises f to the power k (k is a scalar)*

>> f ^ 2

Ans =

    (x ^ 2 + x + 1) ^ 2

f^g	*It elevates a function to another function (fg)*

>> f ^ g

Ans =

    (x ^ 2 + x + 1) ^ (cos (x) + 2 * x ^ 2 - x ^ 3).

(continued)

compose (f, g)	*A function of f and g (f ° g (x) = f (g (x)))*
	`>> compose (f, g)`
	`Ans =`
	`    cos (x) + (cos (x) + 2 * x ^ 2 - x ^ 3) ^ 2 + 2 * x ^ 2 - x ^ 3 + 1`
compose(f,g,h)	*Function of f and g, taking the expression or as the domain of f and g*
	`>> compose (f, g, h)`
	`Ans =`
	`    cos (log (x) - x) + 2 * (x - log (x)) ^ 2 + (x - log (x)) ^ 3 + (cos (log (x)`
g = finverse (f)	*Inverse of the function f*
	`>> finverse (f)` `Warning: finverse(x^2 + x + 1) is not unique.`
	`Ans =`
	`    (4 * x - 3) ^(1/2)/2 - 1/2`

Commands that Handle Variables in the Workspace and Store them in Files

MATLAB has a group of commands that allow you to define and manage variables, as well as store them in MATLAB format files (with extension *.mat*) or in ASCII format, in a simple way. When extensive calculations are performed, it is convenient to give names to intermediate results. These intermediate results are assigned to variables to make it easier to use. Let's not forget that the value assigned to a variable is permanent until it is expressly changed or is out of the present session of work. MATLAB incorporates a group of commands to manage variables among which are the following:

clear	*Clears all variables in the workspace*
clear(v1,v2, ..., vn)	*Deletes the specified numeric variables*
clear('v1', 'v2', ..., 'vn')	*Clears the variables specified in a string*
disp(X)	*Shows an array without including its name*
length(X)	*Shows the length of the vector X and if X is an array, displays its greatest dimension*
load	*It reads all variables from the file MATLAB.mat*
load file	*Reads all variables specified as .mat files*
load file X Y Z	*Reads the variables X, Y, Z of the given .mat file*
load file -ascii	*It reads the file as ASCII whatever its extension*
load file -mat	*It reads the file as .mat whatever its extension*
S = load(...)	*Returns the contents of a file in the variable .mat S*

(continued)

saveas(h,'f.ext')	*Saves the figure or model h as a f.ext file*
saveas(h,'f', 'format')	*Save the figure or model h as the f in the specified format file*
d = size(X)	*Returns the sizes of each dimension in a vector*
[m,n] = size(X)	*Returns the dimensions of the matrix X as two variables named m & n*
[d1,d2,d3,...,dn] = size(X)	*Returns the dimensions of the array X as variable names d1, d2,..., dn*
who	*The variables in the workspace list*
whos	*List of variables in the workspace with your sizes and types*
who('-file', 'fichero')	*List of variables in the given .mat file*
whos('-file', 'fichero')	*List of variables in the given .mat file and their sizes and types*
who('var1', 'var2',...)	*List of the variables string from the given workspace*
who('-file', 'filename', 'var1', 'var2',...)	*List of the variables specified in the string in the given .mat file*
s = who(...)	*The listed variables stored in s*
s = whos(...)	*The variables with their sizes and types stored in s*
who -file filename var1 var2 ...	*List of numerical variables specified in the given .mat file*
whos -file filename var1 var2 ...	*List of numerical variables specified in the file .mat given with their sizes and types*
Workspace	*Shows a browser to manage the workspace*

The *save* command is the essential instrument for storing data in the MATLAB *.mat* file type (only readable by the MATLAB program) and in file type ASCII (readable by any application). By default, the storage of variables often occurs in files formatted using MATLAB *.mat*. To store variables in files formatted in ASCII, it is necessary to use the command *save* with the options that are presented below:

Option	Mode of storage of the data
-append	*The variables are added to the end of the file*
-ascii	*The variables are stored in a file in ASCII format of 8 digits*
-ascii - double	*The variables are stored in a file in ASCII format of 16 digits*
-ascii – tabs	*The variables are stored in a tab-delimited file in ASCII format of 8 digits*
-ascii - double - tabs	*The variables are stored in a tab-delimited file in ASCII format of 16 digits*
-mat	*The variables are stored in a file with binary .mat format*

EXERCISE 2-1

Calculate the value of 7 to the 400th power with 500 exact decimal numbers.

```
>> vpa '7 ^ 400' 500
```

Ans =

3234476509624757991344647769100216810857201398904625400933895331391691459636928060001*10^338

500 figures are not needed to express the exact value of the result. It notes that it is enough with 338 figures.
If you want the result with less accurate figures than it actually is, MATLAB completes the result with powers of 10.
Let's see:

```
>> vpa '7 ^ 400' 45
```

Ans =

1.0945006043361130854242544564866621752 99975487 * 10 ^ 338

EXERCISE 2-2

Calculate the greatest common divisor and least common multiple of the numbers 1000, 500 and 625

```
>> gcd (gcd (1000,500), 625)
```

Ans =

125

As the gcd function only supports two arguments in MATLAB, we have applied the property: *gcd(a, b, c) = gcd (gcd(a, b), c) = gcd(a, gcd (b, c))*. The property is analogous to the least common multiple: *lcm(a, b, c) = lcm (lcm(a, b), c) = lcm (a, lcm (b, c))*. We will make the calculation in the following way:

```
>> lcm(lcm(1000,500), 625)
```

Ans =

5000

EXERCISE 2-3

Is the number 99,991 prime? Find the prime factors of the number 135,678,742.

We divide both numbers into prime factors:

```
>> factor (99991)

Ans =

    99991

>> factor (135678742)

Ans =

    2 1699 39929
```

It is observed that 99991 is a prime number because in attempting to break it down into prime factors, it turns out to be the only prime factor of itself. Observe that the number 135678742 has three prime factors.

EXERCISE 2-4

Find the remainder of dividing 2^{134} by 3. Is the number $2^{32} - 1$ divisible by 17? Also find the number N which divided by 16, 24, 30 and 32 yields a remainder of 5.

The first part of the problem is resolved as follows:

```
>> rem(2^134,3)

Ans =

    0
```

It is observed that 2134 is a multiple of 3.

To see if $2^{32} - 1$ is divisible by 17, we factor it:

```
>> factor(2^32-1)

Ans =

    3 5 17 257 65537
```

Note that 17 is one of its factors, so then it is divisible by 17.

To resolve the last part of the problem, we calculate the least common multiple of all the numbers and add 5.

```
>> N = 5+lcm(16,lcm(24,lcm(30,32)))

N =

    485
```

EXERCISE 2-5

Calculate the value of 100 factorial. Calculate it also with 70 and 200 significant figures.

```
>> factorial(100)

ans =

    9.3326e+157

>> vpa(factorial(100))

ans =

    9.3326215443944102188325606108575*10^157

>> vpa(factorial(100),70)

ans =

    9.332621544439441021883256061085752672409442548549605715091669106910400408*10^157

>> vpa(factorial(100),200)

ans =

    9.3326215443944102188325606108575267240944425485496057150916691040040799506424293714863269
    40304505128980429892969444748982587372043112366414775618770165018132248*10^157
```

EXERCISE 2-6

In base 5 the results of the following operation:

$$a25aaff6 + 6789aba + 1100221 + 35671 - 1250$$
$$16 \qquad 12 \qquad 8 \qquad 3$$

As it is a venture to convert between numbers in different base numbering systems, it will be simplest to convert to base 10 first and then perform the operation to calculate the result in base-5.

```
>>R10=base2dec('a25aaf6',16)+base2dec('6789aba',12)+base2dec('35671',8)
+ base2dec('1100221',3)-1250
```

R10 =

    190096544

```
>> R5 = dec2base (R10, 5)
```

R5 =

    342131042134

EXERCISE 2-7

In base 13, get the result of the following operation:

$$(666551) (aa199800a) + (fffaaa125) / (33331 + 6)$$
$$7 \qquad 11 \qquad 16 \qquad 4$$

We use the strategy of the previous exercise. First, we make the operation with all the numbers to base 10 and then find the result for base 13.

```
>> R10 = vpa (base2dec('666551',7) * base2dec('aa199800a',11) + 79 * base2dec('fffaaa125',16)
/ (base2dec ('33331', 4) + 6))
```

R10 =

    275373340490851.53125

```
>> R13 = dec2base (275373340490852,13)
```

R13 =

    BA867963C1496

EXERCISE 2-8

Perform the following operations with rational numbers:

a. 3/5 + 2/5 + 7/5

b. 1/2 + 1/3 + 1/4 + 1/5 + 1/6

c. 1/2-1/3 + 1/4 - 1/5 + 1/6

d. (2/3-1/6)-(4/5+2+1/3) + (4-5/7)

a.

```
>> format rat
>> 3/5 + 2/5 + 7/5
```

Ans =

    12/5

b.

```
>> 1/2 + 1/3 + 1/4 + 1/5 + 1/6
```

Ans =

    29/20

c.

```
>> 1/2-1/3 + 1/4 - 1/5 + 1/6
```

Ans =

    23/60

d.

```
>> (2/3-1/6)-(4/5+2+1/3) + (4-5/7)
```

Ans =

    137/210

Alternatively, also the operations can be made as follows:

```
>> simplify (sym(3/5+2/5+7/5))
```

Ans =

    12/5

```
>> simplify (sym(1/2+1/3+1/4+1/5+1/6))

Ans =

    29/20

>> simplify (sym(1/2-1/3+1/4-1/5+1/6))

Ans =

    23/60

>> simplify (sym ((2/3-1/6)-(4/5+2+1/3) +(4-5/7)))

Ans =

    137/210
```

EXERCISE 2-9

Perform the following rational operations:

a. $3/a+2/a+7/a$

b. $1 / (2a) + 1 / (3a) + 1 / (4a) + 1 / (5a) + 1 / (6a)$

c. $1 / (2a) + 1 / (3b + 1 / (4a) + 1 / (5b) + 1 / (6c))$

To treat operations with expressions that contain symbolic variables a it is necessary to prepend the command **syms a** to declare the variable as symbolic, and then use *simplify or simple*.

a.

```
>> syms a
>> simplify(3/a+2/a+7/a)

Ans =

    12/a

>> 3/a+2/a+7/a

Ans =

    12/a

>> Ra = simple(3/a+2/a+7/a)

RA =

    12/a
```

b.

```
>> simplify (1 /(2*a) + 1 /(3*a) + 1 /(4*a) + 1 /(5*a) + 1 /(6*a))

Ans =

    29 /(20*a)

>> Rb = simple (1 /(2*a) + 1 /(3*a) + 1 /(4*a) + 1 /(5*a) + 1 /(6*a))

RB =

    29 /(20*a)
```

c.

```
>> syms a b c
>> pretty (simplify (1 /(2*a) + 1 /(3*b) + 1 /(4*a) + 1 /(5*b) + 1 /(6*c)))

   3      8        1
  --- + ---- +    --
  4a    15b       6c

>> pretty (simple (1 /(2*a) + 1 /(3*b) + 1 /(4*a) + 1 /(5*b) + 1 /(6*c)))

   3      8        1
  --- + ---- +    --
  4a    15b       6c
```

EXERCISE 2-10

Simplify the following rational expressions:

a. $(1-a^9) / (1-a^3)$

b. $(3a + 2a + 7a) / (a^3 + a)$

c. $1 / (1+a) + 1 / (1+a) + 1 / (1+a)^{2\,3}$

d. $1 + a / (a + b) +^2 / (a + b)^2$

a.

```
>> syms a b
>> pretty (simple ((1-a^9) /(1-a^3)))

   6    3
  a + a + 1
```

b.

```
>> pretty (simple ((3*a+2*a+7*a) /(a^3+a)))

      12
   ------
     2
    a + 1
```

c.

```
>> pretty (simple ((1 + 1 /(1+a) /(1+a) ^ 2 + 1 /(1+a) ^ 3)))

     2
    a + 3 a + 3
   ------------
            3
     (a + 1)
```

d.

```
>> pretty (simple ((1 + a / (a + b) + a ^ 2 / (a + b) ^ 2)))

       2
    2 a + b a
   ---------- + 1
         2
    (a + b)
```

EXERCISE 2-11

Perform the following operations with irrational numbers:

a. $3\sqrt{a} + 2\sqrt{a} - 5\sqrt{a} + 7\sqrt{a}$

b. $\sqrt{2} + 3\sqrt{2} - \sqrt{2}/2$

c. $4a^{1/3} - 3b^{1/3} - 5a^{1/3} - 2b^{1/3} + ma^{1/3}$

d. $\sqrt{3a}\sqrt{27a}$

e. $\sqrt{a}\sqrt[3]{a}$

f. $\sqrt{a\sqrt[5]{a}}$

a.

We use the command *simplify* or the command *simple*.

```
>> syms a b m
>> pretty(simplify(3*sqrt(a) + 2*sqrt(a) - 5*sqrt(a) + 7*sqrt(a)))

      1/2
   7 a
```

b.

```
>> pretty(simplify(sym(sqrt(2)+3*sqrt(2)-sqrt(2)/2)))

      1/2
   7 2
   ------
     2
```

c.

```
>> syms a b m
>> pretty(simplify(4*a^(1/3)- 3*b^(1/3)-5*a^(1/3)- 2*b^(1/3)+m*a^(1/3)))


    1                 1
    -                 -
    3        1/3      3
   a   m - a    - 5 b
```

d.

```
>> pretty(simplify(sqrt(3*a)*sqrt(27*a)))

   9 a
```

e.

```
>> pretty(simplify(a^(1/2)*a^(1/3)))

    5
    -
    6
   a
```

f.

```
>> pretty(simplify(sqrt(a*(a^(1/5)))))
```

```
/   6 \1/2
|   - |
|   5 |
\ a  /
```

EXERCISE 2-12

Perform the following irrational expressions by rationalizing   the denominators:

$$a.\ \frac{2}{\sqrt{2}}\quad b.\ \frac{3}{\sqrt{3}}\quad c.\ \frac{a}{\sqrt{a}}$$

In these cases of rationalization, the simple use of the command *simplify* solves problems. You can also use the command *radsimp*.

a.

```
>> simplify (sym (2/sqrt (2)))
```

Ans =

    2 ^(1/2)

b.

```
>> simplify (sym (3/sqrt (3)))
```

Ans =

    3 ^(1/2)

c.

```
>> syms a
>> simplify (sym (a/sqrt (a)))
```

Ans =

    a^(1/2)

EXERCISE 2-13

Given the vector variables $a = [\pi, 2\pi, 3\pi, 4\pi, 5\pi]$ and $b = [e, 2e, 3e, 4e, 5e]$ calculate $c = $ sine$(a) + b$, $d = \cosh(a)$, $e = $ Ln(b), $f = c * d$, $g = c/d$, $h = d^2$.

```
>> a=[pi,2*pi,3*pi,4*pi,5*pi],b=[exp(1),2*exp(1),3*exp(1),4*exp(1),5*exp(1)]

a =

   3.1416 6.2832 9.4248 12.5664 15.7080

b =

   2.7183 5.4366 8.1548 10.8731 13.5914

>> c=sin(a)+b,d=cosh(a),e=log(b),f=c.*d,g=c./d,h=d.^2

c =

   2.7183 5.4366 8.1548 10.8731 13.5914

d =

   1.0e + 006 *

   0.0000 0.0003 0.0062 0.1434 3.3178

e =

   1.0000 1.6931 2.0986 2.3863 2.6094

f =

   1.0e + 007 *

   0.0000 0.0001 0.0051 0.1559 4.5094

g =

   0.2345 0.0203 0.0013 0.0001 0.0000

h =

   1.0e + 013 *

   0.0000 0.0000 0.0000 0.0021 1.1008
```

EXERCISE 2-14

Given the vector of the first 10 natural numbers, find:

1. The sixth element
2. Its elements located between the fourth and the seventh both inclusive
3. Its elements located between the second and the ninth both including three by three
4. The elements of the number 3, but major to minor

```
>> x =(1:10)

x =

   1    2    3    4    5    6    7    8    9   10

>> x (6)

Ans =

    6
```

We have obtained the sixth element of the vector *x*.

```
>> x(4:7)

Ans =

    4 5 6 7
```

We have obtained the elements of the vector *x* located between the fourth and the seventh, both inclusive.

```
>> x(2:3:9)

Ans =

    2 5 8
```

We have obtained the elements of the vector *x* located between the second and ninth, both inclusive, but separated by three in three units.

```
>> x(9:-3:2)

Ans =

    9 6 3
```

We have obtained the elements of the vector *x* located between the ninth and second, both inclusive, but separated by three in three units and starting at the ninth.

EXERCISE 2-15

Given the 2x3 matrix whose rows consist of the first six odd numbers:

Cancel your element (2, 3), transpose it and attach it the identity matrix of order 3 on your right.

If C is what we call this the matrix obtained previously, build an array D extracting the odd columns of the C matrix, a matrix and formed by the intersection of the first two rows of C and its third and fifth columns, and a matrix F formed by the intersection of the first two rows and the last three columns of the matrix C.

Build the matrix diagonal G such that the elements of the main diagonal are the same as the diagonal main of D.

We build the matrix H, formed by the intersection of the first and third rows of C and its second, third and fifth columns.

We consider first the 2 x 3 matrix whose rows are the 6 consecutive odd first:

```
>> A = [1 3 5; 7 9 11]

A =

    1 3   5
    7 9  11
```

Now we are going to cancel the element (2, 3), that is, its last element:

```
>> A (2,3) = 0

A =

    1 3 5
    7 9 0
```

Then consider the B matrix transpose of A:

```
>> B = A'

B =

    1 7
    3 9
    5 0
```

We now construct a matrix C, formed by the matrix B and the matrix identity of order 3 attached to its right:

```
>> C = [B eye(3)]

C =

    1    7    1    0    0
    3    9    0    1    0
    5    0    0    0    1
```

We are going to build a matrix *D* extracting odd columns of the matrix *C*, a parent *and* formed by the intersection of the first two rows of *C* and its third and fifth columns, and a matrix *F* formed by the intersection of the first two rows and the last three columns of the matrix *C*:

```
>> D = C(:,1:2:5)

D =

   1 1 0
   3 0 0
   5 0 1

>> E = C([1 2],[3 5])

E =

   1 0
   0 0

>> F = C([1 2],3:5)

F =

   1 0 0
   0 1 0
```

Now we build the diagonal matrix *G* such that the elements of the main diagonal are the same as those of the main diagonal of *D*:

```
>> G = diag (diag (D))

G =

   1 0 0
   0 0 0
   0 0 1
```

Then build the matrix *H*, formed by the intersection of the first and third rows of *C* and its second, third and fifth columns:

```
>> H = C([1 3],[2 3 5])

H =

   7 1 0
   0 0 1
```

EXERCISE 2-16

Build an array (*I*),formed by the identity matrix of order 5 x 4 and zero and unit matrices of the same order attached to your right. Remove the first row of *I* and, finally, form the matrix *J* with the odd rows and column pairs and and estimate your order (size).

In addition, construct a random order 3 x 4 matrix *K* and first reverse the order of its ranks, then the order of its columns and then the order of the rows and columns at the same time. Finally, find the matrix *L* of order 4 x 3 whose columns are taking the elements of *K* columns sequentially.

```
>> I = [eye (5.4) zeros (5.4) ones (5.4)]
```

Ans =

```
    1    0    0    0    0    0    0    0    1    1    1    1
    0    1    0    0    0    0    0    0    1    1    1    1
    0    0    1    0    0    0    0    0    1    1    1    1
    0    0    0    1    0    0    0    0    1    1    1    1
    0    0    0    0    0    0    0    0    1    1    1    1
```

```
>> I(1,:)
```

Ans =

```
    1    0    0    0    0    0    0    0    1    1    1    1
```

```
>> J = I (1:2:5, 2:2:12)
```

J =

```
    0    0    0    0    1    1
    0    0    0    0    1    1
    0    0    0    0    1    1
```

```
>> size (J)
```

Ans =

```
    3  6
```

Then we build a random matrix *K* of order *3 x 4* and reverse the order of its ranks, then the order of its columns and then the order of the rows and columns at the same time. Finally, we find the matrix *L* of order 4 x 3 whose columns are taking the elements of *K* columns sequentially.

```
>> K = rand (3.4)
```

K =

```
    0.5269 0.4160 0.7622 0.7361
    0.0920 0.7012 0.2625 0.3282
    0.6539 0.9103 0.0475 0.6326
```

```
>> K(3:-1:1,:)

Ans =

      0.6539 0.9103 0.0475 0.6326
      0.0920 0.7012 0.2625 0.3282
      0.5269 0.4160 0.7622 0.7361

>> K(:,4:-1:1)

Ans =

      0.7361 0.7622 0.4160 0.5269
      0.3282 0.2625 0.7012 0.0920
      0.6326 0.0475 0.9103 0.6539

>> K(3:-1:1,4:-1:1)

Ans =

      0.6326 0.0475 0.9103 0.6539
      0.3282 0.2625 0.7012 0.0920
      0.7361 0.7622 0.4160 0.5269

"L = reshape(K,4,3)

L =

     0.5269 0.7012 0.0475
     0.0920 0.9103 0.7361
     0.6539 0.7622 0.3282
     0.4160 0.2625 0.6326
```

EXERCISE 2-17

Given the square matrix of order 3, whose ranks are the first 9 natural numbers, obtain its inverse and transpose its diagonal. Transform it into a lower triangular matrix and rotate it 90 degrees. Get the sum of the elements in the first row and the sum of the diagonal elements. Extract the subarray whose diagonal are the elements a_{11} and a_{22} and also remove the subarray with diagonal elements a_{11} and a_{33}.

```
>> M = [1,2,3;4,5,6;7,8,9]

M =

   1 2 3
   4 5 6
   7 8 9
```

```
>> A = inv (M)

Warning: Matrix is close to singular or badly scaled.
         Results may be inaccurate. RCOND = 2. 937385e-018

A =

    1.0e + 016 *

    0.3152 - 0.6304   0.3152
   -0.6304   1.2609 - 0.6304
    0.3152 - 0.6304   0.3152

>> B = M'

B =
   1 4 7
   2 5 8
   3 6 9

>> V = diag (M)

V =

    1
    5
    9

>> TI = tril (M)

TI =

   1 0 0
   4 5 0
   7 8 9
>> TS = triu (M)

TS =

   1 2 3
   0 5 6
   0 0 9

>> TR = rot90 (M)

TR =

   3 6 9
   2 5 8
   1 4 7
```

```
>> s = M (1,1) + M (1,2) + M (1.3)

s =

    6

>> sd = M (1,1) + M (2.2) + M (3.3)

SD =

   15

>> SM = M (1:2, 1:2)

SM =

   1 2
   4 5

>> SM1 = M([1 3],[1 3])

SM1 =

   1 3
   7 9
```

EXERCISE 2-18

Given the square matrix of order 3, whose ranks are the 9 first natural numbers (non-zero), identify their values less than 5.

If we now consider the vector whose elements are the first 9 numbers natural (non-zero) and the vector with the same elements from greater to lesser, identify the resulting values to the elements of the second vector and subtract the number 1 if the corresponding element of the first vector is greater than 2, or the number 0 if it is less than or equal to 2.

```
>> X = 5 * ones (3.3); X > = [1 2 3; 4 5 6 and 7 8 9]

Ans =

   1 1 1
   1 1 0
   0 0 0
```

The elements of the array X that are greater or equal to the matrix [1 2 3, 4 5 6, 7 8 9] correspond to a 1 in the matrix response. The rest of the elements correspond to a 0 (the result of the operation would be the same if we compare the matrix [1 2 3; 4 5 6 and 7 8 9], using the expression $X = 5$; $X >= [1 2 3 4 5 6; 7-8-9]$).

```
>> X = 5; X > = [1 2 3; 4 5 6 and 7 8 9]

Ans =

    1 1 1
    1 1 0
    0 0 0
```

Then we meet the second part of the exercise:

```
>> A = 1:9, B = 10-A, and = a > 4, Z = B-(A>2)

A =
    1    2    3    4    5    6    7    8    9
B =
    9    8    7    6    5    4    3    2    1
Y =
    0    0    0    0    1    1    1    1    1
Z =
    9    8    6    5    4    3    2    1    0
```

The values of *Y* equal to 1 correspond to elements of *A* larger than 4. *Z* values result from subtracting 1 from the corresponding elements of *B* if the corresponding element of *A* is greater than 2, or the number 0 if the corresponding element of *A* is less than or equal to 2.

EXERCISE 2-19

Find the matrix difference between a random square matrix of order 4 and a normal random matrix of order 4. Calculate the transpose and the inverse of the above difference. Verify that the reverse is correctly calculated.

```
>> A = rand (4) - randn (4)

A =

    0.9389 - 0.0391    0.4686    0.6633
   -0.5839    1.3050 - 0.0698    1.2727
   -1.2820 - 0.4387 - 0.5693 - 0.0881
   -0.5038 - 1.0834    1.2740    1.2890
```

We calculate the inverse and multiply it by the initial matrix to verify that it is the identity matrix.

```
>> B = inv (A)

B =

    0.9630 - 0.1824    0.1288 - 0.3067
   -0.8999    0.4345 - 0.8475 - 0.0239
   -1.6722    0.0359 - 1.5242    0.7209
    1.2729    0.2585    0.8445 - 0.0767
```

```
>> A * B

Ans =

      1.0000    0.0000        0 - 0.0000
           0    1.0000 - 0.0000    0.0000
     -0.0000 - 0.0000    1.0000    0.0000
     -0.0000    0.0000    0.0000    1.0000

>> B * A

Ans =

      1.0000    0.0000    0.0000 0.0000
     -0.0000    1.0000 - 0.0000 0.0000
     -0.0000    0.0000    1.0000 0.0000
     -0.0000 - 0.0000        0 1.0000

>> A '

Ans =

      0.9389 - 0.5839 - 1.2820 - 0.5038
     -0.0391    1.3050 - 0.4387 - 1.0834
      0.4686 - 0.0698 - 0.5693    1.2740
      0.6633    1.2727 - 0.0881    1.2890
```

EXERCISE 2-20

Given the function $f(x) = x^3$ calculate $f(2)$ and $f(b+2)$. We now consider the function of two variables $f(a, b) = a + b$ and we want to calculate $f(4, b)$, $f(a, 5)$ and $(f(3, 5))$.

```
>  f = 'x ^ 3'

f =

   x ^ 3

>> A = subs(f,2)

A =

   8

>> syms b
>> B = subs (f, b+2)

B =

   (b+2) ^ 3
```

```
>> syms a b
>> subs (a + b, a, 4)

Ans =

    4 + b

>> subs(a+b,{a,b},{3,5})

Ans =

    8
```

EXERCISE 2-21

Find the inverse function of $f(x) = \sin(x^2)$ and verify that the result is correct.

```
>> syms x
>> f = sin(x^2)

f =

   sin(x^2)

>> g = finverse (f)

g =

   asin(x) ^(1/2)

>> compose (f, g)

Ans =

    x
```

EXERCISE 2-22

Given functions $f(x) = \sin(\cos(x^{1/2})$ and $g(x) = \text{sqrt}(\tan(x^2))$ calculate the composite of f and g and the composite g and f. Also calculate the inverse of functions f and g.

```
>> syms x, f = (cos (x ^(1/2)));
>> g = sqrt (tan(x^2));
>> simple (compose(f,g))
```

Ans =

```
    sin (cos (tan(x^2) ^(1/4)))
```

```
>> simple (compose(g,f))
```

Ans =

```
    tan (sin (cos (x ^(1/2))) ^ 2) ^(1/2)
```

```
>> F = finverse (f)
```

F =

```
   acos(asin (x)) ^ 2
```

```
>> G = finverse (g)
```

G =

```
   atan(x^2) ^(1/2)
```

CHAPTER 3

■ ■ ■

Complex Numbers and Functions of Complex Variables

Complex Numbers

Complex numbers are easily implemented in MATLAB in standard binary form $a+bi$ or $a+bj$, where the symbol i or j represents the imaginary unit. It is not necessary to include the product symbol (the asterisk) before the imaginary unit, but if it is included, everything will still work correctly. However, it is important that spaces are not introduced between the imaginary unit and its coefficient.

A complex number can have a symbolic real or imaginary part, and operations on complex numbers can be carried out in any mode of precision that is set with the command *format*. Therefore, it is possible to work with complex numbers in exact rational format via the command *format rat*.

The common operations (sum, difference, product, division and exponentiation) are carried out on complex numbers in the usual way. Examples are shown in Figure 3-1.

```
>> (3+21)+(5-6i)

ans =

  29.0000 - 6.0000i

>> (3+21)-(5-6i)

ans =

  19.0000 + 6.0000i

>> (3+21)*(5-6i)

ans =

  1.2000e+002 -1.4400e+002i

>> (3+21)/(5-6i)

ans =

   1.9672 + 2.3607i

>> (3+21)^(5-6i)

ans =

   7.7728e+006 -1.7281e+006i
```

Figure 3-1.

   Obviously, as the real numbers are a subset of the complex numbers, a function of complex variables will also be valid for real variables.

General Functions of Complex Variables

MATLAB has a range of preset general functions of complex variables, which of course will also be valid for integer, rational, and real variables. The most important functions are presented in the following sections.

Trigonometric Functions of a Complex Variable

Below is a table of the trigonometric functions of a complex variable and their inverses that MATLAB incorporates, illustrated with examples.

Function	Inverse
sin (z) *sine*	**asin(z)** *arcsine*
>> sin(5-6i)	>> asin(1-i)
ans =	ans =
-1 9343e + 002-5 7218e + 001i	0.6662 - 1.0613i
cos (z) *cosine*	**acos (z)** *arccosine*
>> cos(3 + 4i)	>> acos(-i)
ans =	ans =
-27.0349 - 3.8512i	1.5708 + 0.8814i
tan (z) *tangent*	**atan(z) and atan2(z)** *arctangent*
>> tan(pi/4i)	>> atan(-pi*i)
ans =	ans =
0 - 0.6558i	1.5708 - 0.3298i
csc (z) *inverse cosecant*	**acsc (z)** *arccosecant*
>> csc(1-i)	>> acsc(2i)
ans =	ans =
0.6215 + 0.3039i	0 - 0.4812i
sec (z) *secant*	**asec (z)** *arcsecant*
>> sec(-i)	>> asec(0.6481+0i)
ans =	ans =
0.6481	0 + 0.9999i
cot (z) *cotangent*	**acot (z)** *arccotangent*
>> cot(-j)	>> acot(1-6j)
ans =	ans =
0 + 1.3130i	0.0277 + 0.1635i

Hyperbolic Functions of a Complex Variable

Below is a table of the hyperbolic functions of a complex variable and their inverses that MATLAB incorporates, illustrated with examples.

Function	Inverse

sinh(z) *hyperbolic sine*
>> sinh(1+i)
ans =
    0.6350 + 1.2985i
	asinh(z) *arc hyperbolic sine*
	>> asinh(0.6350 + 1.2985i)
	ans =
	    1.0000 + 1.0000i

cosh(z) *hyperbolic cosine*
>> cosh(1-i)
ans =
    0.8337 - 0.9889i
	acosh(z) *arc hyperbolic cosine*
	>> acosh(0.8337 - 0.9889i)
	ans =
	    1.0000 - 1.0000i

tanh(z) *hyperbolic tangent*
>> tanh(3-5i)
ans =
    1.0042 + 0.0027i
	atanh(z) *arc hyperbolic tangent*
	>> atanh(3-41)
	ans =
	    -0.0263 - 1.5708i

csch(z) *hyperbolic cosecant*
>> csch(i)
ans =
    0 - 1.1884i
	acsch (z) *arc hyperbolic cosecant*
	>> acsch(- 1.1884i)
	ans =
	    0 + 1.0000i

sech(z) *hyperbolic secant*
>> sech(i^i)
ans=
    0.9788
	asech(z) *arc hyperbolic secant*
	>> asech(5-0i)
	ans =
	    0 + 1.3694i

coth(z) *hyperbolic cotangent*
>> coth(9+i)
ans =
    1.0000 - 0.0000i
	acoth(z) *arc hyperbolic cotangent*
	>> acoth(1-i)
	ans =
	    0.4024 + 0.5536i

Exponential and Logarithmic Functions of a Complex Variable

Below is a table of exponential and logarithmic functions that MATLAB incorporates, illustrated with examples.

Function	Meaning

exp (z)	*Base e exponential function (e ^ x)*
	
	`>> exp(1-i)`
	
	`ans =`
	
	`    1.4687 - 2.2874i`

log (x)	*Base e logarithm*
	
	`>> log(1.4687-2.2874i)`
	
	`ans =`
	
	`    1.0000 - 1.0000i`

log10 (x)	*Base 10 logarithm*
	
	`>> log10 (100 + 100i)`
	
	`ans =`
	
	`    2.1505 + 0.3411i`

log2 (x)	*Base 2 logarithm*
	
	`>> log2(4-6i)`
	
	`ans =`
	
	`    2.8502 - 1.4179i`

pow2 (x)	*Base 2 power function*
	
	`>> pow2(2.8502-1.4179i)`
	
	`ans =`
	
	`    3.9998 - 6.0000i`

sqrt (x)	*Square root*
	
	`>> sqrt(1+i)`
	
	`ans =`
	
	`    1.0987 + 0.4551i`

Specific Functions of a Complex Variable

MATLAB incorporates a group of functions specifically to work with moduli, arguments, and real and imaginary parts of complex numbers. Among these are the following:

Function	Meaning

abs (Z)	*The modulus (absolute value) of Z*
	`>> abs(12.425-8.263i)`
	`ans =`
	      `14.9217`

angle (Z)	*The argument of Z*
	`>> angle(12.425-8.263i)`
	`ans =`
	      `-0.5869`

conj (Z)	*The complex conjugate of Z*
	`>> conj(12.425-8.263i)`
	`ans =`
	      `12.4250 + 8.2630i`

real (Z)	*The real part of Z*
	`>> real(12.425-8.263i)`
	`ans =`
	      `12.4250`

imag (Z)	*The imaginary part of Z*
	`>> imag(12.425-8.263i)`
	`ans =`
	      `-8.2630`

floor (Z)	*Applies the floor function to real(Z) and imag(Z)*
	`>> floor(12.425-8.263i)`
	`ans =`
	      `12.0000 - 9.0000i`

(continued)

Function	Meaning
ceil (Z)	*Applies the ceil function to real(Z) and imag(Z)*
	`>> ceil(12.425-8.263i)`
	`ans =`
	`    13.0000 - 8.0000i`
round (Z)	*Applies the round function to real(Z) and imag(Z)*
	`>> round(12.425-8.263i)`
	`ans =`
	`    12.0000 - 8.0000i`
fix (Z)	*Applies the fix function to real(Z) and imag(Z)*
	`>> fix(12.425-8.263i)`
	`ans =`
	`    12.0000 8.0000i`

Basic Functions with a Complex Vector Argument

MATLAB enables you to work with complex matrices and vector functions. We must not forget that these functions are also valid for real variables, since the real numbers are a special case of the complex numbers, being complex numbers with zero imaginary part. Below is a table summarizing the specific functions of a complex vector that MATLAB offers. Later, when we tabulate the functions of a complex matrix variable, we will observe that all of them are also valid for vector variables, a vector being a particular case of a matrix.

max (V) *Maximum component (for complex vectors the max is calculated as the component with maximum absolute value)*

```
>> max([1-i 1+i 3-5i 6i])

ans =

     0 + 6.0000i

>> max([1, 0, -23, 12, 16])

ans =

    16
```

min (V) *Minimum component (for complex vectors the min is calculated as the component with minimum absolute value)*

```
>> min([1-i 1+i 3-5i 6i])

ans =

    1.0 - 1.0000i

>> min([1, 0, -23, 12, 16])

ans =

   -23
```

mean (V) *Arithmetic mean of the components of V*

```
>> mean([1-i 1+i 3-5i 6i])

ans =

    1.2500 + 0.2500i

>> mean([1, 0, -23, 12, 16])

ans =

    1.2000
```

median (V) *Median of the components of V*

```
>> median([1-i 1+i 3-5i 6i])

ans =

    2.0000 2.0000i

>> median([1, 0, - 23, 12, 16])

ans =

    1
```

(*continued*)

std (V)   *Standard deviation of the components of V*

```
>> std([1-i 1+i 3-5i 6i])

ans =

    4.7434

>> std([1, 0, -23, 12, 16])

ans =

    15.1888
```

sort (V)   *Sorts the components of V in ascending order. For complex vectors the order is determined by the absolute values of the components.*

```
>> sort([1-i 1+i 3-5i 6i])

ans =

  Columns 1 through 2

    1.0000 - 1.0000i   1.0000 + 1.0000i

  Columns 3 through 4

    3.0000 - 5.0i    6.0000i

>> sort([1, 0, -23, 12, 16])

ans =

    -23 0 1 12 16
```

sum (V)   *Sums the components of V*

```
>> sum([1-i 1+i 3-5i 6i])

ans =

    5.0000 + 1.0000i

>> sum([1, 0, -23, 12, 16])

ans =

    6
```

prod (V)   *Finds the product of the elements of V, so n!= prod(1:n)*

```
>> prod([1-i 1+i 3-5i 6i])

ans =

    60.0000 + 36.0000i

>> prod([1, 0, -23, 12, 16])

ans =

    0
```

(*continued*)

cumsum (V)   *Gives the cumulative sums of V*

```
>> cumsum([1-i 1+i 3-5i 6i])

ans =

   Columns 1 through 2

     1.0000 - 1.0000i   2.0000

   Columns 3 through 4

     5.0000 - 5.0000i 5.0000 + 1.0000i

>> cumsum([1, 0, -23, 12, 16])

ans =

   1 1 -22 -10 -6
```

cumprod (V)   *Gives the cumulative products of V*

```
>> cumprod([1-i 1+i 3-5i 6i])

ans =

   Columns 1 through 2

     1.0000 - 1.0000i   2.0000

   Columns 3 through 4

     6.0000 - 10.0000i 60.0000 + 36.0000i

>> cumprod([1, 0, -23, 12, 16])

ans =

   1    0    0    0    0
```

diff (V)   *Gives the vector of first differences of the components of V $(V_t - V_{t-1})$*

```
>> diff([1-i 1+i 3-5i 6i])

ans =

   0 + 2.0000i   2.0000 - 6.0000i   -3.0000 + 11.0000i

>> diff([1, 0, -23, 12, 16])

ans =

   -1 -23 35 4
```

(*continued*)

gradient (V)   *Gives the gradient of V*

```
> gradient([1-i 1+i 3-5i 6i])

ans =

   Columns 1 through 3

     0 + 2.0000i   1.0000 - 2.0000i   -0.5000 + 2.5000i

   Column 4

     -3.0000 + 11.0000i

>> gradient([1, 0, -23, 12, 16])

ans =

     -1.0000 -12.0000 6.0000 19.5000 4.0000
```

del2 (V)   *Gives the Laplacian of V (5-point discrete)*

```
>> del2([1-i 1+i 3-5i 6i])

ans =

   Columns 1 through 3

     2.2500 - 8.2500i   0.5000 - 2.0000i   -1.2500 + 4.2500i

   Column 4

     -3.0000 + 10.5000i

>> del2 ([1, 0, -23, 12, 16])

ans =

     -25.5000 -5.5000 14.5000 -7.7500 -30.0000
```

fft (V)   *Returns the discrete Fourier transform of V*

```
>> fft([1-i 1+i 3-5i 6i])

ans =

   Columns 1 through 3

     5.0000 + 1.0000i   -7.0000 + 3.0000i   3.0000 - 13.0000i

   Column 4

     3.0000 + 5.0000i

>> fft([1, 0, -23, 12, 16])

ans =

   Columns 1 through 3

     6.0000   14.8435 + 35.7894i   -15.3435 - 23.8824i

   Columns 4 through 5

     -15.3435 + 23.8824i   14.8435 - 35.7894i
```

(continued)

fft2 (V)	*Returns the two-dimensional discrete Fourier transform of V*

```
>> fft2([1-i 1+i 3-5i 6i])

ans =

   Columns 1 through 3

     5.0000 + 1.0000i  -7.0000 + 3.0000i   3.0000 - 13.0000i

   Column 4

     3.0000 + 5.0000i

>> fft2([1, 0, -23, 12, 16])

ans =

   Columns 1 through 3

     6.0000   14.8435 + 35.7894i  -15.3435 - 23.8824i

   Columns 4 through 5

     -15.3435 + 23.8824i    14.8435 - 35.7894i
```

ifft (V)	*Returns the inverse discrete Fourier transform of V*

```
>> ifft([1-i 1+i 3-5i 6i])

ans =

   Columns 1 through 3

     1.2500 + 0.2500i   0.7500 + 1.2500i   0.7500 - 3.2500i

   Column 4

     -1.7500 + 0.7500i

>> ifft([1, 0, -23, 12, 16])

ans =

   Columns 1 through 3

     1.2000    2.9687 - 7.1579i  -3.0687 + 4.7765i

   Columns 4 through 5

     -3.0687 - 4.7765i   2.9687 + 7.1579i
```

(continued)

ifft2 (V)   *Returns the inverse two dimensional discrete Fourier transform of V*

```
>> ifft2([1-i 1+i 3-5i 6i])

ans =

    Columns 1 through 3

       1.2500 + 0.2500i    0.7500 + 1.2500i    0.7500 - 3.2500i

    Column 4

       -1.7500 + 0.7500i

>> ifft2([1, 0, -23, 12, 16])

ans =

    Columns 1 through 3

       1.2000   2.9687 - 7.1579i   -3.0687 + 4.7765i

    Columns 4 through 5

       -3.0687 - 4.7765i    2.9687 + 7.1579i
```

Basic Functions with a Complex Matrix Argument

The functions described in the above table also support as an argument a complex matrix Z, in which case the result is a row vector whose components are the results of applying the function to each column of the matrix. Let us not forget that these functions are also valid for real variables.

---

max (Z)   *Returns a vector indicating the maximal components of each column of the matrix Z (for complex matrices the maximum is determined by the absolute values of the components)*

```
>> Z=[1-i 3i 5;-1+i 0 2i;6-5i 8i -7]

Z =

      1.0000 - 1.0000i        0 + 3.0000i    5.0000
     -1.0000 + 1.0000i        0              0 + 2.0000i
      6.0000 - 5.0000i        0 + 8.0000i   -7.0000

>> Z=[1-i 3i 5-12i;-1+i 0 2i;6-5i 8i -7+6i]

Z =

      1.0000 - 1.0000i    0 + 3.0000i    5.0000 - 12.0000i
     -1.0000 + 1.0000i    0              0 + 2.0000i
      6.0000 - 5.0000i    0 + 8.0000i   -7.0000 + 6.0000i

>> max(Z)

ans =

      6.0000 - 5.0000i    0 + 8.0000i    5.0000 - 12.0000i

>> Z1=[1 3 5;-1 0 2;6 8 -7]

Z1 =

      1    3    5
     -1    0    2
      6    8   -7

>> max(Z1)

ans =

      6    8    5
```

min (Z)   *Returns a vector indicating the minimal components of each column of the matrix Z (for complex matrices the minimum is determined by the absolute values of the components)*

```
>> min(Z)

ans =

      1.0000 - 1.0000i        0          0 + 2.0000i

>> min(Z1)

ans =

     -1    0   -7
```

---

mean (Z)	*Returns the vector of arithmetic means of the columns of the matrix Z*

```
>> mean(Z)

ans =

     2.0000 - 1.6667i   0 + 3.6667i   -0.6667 - 1.3333i

>> mean(Z1)

ans =

     2.0000     3.6667        0
```

median (Z)	*Returns the vector of medians of the columns of the matrix Z*

```
>> median(Z)

ans =

    -1.0000 + 1.0000i   0 + 3.0000i   -7.0000 + 6.0000i

>> median(Z1)

ans =

      1      3      2
```

std (Z)	*Returns the vector of standard deviations of the columns of the matrix Z*

```
>> std(Z)

ans =

     4.7258     4.0415     11.2101

>> std(Z1)

ans =

     3.6056     4.0415     6.2450
```

sort (Z)	*Sorts in ascending order the components of the columns of Z. For complex matrices the ordering is by absolute value*

```
>> sort(Z)

ans =

      1.0000 - 1.0000i   0              0 +  2.0000i
     -1.0000 + 1.0000i   0 + 3.0000i   -7.0000 +  6.0000i
      6.0000 - 5.0000i   0 + 8.0000i    5.0000 - 12.0000i

>> sort(Z1)

ans =

     -1     0    -7
      1     3     2
      6     8     5
```

(*continued*)

sum (Z)	*Returns the sum of the components of the columns of the matrix Z*

```
>> sum(Z)

ans =

    6.0000 - 5.0000i   0 + 11.0000i  -2.0000 - 4.0000i

>> sum(Z1)

ans =

    6    11    0
```

prod (Z)	*Returns the vector of products of the elements of the columns of the matrix Z*

```
>> prod(Z)

ans =

    1.0e+002 *

    0.1000 + 0.1200i        0      -2.2800 + 0.7400i

>> prod(Z1)

ans =

    -6     0    -70
```

cumsum (Z)	*Gives the matrix of cumulative sums of the columns of Z*

```
>> cumsum(Z)

ans =

    1.0000 - 1.0000i   0 + 3.0000i    5.0000 - 12.0000i
    0                  0 + 3.0000i    5.0000 - 10.0000i
    6.0000 - 5.0000i   0 + 11.0000i  -2.0000 -  4.0000i

>> cumsum(Z1)

ans =

    1    3    5
    0    3    7
    6   11    0
```

(*continued*)

cumprod (V)   *Returns the cumulative products of the columns of the matrix Z*

```
>> cumprod(Z)

ans =

    1.0e+002 *
    0.0100 - 0.0100i    0 + 0.0300i    0.0500 - 0.1200i
    0        + 0.0200i   0              0.2400 + 0.1000i
    0.1000 + 0.1200i    0             -2.2800 + 0.7400i

>> cumprod(Z1)

ans =

    1    3    5
   -1    0   10
   -6    0  -70
```

diff (Z)   *Returns the matrix of first differences of the components of the columns of Z*

```
>> diff(Z)

ans =

   -2.0000 + 2.0000i    0 - 3.0000i  -5.0000 + 14.0000i
    7.0000 - 6.0000i    0 + 8.0000i  -7.0000 +  4.0000i

>> diff(Z1)

ans =

   -2    -3    -3

    7     8    -9
```

gradient (Z)   *Returns the matrix of gradients of the columns of Z*

```
>> gradient(Z)

ans =

   -1.0000 + 4.0000i    2.0000 - 5.5000i   5.0000 - 15.0000i
    1.0000 - 1.0000i    0.5000 + 0.5000i       0 + 2.0000i
   -6.0000 + 13.0000i  -6.5000 + 5.5000i  -7.0000 - 2.0000i

>> gradient(Z1)

ans =

    2.0000   2.0000    2.0000
    1.0000   1.5000    2.0000
    2.0000  -6.5000  -15.0000
```

(continued)

87

del2 (V)   *Returns the discrete Laplacian of the columns of the matrix Z*

```
>> del2(Z)

ans =

        3.7500 - 6.7500i    1.5000 - 2.0000i    1.0000 - 7.2500i
        2.0000 - 1.2500i   -0.2500 + 3.5000i   -0.7500 - 1.7500i
        2.0000 - 5.7500i   -0.2500 - 1.0000i   -0.7500 - 6.2500i

>> del2(Z1)

ans =

        2.2500     2.7500    -1.5000
        2.5000     3.0000    -1.2500
       -2.0000    -1.5000    -5.7500
```

fft (Z)   *Returns the discrete Fourier transform of the columns of the matrix Z*

```
>> fft(Z)

ans =

        6.0000 - 5.0000i         0 + 11.0000i   -2.0000 -   4.0000i
        3.6962 + 7.0622i   -6.9282 -   1.0000i    5.0359 - 22.0622i
       -6.6962 - 5.0622i    6.9282 -   1.0000i   11.9641 -   9.9378i

>> fft(Z1)

ans =

        6.0000              11.0000                      0
       -1.5000 + 6.0622i   -1.0000 + 6.9282i    7.5000 - 7.7942i
       -1.5000 - 6.0622i   -1.0000 - 6.9282i    7.5000 + 7.7942i
```

fft2 (Z)   *Returns the two-dimensional discrete Fourier transform of the columns of the matrix Z*

```
>> fft2(Z)

ans =

        4.0000 +   2.0000i   19.9904 - 10.2321i   -5.9904 - 6.7679i
        1.8038 - 16.0000i    22.8827 + 28.9545i  -13.5981 + 8.2321i
       12.1962 - 16.0000i    -8.4019 +  4.7679i  -23.8827 - 3.9545i

>> fft2(Z1)

ans =

       17.0000               0.5000 -  9.5263i    0.5000 +  9.5263i
        5.0000 + 5.1962i     8.0000 + 13.8564i  -17.5000 -  0.8660i
        5.0000 - 5.1962i   -17.5000 +  0.8660i    8.0000 - 13.8564i
```

(continued)

ifft (Z)	*Returns the inverse discrete Fourier transforms of the columns of the matrix Z*

```
>> ifft(Z)

ans =

        2.0000 - 1.6667i        0 + 3.6667i   -0.6667 - 1.3333i
       -2.2321 - 1.6874i   2.3094 - 0.3333i    3.9880 - 3.3126i
        1.2321 + 2.3541i  -2.3094 - 0.3333i    1.6786 - 7.3541i

>> ifft(Z1)

ans =

        2.0000              3.6667                   0
       -0.5000 - 2.0207i   -0.3333 - 2.3094i   2.5000 + 2.5981i
       -0.5000 + 2.0207i   -0.3333 + 2.3094i   2.5000 - 2.5981i
```

ifft2 (Z)	*Returns the inverse two dimensional discrete Fourier transform of the columns of the matrix Z*

```
>> ifft2(Z)

ans =

        0.4444 + 0.2222i   -0.6656 - 0.7520i   2.2212 - 1.1369i
        1.3551 - 1.7778i   -2.6536 - 0.4394i  -0.9335 + 0.5298i
        0.2004 - 1.7778i   -1.5109 + 0.9147i   2.5425 + 3.2172i

>> ifft2(Z1)

ans =

        1.8889              0.0556 + 1.0585i    0.0556 - 1.0585i
        0.5556 - 0.5774i    0.8889 - 1.5396i   -1.9444 + 0.0962i
        0.5556 + 0.5774i   -1.9444 - 0.0962i    0.8889 + 1.5396i
```

General Functions with a Complex Matrix Argument

MATLAB incorporates a broad group of hyperbolic, trigonometric, exponential and logarithmic functions that support a complex matrix as an argument. Obviously, these functions also accept a complex vector as the argument, since a vector is a particular case of a matrix. All functions are applied element-wise to the matrix.

Trigonometric Functions of a Complex Matrix Variable

Below is a table of the trigonometric functions of a complex variable and their inverses that MATLAB incorporates, illustrated with examples. In the examples, the matrices Z and Z1 are those introduced in the first example concerning the sine function.

Trigonometric Functions

sin(z) *sine function*

```
>> Z=[1-i, 1+i, 2i;3-6i, 2+4

i, -i;i,2i,3i]

Z =

     1.0000 - 1.0000i    1.0000 + 1.0000i    0 + 2.0000i
     3.0000 - 6.0000i    2.0000 + 4.0000i    0 - 1.0000i
          0 + 1.0000i         0 + 2.0000i    0 + 3.0000i

>> Z1=[1,1,2;3,2,-1;1,2,3]

Z1 =

     1     1     2
     3     2    -1
     1     2     3

>> sin(Z)

ans =

   1.0e+002 *

     0.0130 - 0.0063i    0.0130 + 0.0063i    0 + 0.0363i
     0.2847 + 1.9969i    0.2483 - 0.1136i    0 - 0.0118i
          0 + 0.0118i         0 + 0.0363i    0 + 0.1002i

>> sin(Z1)

ans =

     0.8415  0.8415    0.9093
     0.1411  0.9093 -  0.8415
     0.8415  0.9093    0.1411
```

cos (z) *cosine function*

```
>> cos(Z)

ans =

   1.0e+002 *

     0.0083 + 0.0099i    0.0083 - 0.0099i    0.0376
    -1.9970 + 0.2847i   -0.1136 - 0.2481i    0.0154
     0.0154              0.0376              0.1007

>> cos(Z1)

ans =

     0.5403   0.5403   -0.4161
    -0.9900  -0.4161    0.5403
     0.5403  -0.4161   -0.9900
```

(continued)

Trigonometric Functions

tan (z) *tangent function*

```
>> tan(Z)

ans =

      0.2718 - 1.0839i    0.2718 + 1.0839i    0 + 0.9640i
     -0.0000 - 1.0000i   -0.0005 + 1.0004i    0 - 0.7616i
           0 + 0.7616i          0 + 0.9640i    0 + 0.9951i

>> tan(Z1)

ans =

      1.5574    1.5574   -2.1850
     -0.1425   -2.1850   -1.5574
      1.5574   -2.1850   -0.1425
```

csc (z) *cosecant function*

```
>> csc(Z)

ans =

      0.6215 + 0.3039i    0.6215 - 0.3039i    0 - 0.2757i
      0.0007 - 0.0049i    0.0333 + 0.0152i    0 + 0.8509i
           0 - 0.8509i          0 - 0.2757i    0 - 0.0998i

>> csc(Z1)

ans =

      1.1884    1.1884    1.0998
      7.0862    1.0998   -1.1884
      1.1884    1.0998    7.0862
```

sec (z) *secant function*

```
>> sec(Z)

ans =

      0.4983 - 0.5911i    0.4983 + 0.5911i    0.2658
     -0.0049 - 0.0007i   -0.0153 + 0.0333i    0.6481
      0.6481                    0.2658         0.0993

>> sec(Z1)

ans =

      1.8508    1.8508   -2.4030
     -1.0101   -2.4030    1.8508
      1.8508   -2.4030   -1.0101
```

(continued)

Trigonometric Functions

cot (z) *cotangent function*

```
>> cot(Z)

ans =

      0.2176 + 0.8680i    0.2176 - 0.8680i    0 - 1.0373i
     -0.0000 + 1.0000i   -0.0005 - 0.9996i    0 + 1.3130i
           0 - 1.3130i          0 - 1.0373i    0 - 1.0050i

>> cot(Z1)

ans =

      0.6421      0.6421    -0.4577
     -7.0153     -0.4577    -0.6421
      0.6421     -0.4577    -7.0153
```

Inverse Trigonometric Functions

asin (z) *arcsine function*

```
>> asin(Z)

ans =

      0.6662 - 1.0613i    0.6662 + 1.0613i    0 + 1.4436i
      0.4592 - 2.5998i    0.4539 + 2.1986i    0 - 0.8814i
           0 + 0.8814i          0 + 1.4436i    0 + 1.8184i

>> asin(Z1)

ans =

      1.5708              1.5708              1.5708 - 1.3170i
      1.5708 - 1.7627i    1.5708 - 1.3170i   -1.5708
      1.5708              1.5708 - 1.3170i    1.5708 - 1.7627i
```

acos (z) *arccosine function*

```
>> acos(Z)

ans =

      0.9046 + 1.0613i    0.9046 - 1.0613i    1.5708 - 1.4436i
      1.1115 + 2.5998i    1.1169 - 2.1986i    1.5708 + 0.8814i
      1.5708 - 0.8814i    1.5708 - 1.4436i    1.5708 - 1.8184i

>> acos(Z1)

ans =

      0                   0                   0 + 1.3170i
      0 + 1.7627i         0 + 1.3170i         3.1416
      0                   0 + 1.3170i         0 + 1.7627i
```

(*continued*)

atan(z) and atan2(z) *arctangent function*

```
>> atan(Z)
```

Warning: Singularity in ATAN. This warning will be removed in a future release.
        Consider using DBSTOP IF NANINF when debugging.
Warning: Singularity in ATAN. This warning will be removed in a future release.
        Consider using DBSTOP IF NANINF when debugging.

```
ans =

    1.0172 - 0.4024i    1.0172 + 0.4024i   -1.5708 + 0.5493i
    1.5030 - 0.1335i    1.4670 + 0.2006i         0 -    Infi
         0 +    Infi   -1.5708 + 0.5493i   -1.5708 + 0.3466i

>> atan(Z1)

ans =

    0.7854    0.7854    1.1071
    1.2490    1.1071   -0.7854
    0.7854    1.1071    1.2490
```

acsc (z) *arccosecant function*

```
>> acsc(Z)

ans =

    0.4523 + 0.5306i    0.4523 - 0.5306i    0 - 0.4812i
    0.0661 + 0.1332i    0.0982 - 0.1996i    0 + 0.8814i
         0 - 0.8814i         0 - 0.4812i    0 - 0.3275i

>> acsc(Z1)

ans =

    1.5708    1.5708    0.5236
    0.3398    0.5236   -1.5708
    1.5708    0.5236    0.3398
```

asec (z) *arcsecant function*

```
>> asec(Z)

ans =

    1.1185 - 0.5306i    1.1185 + 0.5306i    1.5708 + 0.4812i
    1.5047 - 0.1332i    1.4726 + 0.1996i    1.5708 - 0.8814i
    1.5708 + 0.8814i    1.5708 + 0.4812i    1.5708 + 0.3275i

>> asec(Z1)

ans =

         0         0    1.0472
    1.2310    1.0472    3.1416
         0    1.0472    1.2310
```

(continued)

93

acot (z) *arccotangent function*

```
>> acot(Z)

warning: singularity in atan. this warning will be removed in a future release.
        consider using dbstop if naninf when debugging.

ans =

      0.5536 + 0.4024i   0.5536 - 0.4024i   0 - 0.5493i
      0.0678 + 0.1335i   0.1037 - 0.2006i   0 +    infi
           0 -    infi        0 - 0.5493i   0 - 0.3466i

>> acot(Z1)

ans =

      0.7854   0.7854    0.4636
      0.3218   0.4636   -0.7854
      0.7854   0.4636    0.3218
```

Hyperbolic Functions of a Complex Matrix Variable

Below is a table of the hyperbolic functions of a complex variable and their inverses that MATLAB incorporates, illustrated with examples. The matrices Z1 and Z are the same as for the previous examples.

Hyperbolic Functions

sinh (z) *hyperbolic sine function*

```
>> sinh(Z)

ans =

      0.6350 - 1.2985i   0.6350 + 1.2985i   0 + 0.9093i
      9.6189 + 2.8131i  -2.3707 - 2.8472i   0 - 0.8415i
           0 + 0.8415i        0 + 0.9093i   0 + 0.1411i

>> sinh(Z1)

ans =

      1.1752    1.1752    3.6269
     10.0179    3.6269   -1.1752
      1.1752    3.6269   10.0179
```

(continued)

Hyperbolic Functions

cosh (z) *hyperbolic cosine function*

```
>> cosh(Z)

ans =

     0.8337 - 0.9889i    0.8337 + 0.9889i   -0.4161
     9.6667 + 2.7991i   -2.4591 - 2.7448i    0.5403
     0.5403             -0.4161             -0.9900

>> cosh(Z1)

ans =

     1.5431     1.5431     3.7622
    10.0677     3.7622     1.5431
     1.5431     3.7622    10.0677
```

tanh (z) *hyperbolic tangent function*

```
>> tanh(Z)

ans =

     1.0839 - 0.2718i    1.0839 + 0.2718i    0 - 2.1850i
     0.9958 + 0.0026i    1.0047 + 0.0364i    0 - 1.5574i
          0 + 1.5574i         0 - 2.1850i    0 - 0.1425i

>> tanh(Z1)

ans =

     0.7616     0.7616     0.9640
     0.9951     0.9640    -0.7616
     0.7616     0.9640     0.9951
```

csch (z) *hyperbolic cosecant function*

```
>> csch(Z)

ans =

     0.3039 + 0.6215i    0.3039 - 0.6215i    0 - 1.0998i
     0.0958 - 0.0280i   -0.1727 + 0.2074i    0 + 1.1884i
          0 - 1.1884i         0 - 1.0998i    0 - 7.0862i

>> csch(Z1)

ans =

     0.8509     0.8509     0.2757
     0.0998     0.2757    -0.8509
     0.8509     0.2757     0.0998
```

(continued)

Hyperbolic Functions

sech (z) *hyperbolic secant function*

```
>> sech(Z)

ans =

    0.4983 + 0.5911i   0.4983 - 0.5911i   -2.4030
    0.0954 - 0.0276i  -0.1811 + 0.2021i    1.8508
    1.8508            -2.4030             -1.0101

>> sech(Z1)

ans =

    0.6481    0.6481    0.2658
    0.0993    0.2658    0.6481
    0.6481    0.2658    0.0993
```

coth (z) *hyperbolic cotangent function*

```
>> coth(Z)

ans =

    0.8680 + 0.2176i   0.8680 - 0.2176i   0 + 0.4577i
    1.0042 - 0.0027i   0.9940 - 0.0360i   0 + 0.6421i
         0 - 0.6421i        0 + 0.4577i   0 + 7.0153i

>> coth(Z1)

ans =

    1.3130    1.3130    1.0373
    1.0050    1.0373   -1.3130
    1.3130    1.0373    1.0050
```

Inverse Hyperbolic Functions

asinh (z) *arc hyperbolic sine function*

```
>> asinh(Z)

ans =

    1.0613 - 0.6662i   1.0613 + 0.6662i   1.3170 + 1.5708i
    2.5932 - 1.1027i   2.1836 + 1.0969i        0 - 1.5708i
         0 + 1.5708i   1.3170 + 1.5708i   1.7627 + 1.5708i

>> asinh(Z1)

ans =

    0.8814    0.8814    1.4436
    1.8184    1.4436   -0.8814
    0.8814    1.4436    1.8184
```

(*continued*)

Inverse Hyperbolic Functions

acosh (z) *arc hyperbolic cosine function*

```
>> acosh(Z)

ans =

     1.0613 - 0.9046i   1.0613 + 0.9046i   1.4436 + 1.5708i
     2.5998 - 1.1115i   2.1986 + 1.1169i   0.8814 - 1.5708i
     0.8814 + 1.5708i   1.4436 + 1.5708i   1.8184 + 1.5708i

>> acosh(Z1)

ans =

          0          0     1.3170
     1.7627     1.3170     0 + 3.1416i
          0     1.3170     1.7627
```

atanh (z) *hyperbolic arctangent function*

```
>> atanh(Z)

ans =

     0.4024 - 1.0172i   0.4024 + 1.0172i   0 + 1.1071i
     0.0656 - 1.4377i   0.0964 + 1.3715i   0 - 0.7854i
          0 + 0.7854i        0 + 1.1071i   0 + 1.2490i

>> atanh(Z1)

ans =

          inf              inf          0.5493 + 1.5708i
     0.3466 + 1.5708i  0.5493 + 1.5708i     -inf
          inf          0.5493 + 1.5708i  0.3466 + 1.5708i
```

acsch (z) *arc hyperbolic cosecant function*

```
>> acsch(Z)

ans =

     0.5306 + 0.4523i   0.5306 - 0.4523i   0 - 0.5236i
     0.0672 + 0.1334i   0.1019 - 0.2003i   0 + 1.5708i
          0 - 1.5708i        0 - 0.5236i   0 - 0.3398i

>> acsch(Z1)

ans =

     0.8814     0.8814     0.4812
     0.3275     0.4812    -0.8814
     0.8814     0.4812     0.3275
```

(continued)

Inverse Hyperbolic Functions

asech (z) *arc hyperbolic secant function*

```
>> asech(Z)

ans =

     0.5306 + 1.1185i   0.5306 - 1.1185i   0.4812 - 1.5708i
     0.1332 + 1.5047i   0.1996 - 1.4726i   0.8814 + 1.5708i
     0.8814 - 1.5708i   0.4812 - 1.5708i   0.3275 - 1.5708i

>> asech(Z1)

ans =

     0            0            0 + 1.0472i
     0 + 1.2310i  0 + 1.0472i  0 + 3.1416i
     0            0 + 1.0472i  0 + 1.2310i
```

acoth (z) *arc hyperbolic cotangent function*

```
>> acoth(Z)

ans =

     0.4024 + 0.5536i   0.4024 - 0.5536i   0 - 0.4636i
     0.0656 + 0.1331i   0.0964 - 0.1993i   0 + 0.7854i
          0 - 0.7854i        0 - 0.4636i   0 - 0.3218i

>> acoth(Z1)

ans =

        Inf      Inf    0.5493
     0.3466   0.5493     -Inf
        Inf   0.5493    0.3466
```

Exponential and Logarithmic Functions of a Complex Matrix Variable

Below is a table of the exponential and logarithmic functions that MATLAB incorporates, illustrated with examples. The matrices Z1 and Z are the same as for the previous examples.

Function	Meaning

exp (z)	*Base e exponential function (e ^ x)*
	
	`>> exp(Z)`
	
	`ans =`
	
	`    1.4687 - 2.2874i   1.4687 + 2.2874i   -0.4161 + 0.9093i`
	`   19.2855 + 5.6122i  -4.8298 - 5.5921i    0.5403 - 0.8415i`
	`    0.5403 + 0.8415i  -0.4161 + 0.9093i   -0.9900 + 0.1411i`
	
	`>> exp(Z1)`
	
	`ans =`
	
	`    2.7183 2.7183  7.3891`
	`   20.0855 7.3891  0.3679`
	`    2.7183 7.3891 20.0855`

log (x)	*Base e logarithm*
	
	`>> log(Z)`
	
	`ans =`
	
	`    0.3466 - 0.7854i   0.3466 + 0.7854i   0.6931 + 1.5708i`
	`    1.9033 - 1.1071i   1.4979 + 1.1071i        0 - 1.5708i`
	`         0 + 1.5708i   0.6931 + 1.5708i   1.0986 + 1.5708i`
	
	`>> log(Z1)`
	
	`ans =`
	
	`        0      0      0.6931`
	`    1.0986   0.6931      0 + 3.1416i`
	`        0   0.6931   1.0986`

log10 (x)	*Base 10 logarithm*
	
	`>> log10(Z)`
	
	`ans =`
	
	`    0.1505 - 0.3411i   0.1505 + 0.3411i   0.3010 + 0.6822i`
	`    0.8266 - 0.4808i   0.6505 + 0.4808i        0 - 0.6822i`
	`         0 + 0.6822i   0.3010 + 0.6822i   0.4771 + 0.6822i`
	
	`>> log10(Z1)`
	
	`ans =`
	
	`        0      0      0.3010`
	`    0.4771   0.3010      0 + 1.3644i`
	`        0   0.3010   0.4771`

(continued)

Function	Meaning
log2 (x)	*Base 2 logarithm*

```
>> log2(Z)

ans =

      0.5000 - 1.1331i    0.5000 + 1.1331i    1.0000 + 2.2662i
      2.7459 - 1.5973i    2.1610 + 1.5973i         0 - 2.2662i
           0 + 2.2662i    1.0000 + 2.2662i    1.5850 + 2.2662i

>> log2(Z1)

ans =

        0    0        1.0000
   1.5850   1.0000        0 + 4.5324i
        0   1.0000   1.5850
```

| **pow2 (x)** | *Base 2 power function* |

```
>> pow2(Z)

ans =

      1.5385 - 1.2779i    1.5385 + 1.2779i    0.1835 + 0.9830i
     -4.2054 + 6.8055i   -3.7307 + 1.4427i    0.7692 - 0.6390i
      0.7692 + 0.6390i    0.1835 + 0.9830i   -0.4870 + 0.8734i

>> pow2(Z1)

ans =

   2.0000 2.0000 4.0000
   8.0000 4.0000 0.5000
   2.0000 4.0000 8.0000
```

| **sqrt (x)** | *Square root function* |

```
>> sqrt(Z)

ans =

      1.0987 - 0.4551i    1.0987 + 0.4551i    1.0000 + 1.0000i
      2.2032 - 1.3617i    1.7989 + 1.1118i    0.7071 - 0.7071i
      0.7071 + 0.7071i    1.0000 + 1.0000i    1.2247 + 1.2247i

>> sqrt(Z1)

ans =

   1.0000   1.0000   1.4142
   1.7321   1.4142        0 + 1.0000i
   1.0000   1.4142   1.7321
```

Specific Functions of Complex Matrix Variables

MATLAB incorporates a group of functions of a complex variable specifically to work with moduli, arguments, and real and imaginary parts. Among these functions are the following:

Function	Meaning
abs (Z)	*The modulus (absolute value) of Z*

```
>> abs(Z)

ans =

    1.4142    1.4142    2.0000
    6.7082    4.4721    1.0000
    1.0000    2.0000    3.0000

>> abs(Z1)

ans =

    1   1   2
    3  -2  -1
    1   2   3
```

Function	Meaning
angle (Z)	*The argument of Z*

```
>> angle(Z)

ans =

   -0.7854    0.7854    1.5708
   -1.1071    1.1071   -1.5708
    1.5708    1.5708    1.5708

>> angle(Z1)

ans =

    0        0        0
    0        0        3.1416
    0        0        0
```

Function	Meaning
conj (Z)	*The complex conjugate of Z*

```
>> conj(Z)

ans =

    1.0000 + 1.0000i    1.0000 - 1.0000i    0 - 2.0000i
    3.0000 + 6.0000i    2.0000 - 4.0000i    0 + 1.0000i
         0 - 1.0000i         0 - 2.0000i    0 - 3.0000i

>> conj(Z1)

ans =

    1   1   2
    2  -3  -1
    1   2   3
```

(continued)

Function	Meaning
real (Z)	*The real part of Z*

```
>> real(Z)

ans =

        1    1    0
        3    2    0
        0    0    0

>> real(Z1)

ans =

        1  1  2
        2 -3 -1
        1  2  3
```

imag (Z)	*The imaginary part of Z*

```
>> imag(Z)

ans =

       -1   1   2
       -4   6  -1
        1   2   3

>> imag(Z1)

ans =

        0 0 0
        0 0 0
        0 0 0
```

floor (Z)	*Applies the floor function to real(Z) and imag(Z)*

```
>> floor(12.357*Z)

ans =

      12.0000 - 13.0000i   12.0000 + 12.0000i   0 + 24.0000i
      37.0000 - 75.0000i   24.0000 + 49.0000i   0 - 13.0000i
            0 + 12.0000i          0 + 24.0000i   0 + 37.0000i

>> floor(12.357*Z1)

ans =

      12   12    24
      37   24   -13
      12  -24   -37
```

(continued)

Function	Meaning
ceil (Z)	*Applies the ceil function to real(Z) and imag(Z)*

```
>> ceil(12.357*Z)

ans =

13.0000 - 12.0000i   13.0000 + 13.0000i   0 + 25.0000i
38.0000 - 74.0000i   25.0000 + 50.0000i   0 - 12.0000i
       0 + 13.0000i          0 + 25.0000i   0 + 38.0000i

>> ceil(12.357*Z1)

ans =

    13  13   25
    38  25  -12
    13  25   38
```

round (Z)	*Applies the function round to real(Z) and imag(Z)*

```
>> round(12.357*Z)

ans =

    12.0000 - 12.0000i   12.0000 + 12.0000i    0 + 25.0000i
    37.0000 - 74.0000i   25.0000 + 49.0000i    0 - 12.0000i
           0 + 12.0000i          0 + 25.0000i    0 + 37.0000i

>> round(12.357*Z1)

ans =

    12 -12 -25
    37  25 -12
    12  25  37
```

fix (Z)	*Applies the function fix to real(Z) and imag(Z)*

```
>> fix(12.357*Z)

ans =

    12.0000 - 12.0000i   12.0000 + 12.0000i    0 + 24.0000i
    37.0000 - 74.0000i   24.0000 + 49.0000i    0 - 12.0000i
           0 + 12.0000i          0 + 24.0000i    0 + 37.0000i

>> fix(12.357*Z1)

ans =

    12  12  24
    24 -37  12
    12 -24 -37
```

(continued)

Operations with Real and Complex Matrix Variables

MATLAB includes the usual operations of sum, difference, product, power, exponentiation and inversion for complex matrix variables. Obviously all these operations will also be valid for real matrix variables. The following table summarizes the operations that are valid both for numerical real and complex matrix variables and algebraic matrix variables.

A + B	*Matrix sum*

```
>> A=[1+i, 1-i, 2i; -i, -3i, 6-5i;2+3i, 2-3i, i]

A =

     1.0000 + 1.0000i   1.0000 - 1.0000i        0 + 2.0000i
          0 - 1.0000i        0 - 3.0000i   6.0000 - 5.0000i
     2.0000 + 3.0000i   2.0000 - 3.0000i        0 + 1.0000i

>> B=[i, -i, 2i; 1-i, 7-3i, 2-5i;8-6i, 5-i, 1+i]

B =

          0 + 1.0000i        0 - 1.0000i        0 + 2.0000i
     1.0000 - 1.0000i   7.0000 - 3.0000i   2.0000 - 5.0000i
     8.0000 - 6.0000i   5.0000 - 1.0000i   1.0000 + 1.0000i

>> A1=[1 6 2;3 5 0; 2 4 -1]

A1 =

     1     6     2
     3     5     0
     2     4    -1

>> B1=[-3 -6 1;-3 -5 2; 12 14 -10]

B1 =

     -3    -6     1
     -3    -5     2
     12    14   -10

>> A+B

ans =

      1.0000 + 2.0000i   1.0000 - 2.0000i        0 +  4.0000i
      1.0000 - 2.0000i   7.0000 - 6.0000i   8.0000 - 10.0000i
     10.0000 - 3.0000i   7.0000 - 4.0000i   1.0000 +  2.0000i

>> A1+B1

ans =

     -2     0     3
      0     0     2
     14    18   -11
```

(*continued*)

A - B *Difference of matrices*

```
>> A-B

ans =

      1.0000             1.0000                    0
     -1.0000            -7.0000              4.0000
     -6.0000 + 9.0000i  -3.0000 - 2.0000i  -1.0000

>> A1-B1

ans =

    4    12    1

    6    10   -2

  -10   -10    9
```

A * B *Product of matrices*

```
>> A * B

ans =

     11.0000 + 15.0000i    7.0000 -  1.0000i   -7.0000 -  3.0000i
     16.0000 - 79.0000i   15.0000 - 52.0000i   -2.0000 -  5.0000i
      2.0000 +  5.0000i    9.0000 - 24.0000i  -18.0000 - 11.0000i

>> A1*B1

ans =

     3    -8    -7
   -24   -43    13
   -30   -46    20
```

A^n *nth power of the matrix A*

```
>> A^3

ans =

   1.0e+002 *

   0.1000 - 0.3400i  -0.3200 - 0.1200i   0.3400 - 0.3600i
   0.0900 - 0.0300i  -1.0700 + 0.2100i  -2.2500 - 0.6700i
   0.3700 - 0.7900i  -1.0300 - 0.0300i  -0.0700 - 0.3700i

>> A1^3

ans =

   155   358    46
   159   347    30
   106   232    19
```

(continued)

P^A   *Scalar p raised to the power of the matrix A*

```
>> 3^A

ans =

        0.0159 - 1.2801i   -0.5297 +  2.8779i   -1.9855 +  3.0796i
      -10.3372 + 0.4829i   17.0229 + 12.9445i   14.7327 + 20.1633i
       -5.0438 + 0.2388i    7.0696 +  6.9611i    5.7189 +  9.5696i

>> 3^A1

ans =

1.0e+003 *

    2.2230    4.9342    0.4889
    2.1519    4.7769    0.4728
    1.4346    3.1844    0.3156
```

A'   *Transpose of the matrix A*

```
>> A'

ans =

     1.0000 - 1.0000i        0 + 1.0000i   2.0000 - 3.0000i
     1.0000 + 1.0000i        0 + 3.0000i   2.0000 + 3.0000i
          0 - 2.0000i   6.0000 + 5.0000i        0 - 1.0000i

>> A1'

ans =

     1     3     2
     6     5     4
     2     0    -1
```

(*continued*)

A^-1   *Inverse of the matrix A*

```
>> A^-1

ans =

     -2.5000 + 2.0000i  -0.0500 + 0.6500i   0.8500 - 1.0500i
      0.5000 + 3.0000i   0.5500 + 0.3500i  -0.3500 - 0.9500i
     -1.0000 - 1.0000i  -0.2000 + 0.1000i   0.4000 + 0.3000i

>> A1^-1

ans =

     -0.2941    0.8235   -0.5882
      0.1765   -0.2941    0.3529
      0.1176    0.4706   -0.7647

>> A*A^-1

ans =

      1.0000             0.0000 - 0.0000i  -0.0000 + 0.0000i
     -0.0000 - 0.0000i   1.0000 + 0.0000i   0.0000
      0.0000 + 0.0000i   0.0000             1.0000 + 0.0000i

>> A1*A1^-1

ans =

      1.0000   -0.0000        0
     -0.0000    1.0000        0
     -0.0000   -0.0000   1.0000
```

A\B   *If A is square A\B = (A⁻¹) * B and if A is not square, A\B is the solution in the sense of least-squares of the system AX = B*

```
>> A\B

ans =

     -0.9000 - 15.3000i   6.8000 + 1.1000i   1.0500 - 3.6500i
    -10.6000 -  5.2000i   5.2000 - 4.1000i  -2.5500 - 2.3500i
      5.9000 -  0.7000i   0.2000 + 3.4000i   2.2000 - 0.1000i

>> A1\B1

ans =

     -8.6471 -10.5882   7.2353
      4.5882   5.3529  -3.9412
    -10.9412 -13.7647   8.7059
```

(continued)

B/A	Equivalent to A\B

```
>> B/A

ans =

         3.0000 -  5.0000i  -0.5000 -  1.0000i  -0.5000 +  2.0000i
         5.0000 + 27.0000i   5.6000 +  2.7000i  -3.2000 -  8.9000i
        -2.5000 + 43.5000i   6.3000 +  6.6000i  -2.1000 - 17.2000i

>> A'\B'

ans =

         3.0000 +  5.0000i   5.0000 - 27.0000i  -2.5000 - 43.5000i
        -0.5000 +  1.0000i   5.6000 -  2.7000i   6.3000 -  6.6000i
        -0.5000 -  2.0000i  -3.2000 +  8.9000i  -2.1000 + 17.2000i

>> B1/A1

ans =

        -0.0588   -0.2353   -1.1176
         0.2353   -0.0588   -1.5294
        -2.2353    1.0588    5.5294

>> A1'\B1'

ans =

        -0.0588    0.2353   -2.2353
        -0.2353   -0.0588    1.0588
        -1.1176   -1.5294    5.5294
```

EXERCISE 3-1

Given the complex numbers $z_1 = 1-i$, and $z_2 = 5i$, calculate: $z_1^3 \, z_1^2/z_2^4$, $z_1^{1/2}$, $z_2^{3/2}$, $\ln(z_1+z_2)$, $\sin(z_1-z_2)$, and $\tanh(z_1/z_2)$.

```
>> Z1=1-i

Z1 =

   1.0000 - 1.0000i

>> Z2=5i

Z2 =

        0 + 5.0000i

>> Z1^3
```

```
ans =

  -2.0000 - 2.0000i

>> Z1^2/Z2^4

ans =

      0 - 0.0032i

>> sqrt(Z1)

ans =

  1.0987 - 0.4551i

>> sqrt(Z2^3)

ans =

  7.9057 - 7.9057i

>> log(Z1+Z2)

ans =

  1.4166 + 1.3258i

>> sin(Z1-Z2)

ans =

  1.6974e+002 -1.0899e+002i

>> tanh(Z1/Z2)

ans =

  -0.2052 - 0.1945i
```

EXERCISE 3-2

Perform the following operations with complex numbers:

$$\frac{i^8 - i^{-8}}{3 - 4i} + 1, \ i^{\sin(1+i)}, \ (2 + \ln(i))^{\frac{1}{i}}, \ (1+i)^i \ i^{\ln(1+i)}, \ (1+\sqrt{3i})^{1-i}$$

```
>> (i^8-i^(-8))/(3-4*i) + 1

ans =

    1

>> i^(sin(1+i))

ans =

 -0.16665202215166 + 0.329041394503071i

>> (2+log(i))^(1/i)

ans =

  1.15809185259777 - 1.56388053989023i

>> (1+i)^i

ans =

  0.42882900629437 + 0.15487175246425i

>> i^(log(1+i))

ans =

  0.24911518828716 + 0.15081974884717i

>> (1+sqrt(3)*i)^(1-i)

ans =

  5.34581479196611 + 1.97594883452873i
```

EXERCISE 3-3

Find the real part, imaginary part, modulus and argument of each of the following:

$$i^{3+i}, \ \left(1+\sqrt{3}i\right)^{1-i}, \ i^{i}, \ i^{i}$$

```
>> Z1=i^3*i; Z2=(1+sqrt(3)*i)^(1-i); Z3=(i^i)^i;Z4=i^i;

>> format short

>> real([Z1 Z2 Z3 Z4])
ans =

    1.0000    5.3458    0.0000    0.2079

>> imag([Z1 Z2 Z3 Z4])

ans =

         0    1.9759   -1.0000         0

>> abs([Z1 Z2 Z3 Z4])

ans =

    1.0000    5.6993    1.0000    0.2079

>> angle([Z1 Z2 Z3 Z4])

ans =

         0    0.3541   -1.5708         0
```

EXERCISE 3-4

Consider the matrix *M* defined as the product of the imaginary unit i with the square matrix of order 3 whose elements are, row by row, the first nine positive integers.

Find the square of *M*, its square root and its exponential to base 2 and -2.

Find the element-wise Naperian logarithm of *M* and its element-wise base e exponential.

Find log(*M*) and e^M.

```
>> M=i*[1 2 3;4 5 6;7 8 9]

M =
        0 + 1.0000i      0 + 2.0000i      0 + 3.0000i
        0 + 4.0000i      0 + 5.0000i      0 + 6.0000i
        0 + 7.0000i      0 + 8.0000i      0 + 9.0000i

>> C=M^2

C =

   -30    -36    -42
   -66    -81    -96
  -102   -126   -150

>> D=M^(1/2)

D =

    0.8570 - 0.2210i    0.5370 + 0.2445i    0.2169 + 0.7101i
    0.7797 + 0.6607i    0.9011 + 0.8688i    1.0224 + 1.0769i
    0.7024 + 1.5424i    1.2651 + 1.4930i    1.8279 + 1.4437i

>> 2^M

ans =

    0.7020 - 0.6146i   -0.1693 - 0.2723i   -0.0407 + 0.0699i
   -0.2320 - 0.3055i    0.7366 - 0.3220i   -0.2947 - 0.3386i
   -0.1661 + 0.0036i   -0.3574 - 0.3717i    0.4513 - 0.7471i

>> (-2)^M

ans =

   17.3946 -16.8443i    4.3404 - 4.5696i   -7.7139 + 7.7050i
    1.5685 - 1.8595i    1.1826 - 0.5045i   -1.2033 + 0.8506i
  -13.2575 +13.1252i   -3.9751 + 3.5607i    6.3073 - 6.0038i
```

```
>> log(M)

ans =

        0 + 1.5708i    0.6931 + 1.5708i    1.0986 + 1.5708i
   1.3863 + 1.5708i    1.6094 + 1.5708i    1.7918 + 1.5708i
   1.9459 + 1.5708i    2.0794 + 1.5708i    2.1972 + 1.5708i

>> exp(M)

ans =

   0.5403 + 0.8415i   -0.4161 + 0.9093i   -0.9900 + 0.1411i
  -0.6536 - 0.7568i    0.2837 - 0.9589i    0.9602 - 0.2794i
   0.7539 + 0.6570i   -0.1455 + 0.9894i   -0.9111 + 0.4121i


>> logm(M)

ans =

  -5.4033 - 0.8472i   11.9931 - 0.3109i   -5.3770 + 0.8846i
  12.3029 + 0.0537i  -22.3087 + 0.8953i   12.6127 + 0.4183i
  -4.7574 + 1.6138i   12.9225 + 0.7828i   -4.1641 + 0.6112i

>> expm(M)

ans =

   0.3802 - 0.6928i   -0.3738 - 0.2306i   -0.1278 + 0.2316i
  -0.5312 - 0.1724i    0.3901 - 0.1434i   -0.6886 - 0.1143i
  -0.4426 + 0.3479i   -0.8460 - 0.0561i   -0.2493 - 0.4602i
```

EXERCISE 3-5

Consider the vector sum V of the complex vector $Z = (i, -i, i)$ and the real vector $R = (0,1,1)$. Find the mean, median, standard deviation, variance, sum, product, maximum and minimum of the elements of V, as well as its gradient, its discrete Fourier transform and its inverse.

```
>> Z=[i,-i,i]

Z =

        0 + 1.0000i        0 - 1.0000i        0 + 1.0000i

>> R=[0,1,1]

R =

     0     1     1
```

```
>> V=Z+R

V =

       0 + 1.0000i    1.0000 - 1.0000i    1.0000 + 1.0000i

>> [mean(V),median(V),std(V),var(V),sum(V),prod(V),max(V),min(V)]'

ans =

   0.6667 - 0.3333i
   1.0000 + 1.0000i
   1.2910
   1.6667
   2.0000 - 1.0000i
        0 - 2.0000i
   1.0000 + 1.0000i
        0 - 1.0000i

>> gradient(V)

ans =

   1.0000 - 2.0000i    0.5000    0 + 2.0000i

>> fft(V)

ans =

   2.0000 + 1.0000i  -2.7321 + 1.0000i    0.7321 + 1.0000i

>> ifft(V)

ans =

   0.6667 + 0.3333i    0.2440 + 0.3333i   -0.9107 + 0.3333i
```

EXERCISE 3-6

Given matrices:

$$A1 = \begin{bmatrix} 1 & 0 & 0 \\ 0 & 1 & 0 \\ 0 & 0 & 1 \end{bmatrix} \; A2 = \begin{bmatrix} 0 & 1 & 0 \\ 0 & 0 & 1 \\ 0 & 0 & 0 \end{bmatrix} \; B1 = \begin{bmatrix} 0 & 1 & 2 \\ 0 & -1 & 3 \\ 0 & 0 & 0 \end{bmatrix} \; B2 = \begin{bmatrix} -i & i & -i \\ 0 & 0 & i \\ 0 & 0 & i \end{bmatrix}$$

$$C1 = \begin{bmatrix} 1 & -1 & 0 \\ -1 & sqrt(2)i & -sqrt(2)i \\ 0 & 0 & -1 \end{bmatrix} \; C2 = \begin{bmatrix} 0 & 2 & 1 \\ 1 & 0 & 0 \\ 1 & -1 & 0 \end{bmatrix}$$

First calculate $A = A1 + A2$, $B = B1 - B2$ and $C = C1 + C2$.

Then calculate $AB - BA$, $A^2 + B^2 + C^2$, ABC, $sqrt(A) + sqrt(B) - sqrt(C)$, $(e^B + e^C)$, their transposes and their inverses.

Finally, check that the product of each of the matrices A, B and C with their inverses gives the identity matrix.

```
>> A1=eye(3)

A1 =

     1     0     0
     0     1     0
     0     0     1

>> A2=[0 1 0;0 0 1;0 0 0]

A2 =

     0     1     0
     0     0     1
     0     0     0

>> A= A1+A2

A =

     1     1     0
     0     1     1
     0     0     1

>> B1=[0 1 2;0 -1 3;0 0 0]
```

```
B1 =

    0    1    2
    0   -1    3
    0    0    0

>> B2=[-i i -i;0 0 i;0 0 i]

B2 =

      0 - 1.0000i        0 + 1.0000i        0 - 1.0000i
      0                  0                  0 + 1.0000i
      0                  0                  0 + 1.0000i

>> B=B1-B2

B =

      0 + 1.0000i   1.0000 - 1.0000i   2.0000 + 1.0000i
      0                 -1.0000        3.0000 - 1.0000i
      0                  0                  0 - 1.0000i

>> C1=[1,-1,0;-1,sqrt(2)*i,-sqrt(2)*i;0,0,-1]

C1 =

   1.0000           -1.0000                 0
  -1.0000            0 + 1.4142i       0 - 1.4142i
        0            0                    -1.0000

>> C2=[0 2 1;1 0 0;1 -1 0]

C2 =

    0    2    1
    1    0    0
    1   -1    0

>> C=C1+C2

C =

   1.0000            1.0000            1.0000
        0            0 + 1.4142i       0 - 1.4142i
   1.0000           -1.0000           -1.0000

>> M1=A*B-B*A
```

```
M1 =

     0          -1.0000 - 1.0000i   2.0000
     0               0              1.0000 - 1.0000i
     0               0                   0

>> M2=A^2+B^2+C^2

M2 =

   2.0000          2.0000 + 3.4142i   3.0000 - 5.4142i
        0 - 1.4142i  -0.0000 + 1.4142i   0.0000 - 0.5858i
        0          2.0000 - 1.4142i   2.0000 + 1.4142i

>> M3=A*B*C

M3 =

   5.0000 + 1.0000i  -3.5858 + 1.0000i  -6.4142 + 1.0000i
   3.0000 - 2.0000i  -3.0000 + 0.5858i  -3.0000 + 3.4142i
        0 - 1.0000i        0 + 1.0000i        0 + 1.0000i

>> M4=sqrtm(A)+sqrtm(B)-sqrtm(C)

M4 =

   0.6356 + 0.8361i  -0.3250 - 0.8204i   3.0734 + 1.2896i
   0.1582 - 0.1521i   0.0896 + 0.5702i   3.3029 - 1.8025i
  -0.3740 - 0.2654i   0.7472 + 0.3370i   1.2255 + 0.1048i

>> M5=expm(A)*(expm(B)+expm(C))

M5 =

  14.1906 - 0.0822i   5.4400 + 4.2724i  17.9169 - 9.5842i
   4.5854 - 1.4972i   0.6830 + 2.1575i   8.5597 - 7.6573i
   3.5528 + 0.3560i   0.1008 - 0.7488i   3.2433 - 1.8406i

>> inv(A)

ans =

   1   -1    1
   0    1   -1
   0    0    1
```

```
>> inv(B)

ans =

        0 - 1.0000i  -1.0000 - 1.0000i  -4.0000 + 3.0000i
        0             -1.0000            1.0000 + 3.0000i
        0                    0                0 + 1.0000i

>> inv(C)

ans =

  0.5000    0              0.5000
  0.2500    0 - 0.3536i    -0.2500
  0.2500    0 + 0.3536i    -0.2500

>> [A*inv(A) B*inv(B) C*inv(C)]

ans =

   1    0    0    1    0    0    1    0    0
   0    1    0    0    1    0    0    1    0
   0    0    1    0    0    1    0    0    1

>> A'

ans =

   1    0    0
   1    1    0
   0    1    1

>> B'

ans =

       0 - 1.0000i         0               0
  1.0000 + 1.0000i   -1.0000              0
  2.0000 - 1.0000i    3.0000 + 1.0000i    0 + 1.0000i

>> C'

ans =

  1.0000    0              1.0000
  1.0000    0 - 1.4142i    -1.0000
  1.0000    0 + 1.4142i    -1.0000
```

EXERCISE 3-7

Given the matrices

$$A = \begin{bmatrix} 1 & 2 & 3 \\ 4 & 5 & 6 \\ 7 & 8 & 9 \end{bmatrix} \quad B = \begin{bmatrix} 1+i & 2+i \\ 3+i & 4+i \end{bmatrix}$$

apply the sine function, the base e exponential and logarithm, the square root, the modulus, the argument and the rounding functions.

Calculate e^B and $ln(A)$.

```
>> A=[1 2 3; 4 5 6; 7 8 9]

A =

    1    2    3
    4    5    6
    7    8    9

>> sin(A)

ans =

    0.8415    0.9093    0.1411
   -0.7568   -0.9589   -0.2794
    0.6570    0.9894    0.4121

>> B=[1+i 2+i;3+i,4+i]

B =

   1.0000 + 1.0000i   2.0000 + 1.0000i
   3.0000 + 1.0000i   4.0000 + 1.0000i

>> sin(B)

ans =

   1.2985 + 0.6350i   1.4031 - 0.4891i
   0.2178 - 1.1634i  -1.1678 - 0.7682i
```

```
>> exp(A)

ans =

  1.0e+003 *

    0.0027    0.0074    0.0201
    0.0546    0.1484    0.4034
    1.0966    2.9810    8.1031

>> exp(B)

ans =

   1.4687 +  2.2874i   3.9923 +  6.2177i
  10.8523 + 16.9014i  29.4995 + 45.9428i

>> log(B)

ans =

   0.3466 + 0.7854i   0.8047 + 0.4636i
   1.1513 + 0.3218i   1.4166 + 0.2450i

>> sqrt(B)

ans =

   1.0987 + 0.4551i   1.4553 + 0.3436i
   1.7553 + 0.2848i   2.0153 + 0.2481i

>> abs(B)

ans =

    1.4142    2.2361
    3.1623    4.1231

>> imag(B)

ans =

     1     1
     1     1

>> fix(sin(B))

ans =

   1.0000          1.0000
   0 - 1.0000i  -   1.0000
```

```
>> ceil(log(A))

ans =

    0    1    2
    2    2    2
    2    3    3

>> sign(B)

ans =

   0.7071 + 0.7071i    0.8944 + 0.4472i
   0.9487 + 0.3162i    0.9701 + 0.2425i
```

The exponential, square root and logarithm functions used above apply element-wise to the matrix, and have nothing to do with the matrix exponential and logarithmic functions that are used below.

```
>> expm(B)

ans =

  1.0e+002 *

  -0.3071 + 0.4625i   -0.3583 + 0.6939i
  -0.3629 + 1.0431i   -0.3207 + 1.5102i

>> logm(A)

ans =

  -5.6588 + 2.7896i  12.5041 -  0.4325i   -5.6325 - 0.5129i
  12.8139 - 0.7970i -23.3307 +  2.1623i   13.1237 - 1.1616i
  -5.0129 - 1.2421i  13.4334 -  1.5262i   -4.4196 + 1.3313i
```

EXERCISE 3-8

Solve the following equation in the complex field:

$sin(z) = 2$

```
>> vpa(solve('sin(z) = 2'))

ans =

  1.3169578969248167086250463473308 * i + 1.5707963267948966192313216916398
  1.5707963267948966192313216916398 - 1.3169578969248167086250463473308 * i
```

EXERCISE 3-9

Solve the following equations:

a. $1+x+x^2+x^3+x^4+x^5 = 0$

b. $x^2 +(6-i)x+8-4i = 0$

c. $\tan(Z) = 3i/5$

```
>> solve('1+x+x^2+x^3+x^4+x^5 = 0')

ans =

 -1
 -1/2 - (3-^(1/2) * i) / 2
  1/2 - (3-^(1/2) * i) / 2
 -1/2 + (3 ^(1/2) * i) / 2
  1/2 + (3 ^(1/2) * i) / 2

>> solve ('x ^ 2 +(6-i) * x + 8-4 * i = 0')

ans =

    -4
 i 2

>> vpa (solve ('tan (Z) = 3 * i/5 '))

ans =

0.69314718055994530941723212145818 * i
```

EXERCISE 3-10

Find the following:

a. The fourth roots of - *1* and *1;*

b. The fifth roots of *2 + 2i* and - *1 + i√3;*

c. The real part of *tan(iLn((a+ib) / (a-ib)));*

d. The imaginary part of $Z = (2 + i)^{\cos(4-i)}$.

```
>> solve('x^4+1=0')

ans =

 2^(1/2) * (-i/2 - 1/2)
 2^(1/2) * (i/2 - 1/2)
 2^(1/2) * (1/2 - i/2)
 2^(1/2) * (i/2 + 1/2)

>> pretty(solve('x^4+1=0'))

   +-                    -+
   |    1/2 /   i    1 \   |
   |   2    | - - - - |   |
   |        \   2    2 /   |
   |                      |
   |    1/2 / i     1 \   |
   |   2    | - - - |    |
   |        \ 2     2 /   |
   |                      |
   |    1/2 / 1    i \    |
   |   2    | - - - |    |
   |        \ 2    2 /    |
   |                      |
   |    1/2 / i    1 \    |
   |   2    | - + - |    |
   |        \ 2    2 /    |
   +-                    -+

>> solve('x^4-1=0')

ans =

 -1
  1
 -i
  i

>> vpa(solve('x^5-2-2*i=0'))
```

```
ans =

   0.19259341768888084906125263406469 * i + 1.2159869826496146992458377919696
  -0.87055056329612413913627001747975 * i - 0.87055056329612413913627001747975
   0.55892786746600970394985946846702 * i - 1.0969577045083811131206798770216
   0.55892786746600970394985946846702 - 1.0969577045083811131206798770216 * i
   1.2159869826496146992458377919696 * i + 0.19259341768888084906125263406469

>> vpa(solve('x^5+1-sqrt(3)*i=0'))

ans =

   0.46721771281818786757419290603946 * i + 1.0493881644090691705137652947201
   1.1424056652180689506550734259384 * i - 0.12007167380592154112409047542855
   0.76862922680258900220179378744147 - 0.85364923855044142809268986292246 * i
  -0.99480195671282768870147766609475 * i - 0.57434917749851750339931347338896
   0.23882781722701229856490119703938 * i - 1.1235965399072191281921551333441

>> simplify(vpa(real(tan(i * log((a+i*b)/(a-i*b))))))

ans =

-0.5 * tanh(conj(log((a^2 + 2.0*a*b*i-1.0*b^2)/(a^2 + b^2)))) * i + (0.5 * ((a^2 +
2.0*a*b*i-1.0*b^2)^2 /(a^2 + b^2)^2 - 1) * i) / ((a^2 + 2.0*a*b*i-1.0*b^2)^2 /(a^2 + b^2)^2 + 1))

>> simplify(vpa(imag((2+i)^cos(4-i))))

ans =

-0.62107490808037524310236676683417
```

CHAPTER 4

■ ■ ■

Graphics in MATLAB. Curves, Surfaces and Volumes

Introduction

MATLAB is scientific software that implements high-performance graphics. It allows to you create two and three-dimensional graphs of exploratory data, graph curves in explicit, implicit and polar coordinates, plot surfaces in explicit, implicit, or parametric coordinates, draw mesh and contour plots, represent various geometric objects and create other specialized graphics.

You can freely adjust the graphics parameters, choosing such features as framing and positioning, line characteristics, markers, axes limits, mesh types, annotations, labels and legends. You can export graphics in many different formats. All of these features will be described in this chapter.

Exploratory Graphics

MATLAB incorporates commands that allow you to create basic exploratory graphics, such as histograms, bar charts, graphs, arrow diagrams, etc. The following table summarizes these commands. For all of them, it is necessary to first define the field of variation of the variable.

bar(Y)   *Creates a bar chart relative to the vector of frequencies Y. If Y is a matrix it creates multiple bar charts for each row of Y.*

```
>> x = [1 2 5 8 4 3 4 1 2 3 2];
>> bar (x)
```

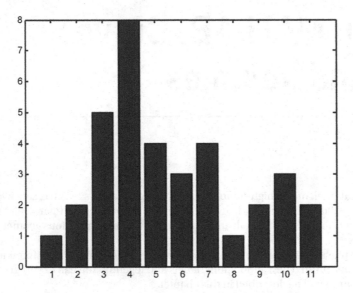

bar(x,Y)   *Creates a bar chart relative to the vector of frequencies Y where x is a vector that defines the location of the bars on the x-axis.*

```
>> x = - 2.9:0.2:2.9;
>> bar (x, exp(-x.*x))
```

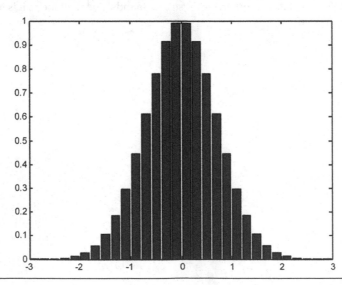

(*continued*)

bar(...,width)   *Creates a bar chart where the bars are given the specified width. By default, the width is 0.8. A width of 1 causes the bars to touch.*

bar(..., 'style')   *Creates a bar chart with the given style of bars. The possible styles are 'group' (the default vertical bar style) and 'stack' (stacked horizontal bars). If the matrix is m× n, the bars are grouped in m groups of n bars.*

```
>> A = [1 6 12 5 7; 3 2 6 5 3];
>> bar (A, 'stack')
>> bar (A, 'group')
```

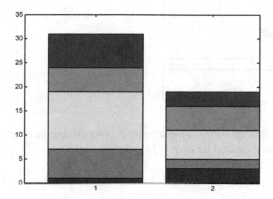

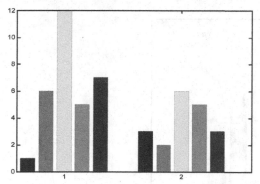

bar(..., color)   *Creates a bar chart where the bars are all of the specified colors (r = red, g = green, b = blue, c = cyan, m = magenta, y = yellow, k = black and w = white).*

(continued)

127

barh(...)   *Creates a horizontal bar chart.*

```
>> barh(A,'group')
```

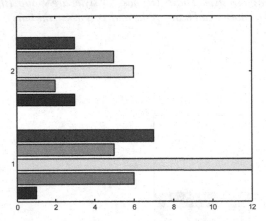

hist(Y)   *Creates a histogram relative to the vector of frequencies Y using 10 equally spaced rectangles. If Y is a matrix, a histogram is created for each of its columns.*

```
>> Y = randn(100);
>> hist(Y)
```

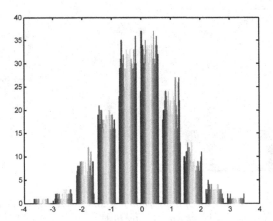

hist(Y,x)   *Creates a histogram relative to the vector of frequencies Y where the number of bins is given by the number of elements in the vector x and the data is sorted according to vector x (if the entries of x are evenly spaced then these are used as the centers of the bins, otherwise the midpoints of successive values are used as the bin edges).*

(continued)

hist(Y,k)	*Creates a histogram relative to the vector of frequencies Y using as many bins as indicated by the scalar k.*

```
>> hist(Y, 8)
```

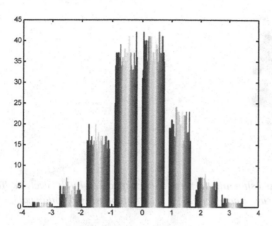

[n,x] = hist(…)	*Returns the vectors n and x with the frequencies assigned to each bin of the histogram and the locations of the centers of each bin.*
ple(X)	*Creates a pie chart relative to the vector of frequencies X.*

```
>> X = [3 5 12 4 7 10];
>> pie(X)
```

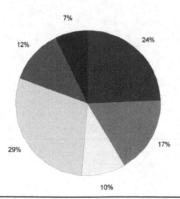

(continued)

pie(X,Y)	*Creates a pie chart relative to the vector of frequencies X by moving out the sectors for which Yi ≠ 0.*

```
>> pie(X,[0 0 1 0 1 1])
```

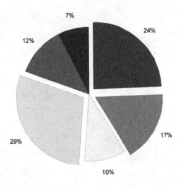

errorbar(x,y,e)	*Plots the function y against x showing the error ranges specified by the vector e. To indicate the confidence intervals, a vertical line of length $2e_i$ is drawn passing through each point (x_i, y_i) with center (x_i, y_i).*

```
>> x = - 4:.2:4;
y = (1/sqrt(2*pi))*exp(-(x.^2)/2);
e = rand(size(x))/10;
errorbar(x,y,e)
```

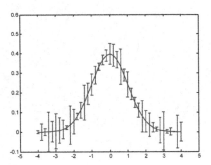

(*continued*)

stem (Y)	*Plots the data sequence Y as stems extending from the x-axis baseline to the points indicated by a small circle.*

```
>> y = randn (50.1); stem (y)
```

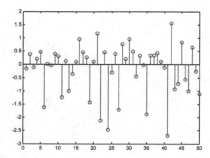

stem(X,Y)	*Plots the data sequence Y as a stem diagram with x-axis values determined by X.*
stairs (Y)	*Draws a stair step graph of the data sequence Y.*
stairs(X,Y)	*Plots a stair step graph of the data Y where the x-values are determined by the vector X.*

```
>> x = -3:0.1:3; stairs(x,exp(-x.^2))
```

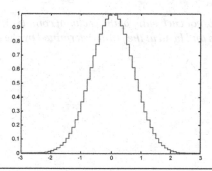

(*continued*)

131

rose (Y)   *Creates an angle histogram showing the distribution of the data Y in 20 angle bins. The angles are given in radians. The radii reflect the number of elements falling into the corresponding bin.*

```
>> y = randn(1000,1) * pi; rose(y)
```

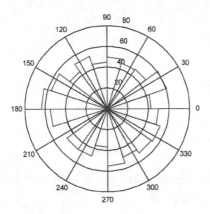

rose(Y,n)   *Plots an angle histogram of the data Y with n equally spaced bins. The default value of n is 20.*

rose(Y,X)   *Plots an angle histogram of the data Y where X specifies the number and location (central angle) of the bins.*

compass (Z)   *Plots a compass diagram of the data Z. For each entry of the vector of complex numbers Z an arrow is drawn with base at the origin and head at the point determined by the entry.*

```
>> z = eig(randn(20,20)); compass(z)
```

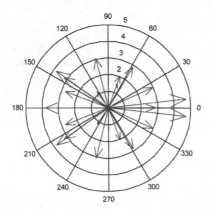

compass(X,Y)   *Equivalent to compass(X+i*Y).*

compass (Z, S) or   *Plots a compass diagram with arrow styles specified by S.*
compass (X, Y , S)

(continued)

feather(Z) or **feather(X,Y) or** **feather(Z,S) or** **feather(X,Y,S)**	*Produces a plot similar to a compass plot, except the arrows now emanate from equally-spaced points along the x-axis instead of from the origin.* `>> z = eig(randn(20,20)); feather(z)` 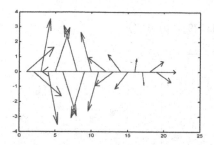

Curves in Explicit, Implicit, Parametric and Polar Coordinates

The most important MATLAB commands for plotting curves in two dimensions in explicit, polar and implied coordinates are presented in the following table.

plot(X,Y)	*Plots the set of points (X, Y), where X and Y are row vectors. For graphing a function y = f (x) it is necessary to specify a set of points (X, f (X)), where X is the range of variation of the variable x. X and Y can be arrays of the same size, in which case a graph is made by plotting the corresponding points (X_i, Y_i) on the same axis. For complex values of X and Y the imaginary parts are ignored. For x = x(t) and y = y(t) with the given parameter t, the specified planar parametric curve graphic variation.* `>> x = 0:0.1:6*pi; y = x.*sin(x); plot(x,y)` 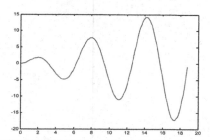

(*continued*)

plot (Y)   *Creates a line plot of the vector Y against its indices. This is useful for plotting time series. If Y is a matrix, plot(Y) creates a graph for each column of Y, presenting them all on the same axes. If the components of the vector are complex, plot(Y) is equivalent to plot(real(Y),imag(Y)).*

>> Y = [1,3,9,27,81,243,729]; plot(Y)

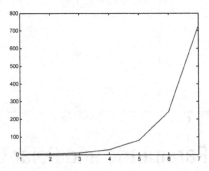

plot (X, Y, S)   *Creates a plot of Y against X as described by plot(X,Y) with the settings defined in S. Usually S consists of two characters between single quotes, the first sets the color of the line graph and the second specifies the marker or line type. The possible values of colors and characters are, respectively, as follows: y (yellow), m (magenta), c (cyan), r (red), g (green), b (blue), w (white), k (black), . (point), o (circle), x (cross), s (square), d (diamond), ^ (upward pointing triangle), v (downward pointing triangle), > (right pointing triangle), < (left pointing triangle), p (pentagram), h (hexagram), + (plus sign), * (asterisk), - (solid line), -- (dashed line),: (dotted line), -. (dash-dot line).*

>> plot([1,2,3,4,5,6,7,8,9],[1, 1/2, 1/3,1/4,1/5,1/6, 1/7,1/8,1/9],'r *')

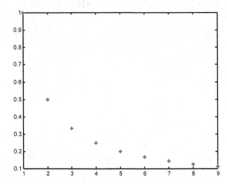

plot (X1,Y1,S1,X2,Y2,S2,...)   *Combines the plots for the triples (Xi, Yi, Si). This is a useful way of representing various functions on the same graph.*

(continued)

fplot ('f', [xmin, xmax])	*Graphs the explicit function $y = f(x)$ in the specified range of variation for x.*

```
>> fplot('x*sin(1/x)', [0,pi/16])
```

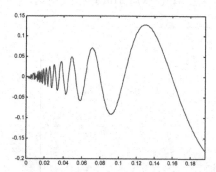

fplot('f', [xmin, xmax, ymin, ymax], S)	*Graphs the explicit function $y = f(x)$ in the specified intervals of variation for x and y, with options for color and characters given by S.*

```
>> fplot('x^2/(x+1)', [-12,12,-8, 8])
```

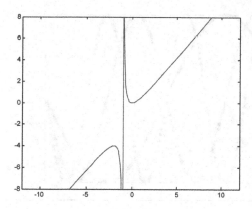

fplot('f', [xmin,xmax],...,t)	*Graphs the function f with relative error tolerance t.*
fplot('f', [xmin, xmax],...,n)	*Graphs the function f with a minimum of $n + 1$ points where the maximum step size is (xmax-xmin)/n.*

(continued)

135

fplot('[f1,f2,...,fn]', [xmin, xmax, ymin, ymax], S)

Graphs the functions f1, f2,..., fn on the same axes in the specified ranges of variation of x and y and with the color and markers given by S.

```
>> fplot('[sin(x), sin(2*x), sin(3*x)]', [0,2*pi])
```

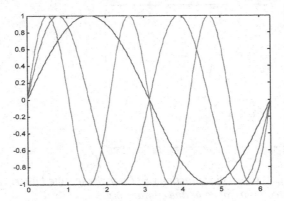

```
>> fplot('[sin (x), sin(2*x), sin(3*x)]', [0, 2 * pi],'k *')
```

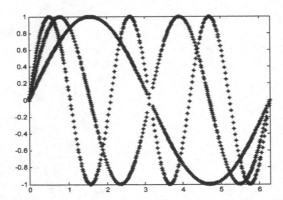

(continued)

ezplot ('f', [xmin xmax])   *Graphs the explicit function $y = f(x)$ or implicit function $f(x,y) = k$ in the given range of variation of x. The range of variation of the variable can be omitted.*

```
>> ezplot('y*x^2+x*y^2=10',[-10,10])
```

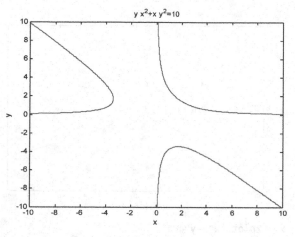

```
>> ezplot('x ^ 2-/(x^2-1)')
```

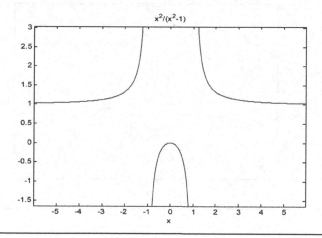

(continued)

ezplot ('f', [xmin, xmax, ymin, ymax])

Graphs the explicit function $y = f(x)$ or the implicit function $f(x,y) = k$ for the given intervals of variation of x and y (which can be omitted).

```
>> ezplot('x^2+y^3=1/2',[-10,10,-8,8])
```

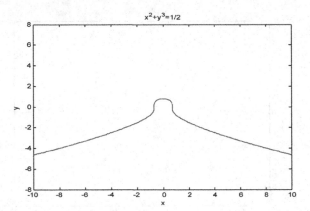

```
>> ezplot('x^2-y^4=1')
```

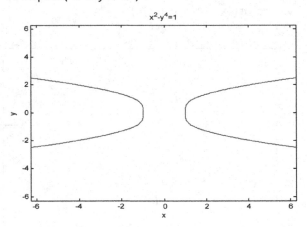

(*continued*)

ezplot(x,y)   *Graphs the planar parametric curve x = x (t) and y = y(t) for 0 ≤ t < 2π.*

```
>> ezplot('4 * cos(t) - cos(4*t)', ' 4 * sin(t) - sin(4*t)')
```

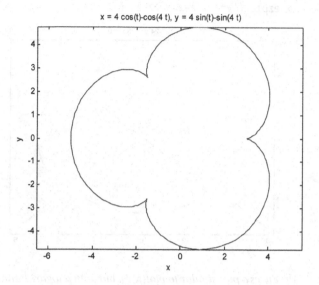

ezplot ('f', [xmin xmax])   *Graphs the planar parametric curve x = x (t) and y = y(t) for xmin < t < xmax.*

```
>> ezplot('t*sin(t)', 't*cos(t)',[-4*pi,4*pi]
```

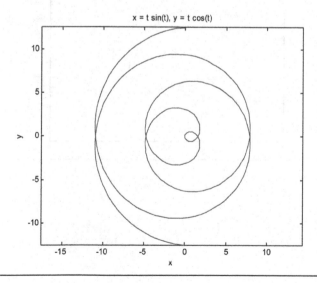

(continued)

139

ezplot ('f')

*Graphs the curve f where the coordinates range over the default domain
[-2π, 2π].*

```
>> ezplot('y^4-x^4-24*y^2+25*x^2=0')
```

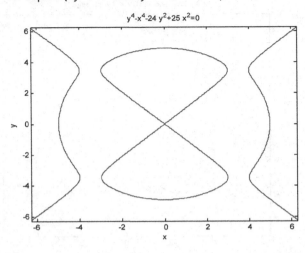

loglog(X,Y)

Produces a plot similar to plot(X,Y), but with a logarithmic scale on the two axes.

```
>> x=0:0.1:pi; y=x.*sin(x); loglog(x,y)
```

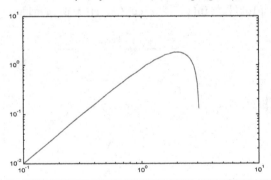

(continued)

semilogx(X,Y)   *Produces a plot similar to plot(X,Y), but with a logarithmic scale on the x-axis and a normal scale on the y-axis.*

```
>> x=0:0.1:pi; y=x.*sin(x); semilogx(x,y)
```

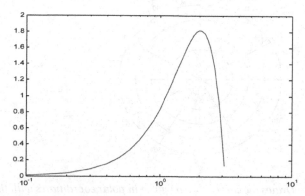

semilogy(X,Y)   *Produces a plot similar to plot(X,Y), but with a logarithmic scale on the y-axis and a normal scale on the x-axis.*

```
>> x=0:0.1:pi; y=x.*sin(x); semilogy(x,y)
```

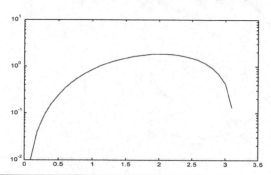

(continued)

141

polar (a, r)	*Draws the curve* $r = r(\alpha)$ *given in polar coordinates.*

```
>> t=0:0.1:2*pi;r=sin(t).*cos(t); polar(t,r)
```

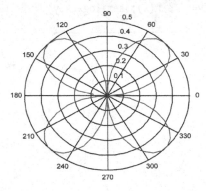

polar (a, r, S)	*Draws the curve* $r = r(\alpha)$ *given in polar coordinates with the style of lines specified by S.*

```
>> t=0:0.05:2*pi;r=sin(t).*cos(t); polar(t,r,'*r')
```

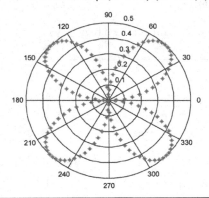

(continued)

ezpolar (r)
ezpolar (r, [a, b])

Draws the curve $r = r(\alpha)$ in polar coordinates where the field of variation of α is given by [a,b], or if it is not stated, is the default range [0, 2π].

```
>> ezpolar ('1 + cos (t)')
```

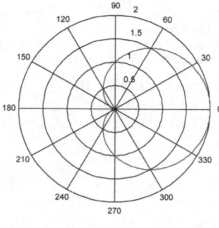

r = 1+cos(t)

fill (X, Y, C)

Draws the filled polygon whose vertices are given by the components (X_i, Y_i) of the specified vectors X and Y. The vector C, which is of the same size as X and Y, specifies the colors assigned to the corresponding points. The C_i values may be: 'r', 'g', 'b', 'c', 'm', 'y', 'w', 'k', whose meanings we already know. If C is a single character, all vertices of the polygon will be assigned the specified color. If X and Y are matrices of the same size then several polygons will be created, each corresponding to the columns of the matrices. In this case, C can be a row vector specifying the color of each polygon, or it can be a matrix specifying the color of the vertices of the polygons.

```
>> t = (1/16:1 / 8:1)'* 2 * pi; x = sin(t); y = cos(t); fill(x, y, 'r')
```

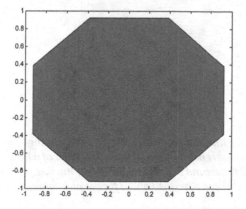

fill(X1,Y1,C1,...)

Draws the filled polygon with vertex coordinates and colors given by (Xi, Yi, Ci).

Three-Dimensional (3D) Curves

MATLAB includes commands that allow you to plot space curves in three dimensions. The following table presents the most important commands.

plot3 (X, Y, Z)	*Draws a 3D line plot by joining the sequence of points determined by (X, Y, Z) by lines, where X, Y and Z are row vectors. X, Y and Z can also be parametric coordinates or matrices of the same size, in which case a graph is made for each triplet of rows, on the same axes. For complex values of X, Y and Z, the imaginary parts are ignored.*

```
>> X = [0 1 1 2; 1 1 2 2; 0 0 1 1];
Y = [1 1 1 1; 1 0 1 0; 0 0 0 0];
Z = [1 1 1 1; 1 0 1 0; 0 0 0 0];
>> plot3 (X, Y, Z)
```

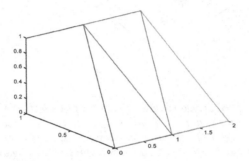

```
>> t = 0:pi/100:20 * pi; plot3 (2 * sin(2*t), 2 * cos(2*t), 4 * t)
```

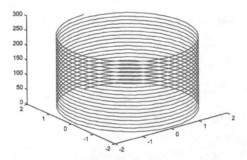

plot3 (X, Y, Z, S)	*Produces the line plot plotting (X,Y,Z) with the settings defined in S. S usually consists of two characters between single quotes, the first of which sets the color of the line graph and the second determines the line or marker properties. The possible settings have already been described above for the plot command.*
plot3(X1,Y1,Z1,S1, X2, Y2,Z2,S2,X3, Y3, Z3, S3,...)	*Combines 3D line plots for the quadruples (Xi, Yi, Zi, Si) on the same axes. This is a useful way of representing various functions on the same graph.*

(continued)

fill3(X,Y,Z,C)

Draws the filled polygon whose vertices are given by the triples of components (Xi, Yi, Zi) of the column vectors X, Y and Z. C is a vector of the same size as X, Y and Z, which specifies the color Ci at each vertex (Xi, Yi, Zi). The Ci values can be 'r,' 'g,' 'b,' 'c,' 'm,' 'y,' 'w,' 'k,' whose meanings we already know. If C is a single character, all vertices will be given this color. If X, Y and Z are matrices of the same size, several polygons corresponding to each triplet column vector (X.j, Y.j, Z.j) will be drawn. In this case, C can be a row vector of elements Cj determining the unique color of each polygon corresponding to (X.j, Y.j, Z.j). C can also be a matrix of the same dimension as X, Y and Z, in which case its elements determine the colors of each vertex (Xijk, Yijk, Zijk) of the set of polygons.

```
>> X = [0 1 1 2; 1 1 2 2; 0 0 1 1];
Y = [1 1 1 1; 1 0 1 0; 0 0 0 0];
Z = [1 1 1 1; 1 0 1 0; 0 0 0 0];
C = [0.5000 1.0000 1.0000 0.5000;
1.0000 0.5000 0.5000 0.1667;
0.3330 0.3330 0.5000 0.5000];
fill3(X,Y,Z,C)
```

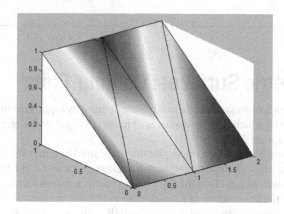

fill3(X1,Y1,Z1,C1, X2, Y2, Z2, C2,...)

Draws the filled polygon whose vertices and colors are given by (Xi, Yi, Zi, Ci).

(continued)

ezplot3(x(t), y(t), z(t))	*Draws the space curve defined by the given three parametric components.*
ezplot3(x(t),y(t),z(t), **[tmin,tmax])**	*Draws the space curve defined by the given three parametric components for the specified range of variation of the parameter.*

```
>> ezplot3('sin (t)', 'cos (t)', ', [0, 6 * pi])
```

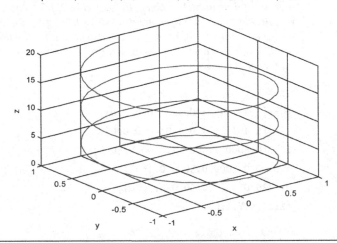

Explicit and Parametric Surfaces: Contour Plots

MATLAB includes commands that allow you to represent surfaces defined by equations of the form $z = f(x,y)$. The first step is to use the command *meshgrid*, which defines the array of points (X, Y) at which the function will be evaluated. Then the command *surf* is used to create the surface.

The command *mesh* is also used to produce a mesh plot that is defined by a function $z = f(x,y)$, so that the points on the surface are represented on a network determined by the z values given by $f(x,y)$ for corresponding points of the plane (x, y). The appearance of a mesh plot is like a fishing net, with surface points forming the nodes of the network.

It is also possible to represent the level curves of a surface by using the command *contour*. These curves are characterized as being the set of points (x,y) in the plane for which the value $f(x,y)$ is some fixed constant.

The following table lists the MATLAB commands which can be used to produce mesh and contour representations of surfaces both in explicit and parametric form.

[X, Y] = meshgrid(x,y)	*Creates a rectangular grid by transforming the monotonically increasing grid vectors x and y into two matrices X and Y specifying the entire grid. Such a grid can be used by the commands surf and mesh to produce surface graphics.*
surf(X,Y,Z,C)	*Represents the explicit surface z = f(x,y) or the parametric surface x = x(t,u), y = y(t,u), z = z(t,u), using the colors specified in C. The C argument can be omitted.*

```
>> [X, Y] = meshgrid(-2:.2:2,-2:.2:2);
Z = X. * exp(-X.^2-Y.^2); surf(X, Y, Z)
```

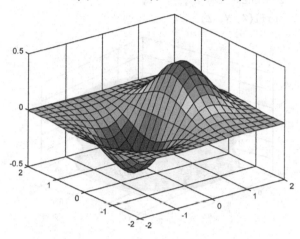

surfc(X,Y,Z,C)	*Represents the explicit surface z = f(x,y) or the parametric surface x = x(t,u), y = y(t,u), z = z(t,u), together with a contour plot of the surface. The contour lines are projected onto the xy-plane.*

```
>> [X, Y] = meshgrid(-2:.2:2,-2:.2:2);
Z = X. * exp(-X.^2-Y.^2); surfc(X, Y, Z)
```

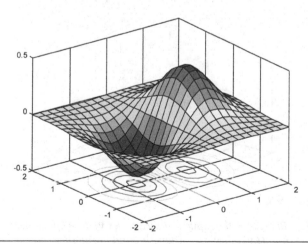

(continued)

147

surfl (X, Y, Z)   *Represents the explicit surface z = f(x,y) or the parametric surface x = x(t,u), y = y(t,u), z = z(t,u), with colormap-based lighting.*

```
>> r =(0:0.1:2*pi)';
t =(-pi:0.1:2*pi);
X = cos(r) * sin(t);
Y = sin(r) * sin(t);
Z = ones(size(r),1)'* t;
surfl(X, Y, Z)
```

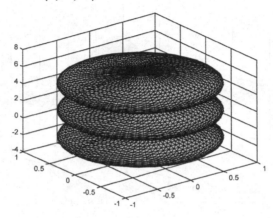

mesh(X,Y,Z,C)   *Represents the explicit surface z = f(x,y) or the parametric surface x = x(t,u), y = y(t,u), z = z(t,u), drawing the grid lines that compose the mesh with the colors specified by C (optional).*

```
>> [X, Y] = meshgrid(-2:.2:2,-2:.2:2);
Z = X. * exp(-X.^2-Y.^2); mesh(X, Y, Z)
```

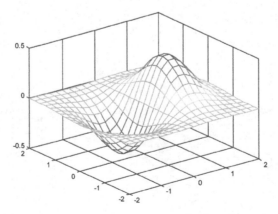

meshz(X,Y,Z,C)   *Represents the explicit surface z = f(x,y) or the parametric surface x = x(t,u), y = y(t,u), z = z(t,u) adding a 'curtain' around the mesh.*

(continued)

148

meshc(X,Y,Z,C)   *Represents the explicit surface z = f(x,y) or the parametric surface x = x(t,u), y = y(t,u), z = z(t,u) together with a contour plot of the surface. The contour lines are projected on the xy-plane.*

```
>> [X, Y] = meshgrid(-2:.2:2,-2:.2:2);
Z = X. * exp(-X.^2-Y.^2); meshc(X, Y, Z)
```

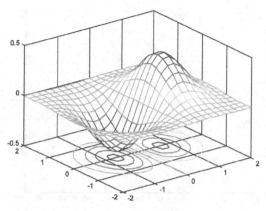

contour (Z)   *Draws a contour plot of the matrix Z, where Z is interpreted as heights of the surface over the xy-plane. The number of contour lines is selected automatically.*

```
>> [X, Y] = meshgrid(-2:.2:2,-2:.2:2);
Z = X. * exp(-X.^2-Y.^2);
>> contour(Z)
```

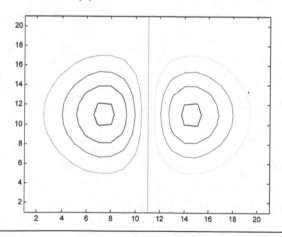

(continued)

contour(Z,n)	*Draws a contour plot of the matrix Z using n contour lines.*

```
>> [X, Y] = meshgrid(-2:.2:2,-2:.2:2);
Z = X. * exp(-X.^2-Y.^2);
>> contour(Z)
```

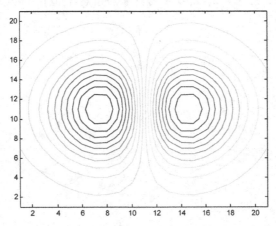

contour (x, y, Z, n)	*Draws a contour plot of the matrix Z with n contour lines and using the x-axis and y-axis values specified by the vectors x and y.*

```
>> r =(0:0.1:2*pi); t =(-pi:0.1:2*pi);
X = cos(r) * cos(t);Y = sin(r) * sin(t);Z = ones(size(r),1)'* t;
>> contour(X, Y, Z)
```

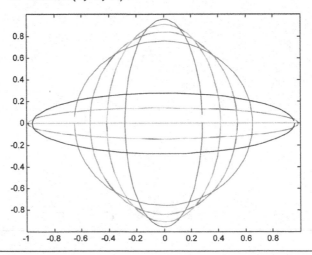

(continued)

contour3 (Z),
contour3 (Z, n) y
contour3 (x, y, Z, n)

Draws three-dimensional contour plots.

```
>> r =(0:0.1:2*pi); t =(-pi:0.1:2*pi);
X = cos (r) * cos(t);Y = sin(r) * sin(t);Z = ones(size(r),1)'* t;
>> contour3(X, Y, Z)
```

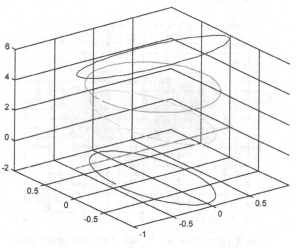

contourf (...)

Draws a contour plot and fills in the areas between the isolines.

```
>> r =(0:0.1:2*pi); t =(-pi:0.1:2*pi);
X = cos(r) * cos(t);Y = sin(r) * sin(t);Z = ones(size(r),1)'* t;
>> contourf(X, Y, Z)
```

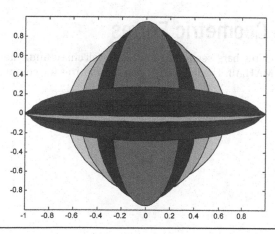

(continued)

| **pcolor (X, Y, Z)** | *Draws a 'pseudocolor' contour plot determined by the matrix (X, Y, Z) using a color representation based on densities. This is often called a density plot.* |

```
>> [X, Y] = meshgrid(-2:.2:2,-2:.2:2);
Z = X. * exp(-X.^2-Y.^2); meshc(X, Y, Z)
>> pcolor(X, Y, Z)
```

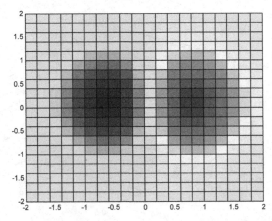

| **trimesh(Tri, X, Y, Z, C)** | *Creates a triangular mesh plot. Each row of the matrix Tri defines a simple triangular face and C defines colors as in surf. The C argument is optional.* |
| **trisurf(Tri,X,Y,Z,C)** | *Creates a triangular surface plot. Each row of the matrix Tri defines a simple triangular face and C defines colors as in surf. The C argument is optional.* |

Three-Dimensional Geometric Forms

The representation of cylinders, spheres, bars, sections, stems, waterfall charts and other three-dimensional geometric objects is possible with MATLAB. The following table summarizes the commands that can be used for this purpose.

bar3 (Y)	*Creates a 3D bar graph relative to the vector of frequencies Y. If Y is a matrix, multiple bar graphs are produced on the same axes, one for each row of Y.*

```
>> bar3(rand(4,4))
```

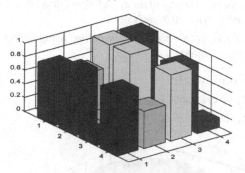

bar3(x,Y)	*Creates a 3D bar graph relative to the vector of frequencies Y where x is a vector that defines the x-axis positions on which the bars are to be located.*
bar3(...,width)	*Creates a 3D bar graph with the specified bar width. By default, the width is 0.8, and a width of 1 causes the bars to touch.*
bar3(...,'style')	*Creates a 3D bar graph with the specified style of bars. The possible styles are 'detached' (default), 'grouped' (grouped vertical bars) and 'stacked' (stacked bars, one for each row in Y).*
bar3(...,color)	*Creates a 3D bar graph where the bars are all of the specified color (r = red, g = green, b = blue, c = cyan, m = magenta, y = yellow, k = black and w = white).*
comet3(z) **comet3(x, y, z)**	*Creates a 3D comet plot animation of the vector z or of the parametric space curve (x(t),y(t),z(t)).*

```
>> t = -pi:pi/500:pi;comet3(sin(5*t),cos(3*t),t)
```

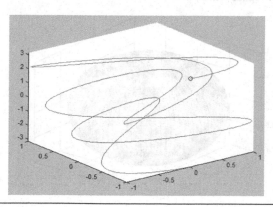

(continued)

[X, Y, Z] = cylinder	*Returns the coordinates of a cylinder centered at the origin of radius 1 and (z-axis aligned) length 1 and with 20 equally spaced points around its circumference.*
[X, Y, Z] = cylinder (r (t))	*Returns the coordinates of the cylinder generated by the curve r.*
[X, Y, Z] = cylinder (r (t), n)	*Returns the coordinates of the cylinder generated by the curve r with n points on the circumference (n = 20 by default).*
cylinder (…)	*The cylinders created above can be plotted using the command surf or with the command cylinder(…).*

```
>> t = 0:pi/10:2*pi;
[X,Y,Z] = cylinder(2+cos(t));
surf(X,Y,Z)
```

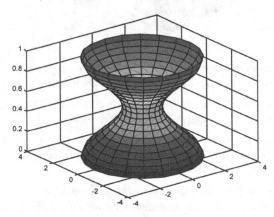

sphere	*Plots the unit sphere with center the origin using 20 × 20 faces.*
sphere(n)	*Plots a unit sphere using n×n faces.*

```
>> sphere(100)
```

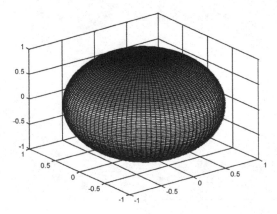

[X, Y, Z] = sphere (n)	*Gives the coordinates of the sphere in three (n + 1)×(n + 1) arrays.*

(continued)

slice(V,sx,sy,sz)	*Draws slices along the x, y, z directions in the volume V at the points in the vectors sx, sy, and sz. V is an m-by-n-by-p volume array containing data values at the default location X = 1:n, Y = 1:m, Z =1:p. Each element in the vectors sx, sy, and sz defines a slice plane in the x-, y-, or z-axis direction.*
slice(X,Y,Z,V,sx,sy,sz)	*Draws slices of the volume V where X, Y, and Z are monotonic orthogonally spaced three-dimensional arrays specifying the coordinates for V. The color at each point is determined by 3-D interpolation into the volume V.*
slice(V,XI,YI,ZI)	*Draws data in the volume V for the slices defined by matrices XI, YI, and ZI which define a surface, and the volume is evaluated at the surface points. XI, YI, and ZI must all be the same size.*
slice(X,Y,Z,V,XI,YI,ZI)	*Draws slices through the volume V along the surface defined by the arrays XI, YI, ZI.*
slice(...,'method')	*Specifies the interpolation method. The options are 'linear,' 'cubic,' or 'nearest.'*

```
>> [x, y, z] = meshgrid(-2:.2:2,-2:.25:2,-2:.16:2);
v = x. * exp(-x.^2-y.^2-z.^2);
slice(x,y,z,v,[-1.2,.8,2],2,[-2,0])
```

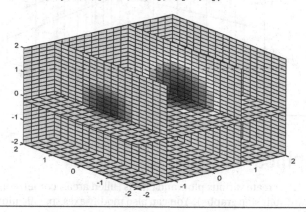

(*continued*)

stem3(Z)	*Plots Z as a sequence of vertical stems with bases on the xy-plane. The base positions are automatically generated.*
stem3(X,Y,Z)	*Plots the sequence Z as vertical stems with xy-plane base positions specified by X and Y.*
stem3(...,'fill')	*Fills the circles at the tips of the stems with color.*
stem3(...,S)	*Creates a 3D stem plot with line style, marker and color specifications S.*

```
>> X = linspace(0,1,10);
Y = X / 2;
Z = sin(X) + cos(Y);
stem3(X,Y,Z,'fill')
```

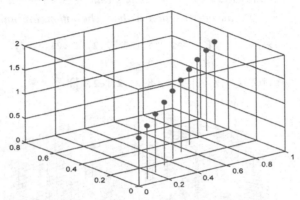

Specialized Graphics

MATLAB provides commands to create various plots and charts (filled areas, comet, contour, mesh, surface and scatter plots, Pareto charts, and stair step graphs). You can also modify axes specifications, and there is an easy to use function plotter. The following table presents the syntax of these commands.

area(Y)	*Creates an area graph displaying the elements of the vector Y as one or more curves, filling the area beneath the curve.*
area(X, Y)	*Identical to plot(X,Y), except the area between 0 and Y is filled.*
area(...,ymin)	*Specifies the base value for the fill area (default 0) .*

```
>> Y = [1, 5, 3; 3, 2, 7; 1, 5, 3; 2, 6, 1]; area(Y)
```

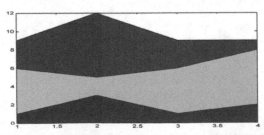

(*continued*)

box on, box off	*Displays/does not display the boundary of the current axes.*
comet(y)	*Creates an animated comet graph of the vector y.*
comet(x, y)	*Plots the comet graph of the vector y versus the vector x.*

```
>> t = - pi:pi/200:pi;comet(t,tan(sin(t))-sin(tan(t)))
```

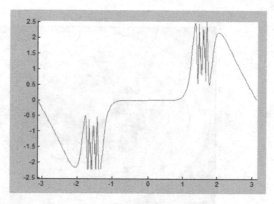

ezcontour(f)	*Creates a contour plot of f(x,y) in the domain $[-2\pi, 2\pi] \times [-2\pi, 2\pi]$.*
ezcontour(f, domain)	*Creates a contour plot of f(x,y) in the given domain.*
ezcontour(...,n)	*Creates a contour plot of f(x,y) over an n×n grid.*

```
>> ezcontour('sqrt(x^2 + y^2)')
```

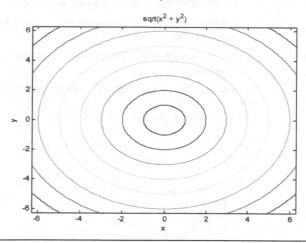

(*continued*)

ezcontourf (f)	*Creates a filled contour plot of f(x,y) in the domain [-2π, 2π] × [-2π, 2π].*
ezcontourf (f, domain)	*Creates a filled contour plot of f(x,y) in the given domain.*
ezcontourf(...,n)	*Creates a filled contour plot of f(x,y) over an n×n grid.*

```
>> ezcontourf('sqrt(x^2 + y^2)')
```

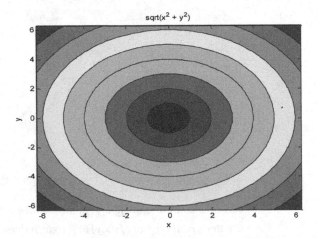

ezmesh(f)	*Creates a mesh plot of f(x,y) over the domain [-2π, 2π] × [-2π, 2π].*
ezmesh(f,domain)	*Creates a mesh plot of f(x,y) over the given domain.*
ezmesh(...,n)	*Creates a mesh plot of f(x,y) using an n×n grid.*
ezmesh (x, y, z)	*Creates a mesh plot of the parametric surface x = x(t,u), y = y(t,u), z = z(t,u), t,u∈ [-2π, 2π].*
ezmesh (x, y, z, domain)	*Creates a mesh plot of the parametric surface x = x(t,u), y = y(t,u), z = z(t,u), t,u∈ domain.*
ezmesh(..., 'circ')	*Creates a mesh plot over a disc centered on the domain.*

```
>> ezmesh ('sqrt(x^2 + y^2)')
```

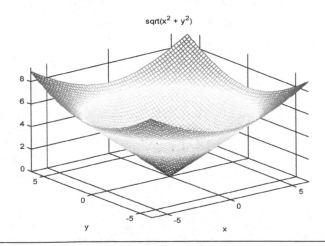

(continued)

ezmeshc (f)
ezmeshc (f, domain)
ezmeshc(...,n)
ezmeshc (x, y, z)
ezmeshc (x, y, z, domain)
ezmeshc(..., 'circ')

Creates a combination of mesh and contour graphs.

```
>> ezmeshc ('sqrt(x^2 + y^2)')
```

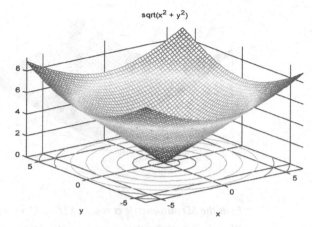

ezsurf (f)
ezsurf (f, domain)
ezsurf(...,n)
ezsurf (x, y, z)
ezsurf (x, y, z, domain)
ezsurf(..., 'circ')

Creates a colored surface plot.

```
>> ezsurf('sqrt(x^2 + y^2)')
```

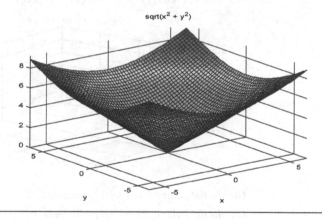

(*continued*)

ezsurfc (f)	*Creates a combination of surface and contour plots.*
ezsurfc (f, domain)	
ezsurfc(...,n)	`>> ezsurfc('sqrt(x^2 + y^2)')`
ezsurfc (x, y, z)	
ezsurfc (x, y, z, domain)	
ezsurfc(..., 'circ')	

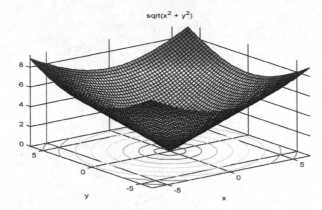

ezplot3 (x, y, z)	*Plots the 3D parametric curve $x = x(t)$, $y(t) = y$, $z(t) = z$ $t \in [-2\pi, 2\pi]$.*
ezplot3 (x, y, z, domain)	*Plots the 3D parametric curve $x = x(t)$, $y(t) = y$, $z(t) = z$ $t \in$ domain.*
ezplot3(..., 'animate')	*Creates a 3D animation of a parametric curve.*

`>> ezplot3('cos(t)','t.*sin(t)','sqrt(t)')`

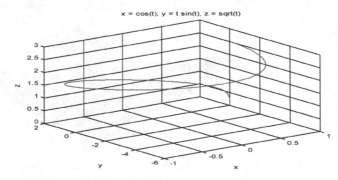

ezpolar(f)	*Graphs the polar curve $r = f(c)$ with $c \in [0, 2\pi]$.*
ezpolar(f, [a, b])	*Graphs the polar curve $r = f(c)$ with $c \in [a, b]$.*

`ezpolar ('sin(2*t). * cos(3*t)', [0 pi])`

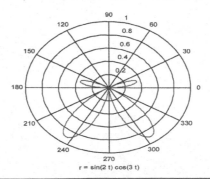

(continued)

| **pareto(Y)** | *Creates a Pareto chart relative to the vector of frequencies Y.* |
| **pareto(X,Y)** | *Creates a Pareto chart relative to the vector of frequencies Y whose elements are given by the vector X.* |

```
>> lines_of_code = [200 120 555 608 1024 101 57 687];
coders =…
{'Fred', 'Ginger', 'Norman', 'Max', 'Julie', 'Wally', 'Heidi', 'Pat'};
Pareto (lines_of_code, coders)
title ('lines of code by programmer')
```

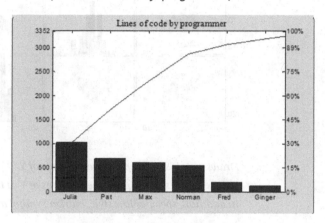

| **pie.3 (X)** | *Creates a 3D pie chart for frequencies X.* |
| **pie.3(X, explode)** | *Creates a detached 3D pie chart.* |

```
>> ft3 ([2 4 3 5], [0 1 1 0], {'North', 'South', 'East', 'West'})
```

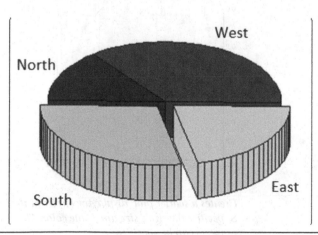

(continued)

plotmatrix(X, Y)   *Creates a scatter plot of the columns of X against the columns of Y.*

```
>> x = randn (50,3); y = x * [- 1 2 1; 2 0 1; 1-2-3;]';
plotmatrix (y)
```

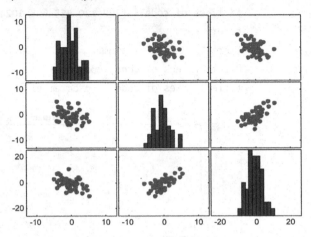

stairs (Y)   *Draws a stair step graph of the elements of Y.*

stairs(X, Y)   *Draws a stair step graph of the elements of Y at the locations specified by X.*

stairs(...,linespec)   *In addition, specifies line style, marker symbol and color.*

```
>> x = linspace(-2*pi,2*pi,40);stairs(x,sin(x))
```

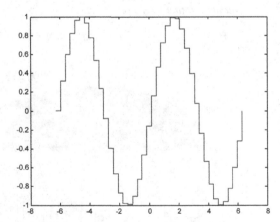

scatter(X,Y,S,C)   *Creates a scatter plot, displaying circles at the locations specified by X and Y.*

scatter(X,Y)   *S specifies the circle size and C the color. The circles can be filled and different*

scatter(X,Y,S)   *markers can be specified.*

scatter(..., marker)

scatter(..., 'filled')

(continued)

scatter3(X,Y,Z,S,C)
scatter3(X,Y,Z)
scatter3(X,Y,Z,S)
scatter3(...,marker)
scatter(...,'filled')

Creates a 3D scatter plot determined by the vectors X, Y, Z. Colors and markers can be specified.

```
>> x=(0:0.1:4);
>> scatter(x,cos(x))
```

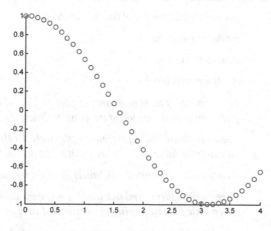

```
>> x=(0:0.1:2*pi);
>> scatter3 (x, cos(x), sin(x))
```

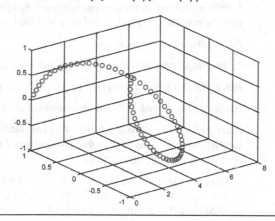

2D and 3D Graphics Options

MATLAB includes many different commands which enable graphics handling, including titles, legends and axis labels, addition of text to plots, and adjustment of coloring and shading. The most important commands are summarized in the following table.

title ('text')	*Adds a title to the top of the current axes.*
xlabel ('text')	*Adds an x-axis label.*
ylabel ('text')	*Adds a y-axis label.*
zlabel ('text')	*Adds a z-axis label.*
clabel(C,h)	*Labels contour lines of a contour plot with a '+', rotating the labels so they are positioned on the inside of the contour lines.*
clabel(C,h,v)	*Labels contour lines of a contour plot only for the levels given by the vector v, rotating the labels so they are positioned on the inside of the contour lines.*
datetick (axis)	*Creates date formatted tick labels for the specified axis ('x', 'y' or 'z').*
datetick (axis, date)	*Creates date formatted tick labels for the specified axis ('x', 'y' or 'z') with the given date format (an integer between 1 and 28).*
legend ('string1', 'string2',...)	*Displays a legend in the current axes using the specified strings to label each set of data.*
legend(h,'string1', 'string2',...)	*Displays a legend on the plot containing the objects identified by the vector h and uses the specified strings to label the corresponding graphics objects.*
legend ('off'),	*Deletes the current axes legend.*
text (x, y, 'text')	*Places the given text at the point (x, y) within a 2D plot.*
text (x, y, z, 'text')	*Places the given text at the point (x, y, z) in a 3D plot.*
gtext ('text')	*Allows you to place text at a mouse-selected point in a 2D plot.*
grid	*Adds grid lines to 2D and 3D plots. **Grid on** adds major grid lines to the axes, **grid off** removes all grid lines from the current axes. The command grid toggles the visibility of the major grid lines.*
hold	*Controls whether the current graph is cleared when you make subsequent calls to plotting functions (the default), or adds a new graph to the current graph, maintaining the existing graph with all its properties. The command **hold on** retains the current graph and adds another graph to it. The command **hold off** resets to default properties before drawing a new graph.*
axis ([xmin xmax ymin ymax zmin zmax])	*Sets the axes limits.*
axis ('auto')	*Computes the axes limits automatically (xmin = min (x), xmax = max(x)).*
axis (axis)	*Freezes the scaling at the current limits, so that if hold is on, subsequent plots use the same limits.*
V = axis	*Returns a row vector V containing scaling factors for the x-, y-, and z-axes. V has four or six components depending on whether the plot is 2D or 3D, respectively.*
axis ('xy')	*Uses Cartesian coordinates with the origin at the bottom left of the graph.*

(continued)

axis ('tight')	*Sets the axis limits to the range of the data.*
axis ('ij')	*Places the origin at the top left of the graph.*
axis ('square')	*Makes the current axes region a square (or a cube when three-dimensional).*
axis ('equal')	*Uses the same scaling factor for both axes.*
axis ('normal')	*Removes the square and equal options.*
axis ('off')	*Turns off all axis lines, tick marks, and labels, keeping the title of the graph and any text.*
axis ('on')	*Turns on all axis lines, tick marks, and labels.*
subplot (m, n, p)	*Divides the current figure into an m×n grid and creates axes in the grid position specified by p. The grids are numbered by row, so that the first grid is the first column of the first row, the second grid is the second column of the first row, and so on.*
plotyy(X1,Y1,X2,Y2)	*Plots X1 versus Y1 with y-axis labeling on the left and plots X2 versus Y2 with y-axis labeling on the right.*
plotyy(X1,Y1,X2,Y2,) 'function')	*Same as the previous command, but using the specified plotting function (plot, loglog, semilogx, semilogy, stem or any acceptable function h = function(x,y)) to plot the graph.*
plotyy(X1,Y1,X2,Y2, 'function1', 'function2')	*Uses function1(X1,Y1) to plot the data for the left axis and function2(X2,Y2) to plot the data for the right axis.*
axis ([xmin xmax ymin ymax zmin zmax])	*Sets the x-, y-, and z-axis limits. Also accepts the options 'ij', 'square,' 'equal', etc., identical to the equivalent two-dimensional command.*
view ([x, y, z])	*Sets the viewing direction to the Cartesian coordinates x, y, and z.*
view([as, el])	*Sets the viewing angle for a three-dimensional plot. The azimuth, az, is the horizontal rotation about the z-axis as measured in degrees from the negative y-axis. Positive values indicate counterclockwise rotation of the viewpoint. el is the vertical elevation of the viewpoint in degrees. Positive values of elevation correspond to moving above the object; negative values correspond to moving below the object.*
hidden	*Hidden line removal draws only those lines that are not obscured by other objects in a 3-D view. The command hidden on hides such obscured lines while hidden off shows them.*
shading	*Controls the type of shading of a surface created with the commands surf, mesh, pcolor, fill and fill3. The option **shading flat** gives a smooth shading, **shading interp** gives a dense shadow and **shading faceted** (default) yields a standard shading.*
colormap (M)	*Sets the colormap to the matrix. M must have three columns and only contain values between 0 and 1. It can also be a matrix whose rows are vectors of RGB type [r g b]. There are some pre-defined arrays M, which are as follows: jet (p), HSV (p), hot (p), cool (p), spring (p), summer (p), autumn (p), winter (p), gray (p), bone (p), copper (p), pink (p), lines (p). All arrays have 3 columns and p rows. For example, the syntax colormap (hot (8)) sets hot (8) as the current colormap.*

(continued)

brighten (p)	*Adjusts the brightness of the figure. If $0 < p < 1$, the figure will be brighter, and if $-1 < p < 0$ the figure will be darker.*
image (A)	*Creates an image graphics object by interpreting each element in a matrix as an index into the figure's colormap or directly as RGB values, depending on the data specified.*
pcolor (A)	*Produces a pseudocolor plot, i.e. a rectangular array of cells with colors determined by A. The elements of A are linearly mapped to an index into the current colormap.*
caxis ([cmin cmax])	*Sets the color limits to the specified minimum and maximum values. Data values less than cmin or greater than cmax map to cmin and cmax, respectively. Values between cmin and cmax linearly map to the current colormap.*
h = figure	*Creates a figure graphics object with name h.*
figure(h)	*Makes the figure identified by h the current figure, makes it visible, and attempts to raise it above all other figures on the screen. The current figure is the target for graphics output.*
	The command close(h) deletes the figure identified by h. The command whitebg(h) complements all the colors of the figure h. The clf command closes the current figure. The command graymon sets defaults for graphics properties to produce more legible displays for grayscale monitors. The refresh command redraws the figure.
e = axes	*Creates axes objects named e.*
axes(e)	*Makes the existing axes e the current axes and brings the figure containing it into focus. The command gca returns the name of the current axes. The command cla deletes all objects related to the current axes.*
l = line(x,y) or **l = line (x, y, z)**	*Creates, as an object of name l, the line joining the points X, Y in the plane or the points X, Y, Z in space.*
p = (X, Y, C) patch or **patch(X,Y,Z,C)**	*Creates an opaque polygonal area p that is defined by the set of points (X, Y) in the plane or (X, Y, Z) in space, and whose color is given by C.*
s = surface(X,Y,Z,C)	*Creates the parametric surface s defined by X, Y and Z and whose color is given by C.*
i = image (C)	*Creates an image i from the matrix C. Each element of C specifies the color of a rectangular segment in the image.*
t = text (x, y, 'string') or **t = text (x, y, z, 'string')**	*Creates the text t defined by the chain, located at the point (x, y) in the plane, or at the point (x, y, z) in space.*
set (h, 'property1', **'property2',...)**	*Sets the named properties for the object h (gca for limits of axes), gcf, gco, gcbo, gcbd, colors, etc.*
get (h, 'property')	*Returns the current value of the given property of the object h.*
object = gco	*Returns the name of the current object.*

(continued)

rotate(h, v, α,[p, q, r])		*Rotates the object h by an angle α about an axis of rotation described by the vector v from the point (p, q, r).*
reset (h)		*Updates all properties assigned to the object h replacing them with their default values.*
delete (h)		*Deletes the object h.*

In addition, the most typical properties of graphics objects in MATLAB are the following:

Object	Properties	Possible values
Figure	*Color (background color)*	*'y,' 'm,' 'c,' 'r,' 'g,' 'b,' 'w,' 'k'*
	ColorMap (map color)	*hot(p), gray(p), pink(p),....*
	Position (figure position)	*[left, bottom, width, height]*
	Name (figure name)	*string name*
	MinColorMap (min. color no.)	*minimum number of colors for map*
	NextPlot (graph. mode following.)	*new, add, replace*
	NumberTitle (no. in the figure title)	*on, off*
	Units (units of measurement)	*pixels, inches, centimeters, points*
	Resize (size figure with mouse)	*on (can be changed), off (cannot be changed)*
Axes	*Box (box axes)*	*on, off*
	Color (color of the axes)	*'y,' 'c,' 'r,' 'g,' 'b,' 'w,' 'k'*
	P:System.Windows.Forms.DataGrid. GridLineStyle (line for mesh)	*'-,' '--,' ';,' '-.'*
	Position (origin position)	*[left, bottom, width, height]*
	TickLength (distance between marks)	*a numeric value*
	TickDir (direction of marks)	*in, out*
	Units (units of measurement)	*pixels, inches, centimeters, points*
	View (view)	*[azimuth, elevation]*
	FontAngle (angle of source)	*normal, italic, oblique*
	FontName (name of source)	*the name of the source text*
	FontSize (font size)	*numeric value*
	T:System.Windows.FontWeight (weight)	*light, normal, demi, bold*
	DrawMode property (drawing mode)	*normal, fast*
	Xcolor, Ycolor, Zcolor (axes color)	*[min, max]*
	XDir, Jdir, ZDir (axes direction)	*normal (increasing from left to right), reverse*
	XGrid, YGrid, Zgrid (grids)	*on, off*
	XLabel, YLabel, Zlabel (tags)	*string containing the text of labels*

(continued)

Object	Properties	Possible values
	XLim, YLim, ZLim (limit values)	*[min, max] (range of variation)*
	XScale, YScale, ZScale (scales)	*linear, log (log)*
	XTick,YTick,ZTick (marks)	*[m1,m2,...] (position of marks on axis)*
Line	*Color (color of the line)*	*'y,' 'm,' 'c,' 'r,' 'g,' 'b,' 'w,' 'k'*
	LineStyle (line style)	*'-,' '--,' ',' '-,' '+,' '*,' ',' 'x'*
	LineWidth (line width)	*numeric value*
	Visible (visible line or not displayed.)	*on, off*
	Xdata, Ydata, Zdata (coordinates.)	*set of coordinates of the line*
Text	*Color (text color)*	*'y,' 'm,' 'c,' 'r,' 'g,' 'b,' 'w,' 'k'*
	FontAngle (angle of source)	*normal, italic, oblique*
	FontName (name of source)	*the name of the source text*
	FontSize (font size)	*numeric value*
	T:System.Windows.FontWeight (weight)	*light, normal, demi, bold*
	HorizontalAlignment (hor. setting.)	*left, center, right*
	VerticalAlignment (adjust to vert.)	*top, cap, middle, baseline, bottom*
	Position (position on screen)	*[x, y, z] (text coordinates)*
	Rotation (orientation of the text)	*0, ±90, ±180, ±270*
	Units (units of measurement)	*pixels, inches, centimeters, points*
	String (text string)	*the text string*
Surface	*CDATA (color of each point)*	*color matrix*
	Edgecolor (color grids)	*'y;'m'..., none, flat, interp*
	Facecolor (color of the faces)	*'y;'m'..., none, flat, interp*
	LineStyle (line style)	*'-,' '--,' ',' '-,' '+,' '*,' ',' 'x'*
	LineWidth (line width)	*numeric value*
	MeshStyle (lines in rows and col.)	*row, Columbia, both*
	Visible (visible line or not displayed.)	*on, off*
	Xdata, Ydata, Zdata (coordinates)	*set of coordinates of the surface*
Patch	*CDATA (color of each point)*	*color matrix*
	Edgecolor (color of the axes)	*'y;'m'..., none, flat, interp*
	Facecolor (color of the faces)	*'y;'m'..., none, flat, interp*
	LineWidth (line width)	*numeric value*
	Visible (visible line or not displayed.)	*on, off*
	Xdata, Ydata, Zdata (coordinates)	*set of coordinates of the surface*
Image	*CDATA (color of each point)*	*color matrix*
	Xdata, Ydata (coordinates)	*set of coordinates of the image*

Here are some illustrative examples.

```
>> x=linspace(0,2,30);
y=sin(x.^2);
plot(x,y)
text(1,0.8, 'y=sin(x^2)')
hold on
z=log(sqrt(x));
plot(x,z)
text(1,-0.1, 'y=log(sqrt(x))')
xlabel('x-axis');
ylabel('y-axis');
title(Sinoidal and logarithmic graphs');
```

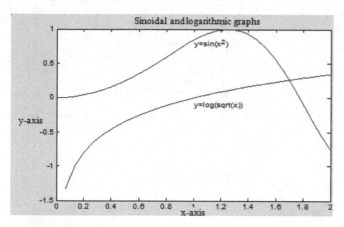

```
>> subplot(2,2,1);
ezplot('sin(x)',[-2*pi 2*pi])
subplot(2,2,2);
ezplot('cos(x)',[-2*pi 2*pi])
subplot(2,2,3);
ezplot('csc(x)',[-2*pi 2*pi])
subplot(2,2,4);
ezplot('sec(x)',[-2*pi 2*pi])
```

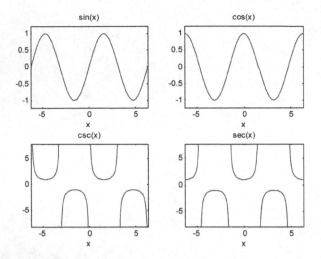

```
>> [X,Y] = meshgrid(-2:0.05:2);
Z=X^2-Y.^2;
subplot(2,2,1)
surf(X,Y,Z)
subplot(2,2,2)
surf(X,Y,Z),view(-90,0)
subplot(2,2,3)
surf(X,Y,Z),view(60,30)
subplot(2,2,4)
surf(X,Y,Z), view (- 10, 30)
```

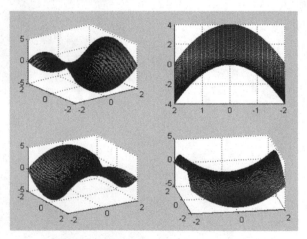

```
>> [X,Y]=meshgrid(-2:0.05:2);
Z=X.^2-Y.^2;
surf(X,Y,Z),shading interp,brighten(0.75),colormap(gray(5))
```

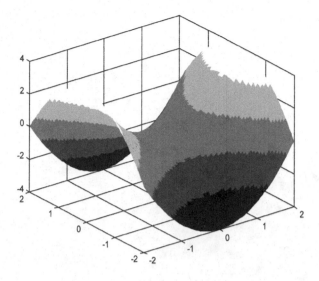

EXERCISE 4-1

Represent the surface defined by the equation:

$$f(x,y) = \frac{(x-1)^2 y^2}{(x-1)^2 + y^2}$$

```
>> [x,y]=meshgrid(0:0.05:2,-2:0.05:2);
>> z=y.^2.*(x-1).^2./(y.^2+(x-1).^2);
>> mesh(x,y,z),view([-23,30])
```

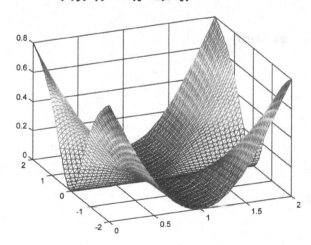

We could also have represented the surface in the following form:

```
>> ezsurf('y^2*(x-1)^2/(y^2+(x-1)^2)')
```

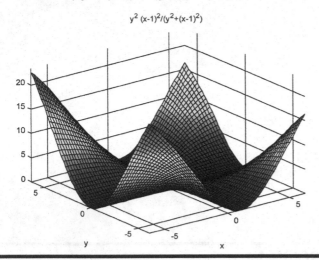

EXERCISE 4-2

Let the function f:R^2→ R be defined by:

$$f(x,y) = \frac{(1-\cos(x))\sin(y)}{x^3 + y^3}.$$

Represent it graphically in a neighborhood of (0,0).

```
>> [x,y]=meshgrid(-1/100:0.0009:1/100,-1/100:0.0009:1/100);
>> z=(1-cos(x)).*sin(y)./(x.^3+y.^3);
>> surf(x,y,z)
>> view([50,-15])
```

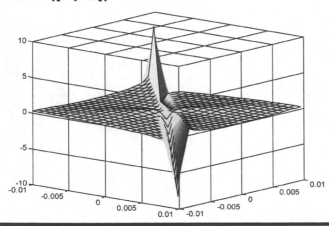

EXERCISE 4-3

Plot the following two curves, given in polar coordinates, next to each other:

$$r = \sqrt{\cos(2a)} \text{ and } r = \sin(2a).$$

Also find the intersection of the two curves.

```
>> a=0:.1:2*pi;
>> subplot(1,2,1)
>> r=sqrt(cos(2*a));
>> polar(a,r)
>> title('r=sqrt(cos(2a))')
>> subplot (1,2,2)
>> r=sin(2*a);
>> polar (a, r)
>> title('r=sin(2a)')
```

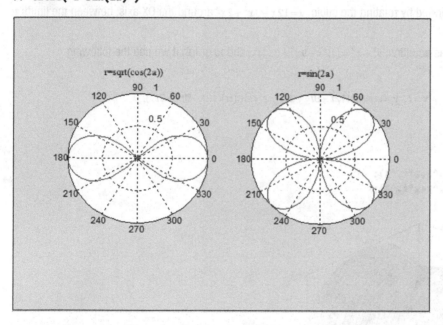

To find the intersection of the two curves, we draw them both on the same axes.

```
>> a=0:.1:2*pi;
>> r=sqrt(cos(2*a));
>> polar(a,r)
>> hold on;
>> r=sin(2*a);
>> polar(a,r)
```

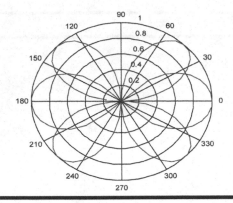

EXERCISE 4-4

Represent the surface generated by rotating the cubic $y = 12x - 9x^2 + 2x^3$ around the OX axis, between the limits $x = 0$ and $x = 5/2$.

The surface of revolution has equation $y^2 + z^2 = (12x - 9x^2 + 2x^3)^2$, and to graph it we use the following parameterization:

$$x = t, \ y = \cos(u)(12t - 9t^2 + 2t^3), \ z = \sin(u)(12t - 9t^2 + 2t^3).$$

```
>> t=(0:.1:5/2);
>> u=(0:.5:2*pi);
>> x=ones(size(u))'*t;
>> y=cos(u)'*(12*t-9*t.^2+2*t.^3);
>> z=sin(u)'*(12*t-9*t.^2+2*t.^3);
>> surf(x,y,z)
```

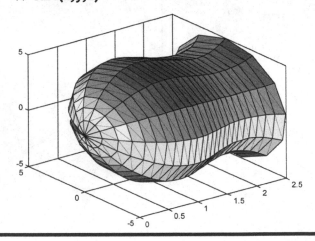

EXERCISE 4-5

Plot the surfaces produced by rotating the ellipse $\dfrac{x^2}{4}+\dfrac{y^2}{9}=1$ *around the X axis and around the Y axis.*

We represent the generated figures alongside each other, but only the positive halves of each figure. The equation of the surface of revolution around the X axis is $y^2+z^2=9(1-x^2/4)$, and is given parametrically by:

$$x=t,\; y=3\cos(u)(1-4t^2)^{\frac{1}{2}},\; z=3.$$

The equation of the surface of revolution around the Y axis is $x^2+z^2=4(1-y^2/4)$ and has the parameterization:

$$x=3\cos(u)(1-9t^2)^{\frac{1}{2}},\; y=t\; z=3\sin(u)(1-9t^2)^{\frac{1}{2}}.$$

```
>> t=(0:.1:2);
>> u=(0:.5:2*pi);
>> x=ones(size(u))'*t;
>> y=cos(u)'*3*(1-t.^2/4).^(1/2);
>> z=sin(u)'*3*(1-t.^2/4).^(1/2);
>> subplot(1,2,1)
>> surf(x,y,z)
>> subplot(1,2,2)
>> x=cos(u)'*3*(1-t.^2/4).^(1/2);
>> y=ones(size(u))'*t;
» z=sin(u)'*3*(1-t.^2/4).^(1/2);
» surf(x,y,z)
```

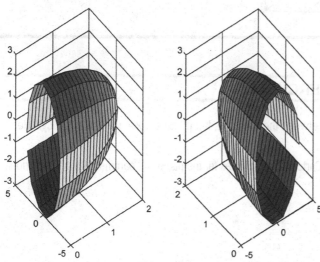

175

EXERCISE 4-6

Represent the intersection of the paraboloid $x^2 + y^2 = 2z$ with the plane $z = 2$.

```
>> [x,y]=meshgrid(-3:.1:3);
>> z=(1/2)*(x.^2+y.^2);
>> mesh(x,y,z)
>> hold on;
>> z=2*ones(size(z));
>> mesh(x,y,z)
>> view(-10,10)
```

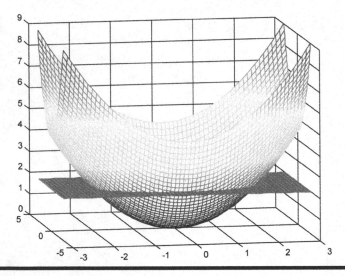

EXERCISE 4-7

Represent the volume in the first octant enclosed between the XY plane, the plane $z = x + y + 2$ and the cylinder $x^2 + y^2 = 16$.

We graphically represent the enclosed volume using Cartesian coordinates for the plane and parameterizing the cylinder.

```
>> t=(0:.1:2*pi);
>> u=(0:.1:10);
>> x=4*cos(t)'*ones(size(u));
>> y=4*sin(t)'*ones(size(u));
>> z=ones(size(t))'*u;
>> mesh(x,y,z)
>> hold on;
>> [x,y]=meshgrid(-4:.1:4);
>> z=x+y+2;
>> mesh(x,y,z)
```

```
>> set(gca,'Box','on');
>> view(15,45)
```

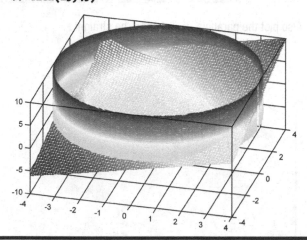

EXERCISE 4-8

Represent the volume bounded by the paraboloid $x^2 + 4y^2 = z$ and laterally by the cylinders $y^2 = x$ and $x^2 = y$.

```
>> [x,y]=meshgrid(-1/2:.02:1/2,-1/4:.01:1/4);
>> z=x^2+4*y.^2;
>> mesh(x,y,z)
>> hold on;
>> y=x.^2;
>> mesh(x,y,z)
>> hold on;
>> x=y.^2;
>> mesh(x,y,z)
>> set(gca,'Box','on')
>> view(-60,40)
```

EXERCISE 4-9

Plot the parabolas $y^2 = x$ *and* $x^2 = y$ on the same axes. Also plot the parabola $y^2 = 4x$ and the straight line $x + y = 3$ on the same axes.

```
>> fplot('[x^2,sqrt(x)]',[0,1.2])
```

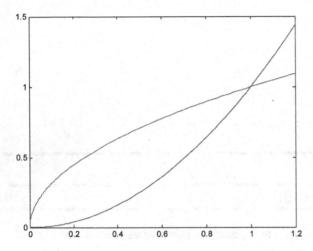

```
>> fplot('[(4*x)^(1/2),3-x]',[0,4,0,4])
```

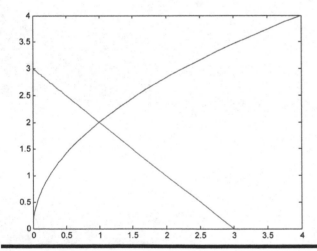

EXERCISE 4-10

Plot the curves defined by the following implicit equations:

$$x^5 - x^2y^2 + y^5 = 0$$

$$x^4 + x^2y - y^5 + y^4 = 0$$

```
>> ezplot('x^5-x^2*y^2+y^5', [-1,1,-1,1])
```

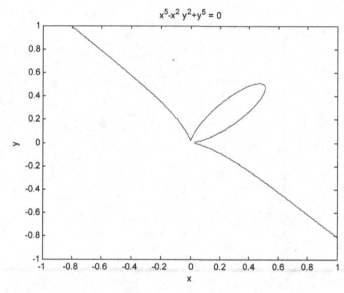

```
>> ezplot('x^4+x^2*y-y^3+y^4', [-1/2,1/2,-1/2,3/2])
```

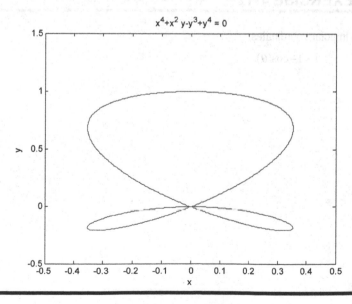

EXERCISE 4-11

Plot the curve given by the following parametric equations:

$$x(t) = t\sin(t)$$

$$y(t) = t\cos(t)$$

```
>> ezplot('t * sin(t) ',' t * cos(t)')
```

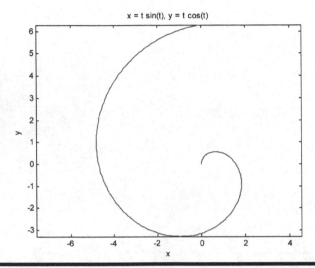

EXERCISE 4-12

Plot the curve given by the following equation in polar coordinates:

$$r = 1 - \cos(\theta).$$

```
>> ezpolar ('1 - cos (t)')
```

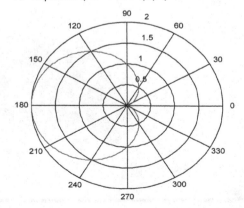

EXERCISE 4-13

Plot the space curve defined by the following parametric parametric equations:

$$x = \cos(t), y = \sin(t), z = t.$$

```
>> ezplot3('cos(t)','sin(t)','t',[0,6*pi])
```

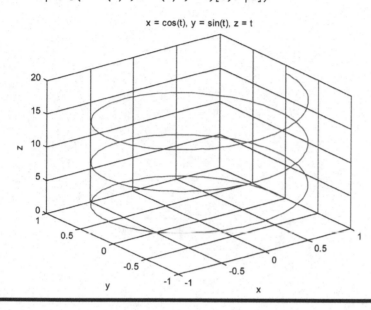

■ ■ ■

CHAPTER 5

Limits of Sequences and Functions. Continuity in One and Several Variables

Limits

MATLAB incorporates features that allow you to work with limits of sequences and functions. In addition to calculating limits of sequences and functions, one can use these commands to analyze the continuity and differentiability of functions, as well as the convergence of numerical series and power series. The following table summarizes the most common MATLAB functions relating to limits.

limit (sequence, inf)	*Calculates the limit of the sequence, indicated by its general term, as n tends to infinity*

```
>> syms n
>> limit(((2*n-3)/(3*n-7))^4, n,inf)

ans =

16 /81
```

limit(function, x, a)	*Calculates the limit of the function of the variable x, as the variable x tends towards the value a*

```
>> syms x
limit((x-1)/(x^(1/2)-1),x,1)

ans =

2
```

limit(function, a)	*Calculates the limit of the function of the variable x, as the variable x tends towards the value a*

```
>> limit((x-1)/(x^(1/2)-1),1)

ans =

2
```

(continued)

limit (function, x, a, 'right')	*Calculates the limit of the function of the variable x, indicated by its analytical expression, as the variable x tends to a from the right*

```
>> syms x
limit((exp(1/x)),x,0,'right')

ans =

Inf
```

limit (function, x, a, 'left')	*Calculates the limit of the function of the variable x, indicated by its analytical expression, as the variable x tends to a from the left*

```
>> limit((exp(1/x)),x,0,'left')

ans =

0
```

As a first example, we calculate the following sequential limits:

$$\lim_{n\to\infty}\left(\frac{3+n}{-1+n}\right)^{n}, \quad \lim_{n\to\infty}\left(1-\frac{2}{3+n}\right)^{n}, \quad \lim_{n\to\infty}\sqrt[n]{\frac{1}{n}}, \quad \lim_{n\to\infty}\frac{-\sqrt[3]{n}+\sqrt[3]{1+n}}{-\sqrt{n}+\sqrt{1+n}}, \quad \lim_{n\to\infty}\frac{n!}{n^{n}}$$

```
>> syms n

>> limit(((n+3)/(n-1))^n, inf)

ans =

exp(4)

>> limit((1-2/(n+3))^n, inf)

ans =

1/exp(2)

>> limit((1/n)^(1/n), inf)

ans =

1

>> limit(((n+1)^(1/3)-n^(1/3))/((n+1)^(1/2)-n^(1/2)),inf)

ans =

0

>> limit((n^n*exp(-n)*sqrt(2*pi*n))/n^n, n,inf)

ans =

0
```

184

In the last limit we have used Sterling's formula to approximate the factorial.

$$n! \approx n^n e^{-n} \sqrt{2\pi n}$$

As a second example, we calculate the following functional limits:

$$\lim_{x \to 1} \frac{|x|}{\sin(x)}, \ \lim_{x \to 3} |x^2 - x - 7|, \ \lim_{x \to 1} \frac{|x-1|}{x^n - 1}, \ \lim_{x \to 1} \sqrt[x]{e}$$

```
>> limit(abs(x)/sin(x),x,0)

ans =

NaN

>> syms x
>> limit(abs(x)/sin(x),x,0)

ans =

NaN

>> limit(abs(x)/sin(x),x,0,'left')

ans =

-1

>> limit(abs(x)/sin(x),x,0,'right')

ans =

1

>> limit(abs(x^2-x-7),x,3)

ans =

1

>> limit((x-1)/(x^n-1),x,1)

ans =

1/n

>> limit(exp(1)^(1/x),x,0)

ans =

NaN
```

```
>> limit(exp(1)^(1/x),x,0,'left')

ans =

0

>> limit(exp(1)^(1/x),x,0,'right')

ans =

Inf
```

Sequences of Functions

You can also use the MATLAB commands for limits of sequences and functions described in the preceding table to study the convergence of sequences of functions.

As a first example, consider the sequence of functions defined by $g_n(x) = (x^2+nx)/n$ with $x \in R$.

A sensible first approach is to graph the sequence of functions to get an idea of what the limit function might be. To graph these functions we can use both the command *plot* and the command *fplot*.

If we use the command *fplot*, the syntax for the simultaneous graphical representation of the first nine functions of the sequence on the same axes would be as follows:

```
>> fplot('[(x^2+x),(x^2+2*x)/2,(x^2+3*x)/3,(x^2+4*x)/4,(x^2+5*x)/5,(x^2+5*x)/5,(x^2+6*x)/6,(x^2+7*x)/7,
(x^2+8*x)/8,(x^2+9*x)/9]',[-2,2,-2,2])
```

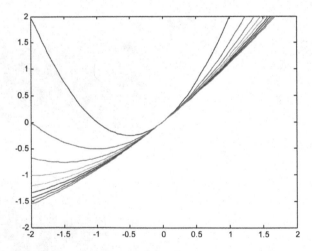

Graphically this indicates that the sequence of functions converges to the identity function $f(x) = x$.

We can corroborate this fact by using the command *limit* with the following syntax:

```
>> syms x n
>> limit((x^2+n*x)/n,n,inf)

ans =

x
```

As a second example, we consider the sequence of functions $g_n(x) = (x^n)/n$ with $x \in [0,1]$.

```
>> limit(x.^n/n,n,inf);x(1)

ans =

0
```

Below is the graphical representation of the sequence of functions, which verifies the result.

```
>> fplot('[x,x^2/2,x^3/3,x^4/4,x^5/5,x^6/6,x^7/7,x^8/8,x^9/9,x^10/10]',[0,1,-1/2,1])
```

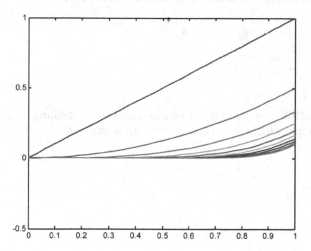

Continuity

The calculation of limits is a necessary tool when dealing with the concept of continuity. Formally, a function *f* is continuous at the point $x = a$ if we have:

$$\lim_{x \to a} f(x) = f(a)$$

If this is not the case, we say the function is discontinuous at a. Thus, for a function f to be continuous at $x = a$, f must be defined at a, and its value at a must be equal to the limit of f at the point a. If the limit of $f(x)$ as $x \to a$ exists, but is different from $f(a)$ (or $f(a)$ is not defined), then f is discontinuous at a, and f is said to have an avoidable discontinuity at a. The discontinuity can be avoided by appropriately redefining the function at a.

If the two lateral limits of f at a (finite or infinite) exist, but are different, then the discontinuity of f at a is said to be of the "first kind". The difference between the values of two different lateral limits is called "the jump". If the difference is finite, the discontinuity is said to be "of the first kind with finite jump". If the difference is infinite, that discontinuity is said to be "of the first kind with infinite jump". If at least one of the lateral limits does not exist, the discontinuity is said to be "of the second kind".

As a first example, we consider the continuity in R-{0} of the function $f(x) = sin(x)/x$. We will check that. $\lim_{x \to a} f(x) = f(a)$.

```
>> syms x a
>> limit (sin (x) / x, x, a)

ans =

sin(a) /a
```

A problem arises at the point $x = 0$, at which the function f is not defined. Therefore, the function is discontinuous at $x = 0$. This discontinuity can be avoided by defining the function at $x = 0$ to have a value equal to $\lim_{x \to 0} f(x)$.

```
>> limit (sin(x) / x, x, 0)

ans =

1
```

Therefore, the function $f(x) = sin(x)/x$ presents an avoidable discontinuity at $x = 0$ that is avoided by defining $f(0) = 1$. At all other points the function is continuous. The graph of the function corroborates these findings.

```
>> fplot ('sin (x) / x', [- 6 * pi, 6 * pi])
```

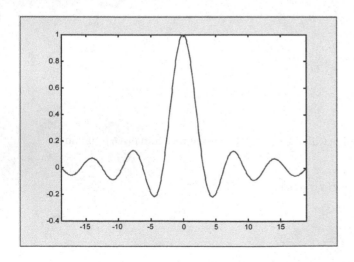

As a second example, we observe that the function $f(x) = \sqrt[x]{e}$ is not continuous at the point $x = 0$ since the lateral boundaries do not match (one is zero and the other infinite).

```
>> syms x

>> limit((exp(1/x)),x,0,'right')

ans =

inf

>> limit((exp(1/x)),x,0, 'left')

ans =

0
```

As a third example, we examine the continuity of the function $f(x) = sin\ (1/x)$. The function f is continuous at any non-zero point, since $\lim_{x \to a} f(x) = f(a)$:

```
>> syms x a

>> limit(sin(1/x),x,a)

ans =

sin(1/a)
```

We now consider the point $x = 0$, at which the function f is not defined. Therefore, the function is discontinuous at $x = 0$. To try to avoid the discontinuity, we calculate:

```
>> limit(sin(1/x),x,0)

ans =

limit(sin(1/x), x = 0)

>> limit(sin(1/x),x,0,'left')

ans =

NaN

>> limit(sin(1/x),x,0,'right')

ans =

NaN
```

We see that at $x = 0$, the function has a discontinuity of the second kind. The graphical representation confirms this result.

```
>> fplot('sin(1/x)',[-pi/6,pi/6])
```

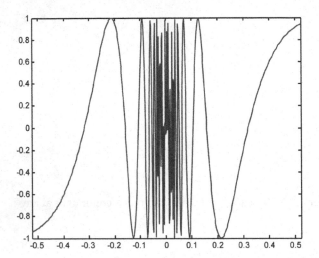

Limits in Several Variables. Iterated and Directional Limits

The generalization of the concept of limit to several variables is quite simple. A sequence of m-dimensional points $\{(a_{1n},a_{2n},...,a_{mn})\}$, with n running through the natural numbers, has as limit the m-dimensional point $(a_{1},..., a_{m})$ if, and only if:

```
Limit[{a₁ₙ}] = a₁, Limit[{a₂ₙ}] = a₂, ..., Limit[{aₘₙ}] = aₘ
n→∞                n→∞                    n→∞
```

This characterization theorem allows us to calculate limits of sequences of m-dimensional points.

There is another theorem similar to the above for the characterization of limits of functions between spaces of more than one dimension. This theorem is used to enable the calculation of limits of multivariable functions.

If $f:R^n \rightarrow R^m$ is a function whose m components are $(f_1,f_2,...,f_m)$. Then it follows that:

```
Limit (f₁(x₁,x₂,..,xₘ),f₂(x₁,x₂,..,xₘ),...,fₙ(x₁,x₂,..,xₘ)) = (l₁,l₂,..,lₙ)  as
x₁→a₁, x₂→a₂,..., xₘ→aₘ
```

if and only if

```
Limit (f₁(x₁,x₂,...,xₘ)) = l₁, Limit(f₂(x₁,x₂,...,xₘ)) = l₂,..., Limit(fₙ(x₁,x₂,...,xₘ)) = lₙ as
x₁→a₁,...,xₘ→aₘ
```

As a first example, we calculate the following three-dimensional limit:

$$\lim_{n\to\infty}\left[\frac{1+n}{n},\left(1+\frac{1}{n}\right)^{2n},\frac{n}{2n-1}\right]$$

```
>> syms n
>> V=[limit((n+1)/n,inf),limit((1+1/n)^(2*n),inf),limit(n/(2*n-1),inf)]

V =

[1, exp(2), 1/2]
```

As a second example, we calculate the following limit:

$$\lim_{n\to\infty}\left[\sqrt[n]{\frac{n}{1+n^2}}, \sqrt[n]{\frac{1}{n}}, \sqrt[n]{5n}, \frac{1+n^2}{n^2}\right]$$

```
>> syms n
>> V1=[limit((n/(n^2+1))^(1/n),inf),limit((1/n)^(1/n),inf),
       limit((5*n)^(1/n),inf),limit((n^2+1)/n^2,inf)]

V1 =

[1, 1, 1, 1]
```

As a third example, we calculate $\lim_{x\to 0} f(x)$ for the function $f{:}R \to R^2$ defined by:

$$f(x)=\left(\frac{\sin(x)}{x}, \sqrt[x]{1+x}\right)$$

```
>> syms x
>> V3=[limit(sin(x)/x,x,0),limit((1+x)^(1/x),x,0)]

V3 =

[1, exp(1)]
```

As fourth example, we find $\lim_{(x,y)\to(0,0)} f(x,y)$ for the function $f{:}R \to R^2$ defined by:

$$f(x,y)=\left[\frac{2(1-\cos(y))}{y^2} + \frac{\sin(x)}{x}, \sqrt[x]{1+x} - \frac{\tan(y)}{y}\right]$$

```
>> [limit(limit(sin(x)/x+2*(1-cos(y))/y^2,x,0),y,0),
    [limit(limit(((1+x)^(1/x)-tan(y)/y),x,0),y,0)]

ans =

[2, exp(1) - 1]
```

Given a function $f: R^n \to R$ an *iterated limit of* $f(x_1,x_2,...,x_n)$ *at the point* $(a_1,a_2,...,a_n)$ is the value of the following limit, if it exists:

$$\text{Lim}_{x_1 \to a_1} (\text{Lim}_{x_2 \to a_2} (... (\text{Lim}_{x_n \to a_n} f(x_1,x_2,..,x_n))...))$$

or any of the other permutations of the limits on x_i with i = 1, 2,...,*n*.

The *directional limit of* f *at the point* $(a_1,..., a_n)$, depending on the direction of the curve h(t) =(h$_1$(t) , h$_2$(t),..., h$_n$(t)), such that h(t$_0$) =(a$_1$,a$_2$,...,a$_n$), is the value:

$$\text{Lim}_{t \to t0} (f(h(t))) = \text{Lim}_{(x_1,x_2,...,x_n) \to (a_1, a_2,...,a_n)} f(x_1,x_2,...,x_n)$$

A necessary condition for a function of several variables to have a limit at a point is that all the iterated limits have the same value (which will be equal to the value of the limit of the function, if it exists). The directional limits of a function at a point may be different for different curves, and some of the directional limits may not exist. Another necessary condition for a function of several variables to have a limit at a point is that all directional limits, approaching along any curve, have the same value (and this common value will be equal to the value of the limit of the function, if it exists). Therefore, to prove that a function has no limit it is enough to show that the iterated limits do not exist, or if they exist, are not the same, or that two directional limits are different, or a directional limit doesn't exist. Another practical procedure to calculate the limit of a function of several variables is to change the coordinates from Cartesian to polar, which can facilitate the limit operation.

As first example, we calculate $\lim_{(x,y) \to (0,0)} f(x,y)$ for $f: R^2 \to R$ defined by:

$$f(x,y) = \frac{xy}{x^2+y^2}$$

```
>> syms x y
>> limit(limit((x*y)/(x^2+y^2),x,0),y,0)

ans =

0

>> limit(limit((x*y)/(x^2+y^2),y,0),x,0)

ans =

0
```

We see that the iterated limits are the same. Next we calculate the directional limits according to the family of straight lines y = *mx*:

```
>> syms m
>> limit((m*x^2)/(x^2+(m^2)*(x^2)),x,0)

ans =

m/(1+m^2)
```

We see that the directional limits depend on the parameter m, which will be different for different values of m (for the different considered straight lines). Thus, we conclude that the function has no limit at (0,0).

The result can be graphically illustrated as a surface as follows.

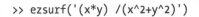

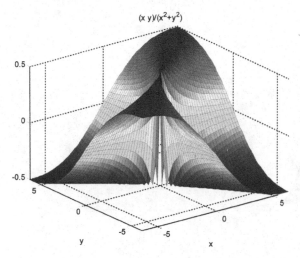

We observe that in a neighborhood of (0,0), the function has no limit.

As second example, we consider $\lim\limits_{(x,y)\to(0,0)} f(x,y)$ for the function $f\colon R^2 \to R$ defined by:

$$f(x,y) = \frac{(y^2 - x^2)^2}{x^2 + y^4}$$

```
>> syms x y
>> limit(limit((y^2-x^2)^2/(y^4+x^2),x,0),y,0)

ans =

1

>> limit(limit((y^2-x^2)^2/(y^4+x^2),y,0),x,0)

ans =

0
```

As the iterated limits are different, we conclude that the function has no limit at the point (0,0).

If we graph the surface in a neighborhood of (0,0) we can observe its behavior at that point.

```
>> ezsurf('(y^2-x^2)^2/(y^4+x^2)',[-1 1], [-1 1])
```

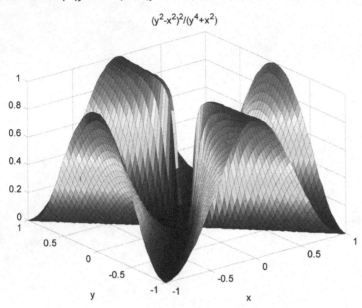

$(y^2-x^2)^2/(y^4+x^2)$

Continuity in Several Variables

Generalizing the definition of continuity in one variable we can easily formalize the concept of continuity in several variables. A function f: $R^n \to R^m$ is said to be continuous at the point $(a_1, a_2, ..., a_n)$ if:

$$\text{Lim } f(x_1, x_2, ..., x_n) = f(a_1, a_2, ..., a_n)$$
$$x_1 \to a_1, \; x_2 \to a_2, ..., \; x_n \to a_n$$

As a first example, we examine the continuity at the point (1,2) of the function:

$$f(x,y) = x^2 + 2y \text{ if } (x,y) \neq (1,2) \text{ and } f(1,2) = 0.$$

```
>> limit(limit((x^2+2*y),x,1),y,2)

ans =

5

>> limit(limit((x^2+2*y),y,2),x,1)

ans =

5
```

We see that if the limit at (1,2) exists, then it should be 5. But the function has value 0 at the point (1,2). Thus, the function is not continuous at the point (1,2).

As a second example, we study the continuity in all of R² of the function $f(x,y)=x^2+2y$.

```
>> syms x y a b
>> limit(limit((x^2+2*y),x,a),y,b)

ans =

a^2 + 2*b

>> limit(limit((x^2+2*y),y,b),x,a)

ans =

a^2 + 2*b

>> f='x^2+2*y'

f =

x^2+2*y

>> subs(f,{x,y},{a,b})

ans =

a^2 + 2*b
```

We see that the iterated limits coincide and their common value coincides with the value of the function at the generic point (a, b) in R², i.e. $\lim_{(x,y)\to(a,b)} f(x,y)=f(a,b)$.

If we graphically represent the surface, we see that the function is continuous across its domain of definition.

```
>> ezsurf('x^2+2*y')
```

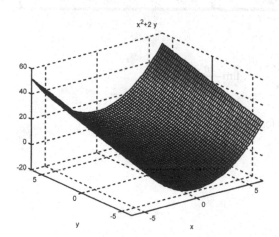

EXERCISE 5-1

Calculate the following limits:

$$\lim_{n\to\infty}\frac{1+7n^2+3n^3}{5-8n+4n^3}, \quad \lim_{n\to\infty}\left[\left(\frac{1+n}{2}\right)^4\frac{1+n}{n^5}\right], \quad \lim_{n\to\infty}\sqrt[n]{\frac{1+n}{n^2}}$$

The first limit presents a typical uncertainty of the type ∞/∞ :

```
>> limit((3*n^3+7*n^2+1)/(4*n^3-8*n+5),n,inf)
```

ans =

3/4

The last two limits are of the type $\infty.0$ and ∞^0 :

```
>> limit(((n+1)/2)*((n^4+1)/n^5), inf)
```

ans =

1/2

```
>> limit(((n+1)/n^2)^(1/n), inf)
```

ans =

1

EXERCISE 5-2

Calculate the following limits:

$$\lim_{x\to2}\frac{x-\sqrt{x+2}}{-3+\sqrt{4x+1}}, \quad \lim_{x\to0}\sqrt[x]{x+1}, \quad \lim_{x\to0}\frac{\sin\left[(ax)^2\right]}{x^2}, \quad \lim_{x\to0}\frac{e^x-1}{\log(x+1)}$$

Here we have three indeterminates of the type *0/0* and one of the form 1^∞ :

```
>> syms x
```

```
>> limit((x-(x+2)^(1/2))/((4*x+1)^(1/2)-3),2)
```

ans =

9/8

```
>> limit((1+x)^(1/x))

ans =

exp(1)

>> syms x a, limit(sin(a*x)^2/x^2,x,0)

ans =

a^2

>> limit((exp(1)^x-1)/log(1+x))

ans =

log(3060513257434037/1125899906842624)

>> vpa(limit((exp(1)^x-1)/log(1+x)))

ans =

1.0000000000000001101889132838495
```

EXERCISE 5-3

Calculate the limit of the following sequence of functions:

$$g_n(x) = \frac{x^n}{(1+x^n)} \quad x > 0$$

We will start by graphically representing the functions to predict the possible limit.

```
>> fplot('[x/(1+x),x^2/(1+x^2),x^3/(1+x^3),x^4/(1+x^4),x^5/(1+x^5),
x^6/(1+x^6),x^7/(1+x^7),x^8/(1+x^8),x^9/(1+x^9),x^10/(1+x^10)]',[0,1,-1/2,1])
```

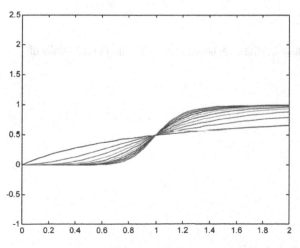

This tells us that, intuitively, the limit is the x-axis (i.e. the function $f(x) = 0$) for values of x in [0,1], the value 0.5 for $x = 1$ and the function $f(x) = 1$ for $x > 1$. Let's see:

```
>> vpa(simplify(limit(x^n/(1+x^n),n,inf)))

ans =

piecewise([x = 1.0, 0.5], [1.0 < x, 1.0], [x < 1.0, 0.0])
```

MATLAB tells us that the limit function is:

$$f(x)=\begin{cases}0 & if & 0<x<1\\0.5 & if & x=1\\1 & if & x>1\end{cases}$$

EXERCISE 5-4

Find $\lim_{(x,y)\to(0,0)} f(x,y)$ for the function f:R² → R defined by:

$$f(x,y)=\frac{(y^2-x)^2}{x^2+y^4}$$

```
>> syms x y m, limit(limit((y^2-x)^2/(y^4+x^2),y,0),x,0)

ans =

1

>> limit(limit((y^2-x)^2/(y^4+x^2),x,0),y,0)

ans =

1
```

We see that the iterated limits are the same. We then calculate the directional limits according to the family of straight lines $y = mx$:

```
>> limit(((m*x)^2-x)^2/((m*x)^4+x^2),x,0)

ans =

1
```

The directional limits according to the family of straight lines $y = mx$ do not depend on m and coincide with the iterated limits. We now find the directional limits according to the family of parabolas $y \wedge 2 = mx$:

```
>> limit(((m*x)-x)^2/((m*x)^2+x^2),x,0)

ans =

(m - 1)^2/(m^2 + 1)
```

The directional limits according to this family of parabolas depend on the parameter, and so they are different. This leads us to conclude that the function has no limit at (0,0).

EXERCISE 5-5

Find $\lim\limits_{(x,y)\to(0,0)} f(x,y)$ for the function f:R$^2 \to$ R defined by:

$$f(x,y)=\frac{(y^2-x)^2}{x^2+y^4}$$

```
>> syms x y, limit(limit((x^2*y)/(x^2+y^2),x,0),y,0)

ans =

0

>> limit(limit((x^2*y)/(x^2+y^2),x,0),y,0)

ans =

0

>> limit(((x^2)*(m*x))/(x^2+(m*x)^2),x,0)

ans =

0

>> limit(((m*y)^2)*y/((m*y)^2+y^2),y,0)

ans =

0
```

We see that the iterated limits and the directional limits according to the given families of lines and parabolas all coincide and are equal to zero. This leads us to suspect that the limit of the function may be zero. To confirm this, we transform to polar coordinates and find the limit:

```
>> syms a r;
>> limit(limit(((r^2) * (cos(a)^2) * (r) * (sin(a))) / ((r^2) * (cos(a) ^ 2) +(r^2) *
(sin(a)^2)), r, 0), a, 0)

ans =

0
```

We therefore conclude that the limit of the function is zero at the point (0,0).

This is an example where as a last resort we had to transform to polar coordinates. We used families of lines and parabolas for our directional limits, but other curves could have been used. A change to polar coordinates can be crucial in determining the limits of functions of several variables. As we have seen, there are sufficient criteria for a function to have no limit at a point, but there are no necessary and sufficient conditions to ensure the existence of a limit.

EXERCISE 5-6

Find $\lim\limits_{(x,y)\to(0,0)} f(x,y)$ for f: R^2 → R defined by:

$$f(x,y)=\frac{(x-1)^2 y^2}{(x-1)^2 + y^2}$$

```
>> syms x y m a r
>> limit (limit (y ^ 2 *(x-1) ^ 2 / (y ^ 2 +(x-1) ^ 2), x, 0), y, 0)

ans =

0

>> limit (limit (y ^ 2 *(x-1) ^ 2 / (y ^ 2 +(x-1) ^ 2), y, 0), x, 0)

ans =

0

>> limit ((m*x) ^ 2 *(x-1) ^ 2/((m*x) ^ 2 +(x-1) ^ 2), x, 0)

ans =

0
```

```
>> limit ((m*x) *(x-1) ^ 2/((m*x) +(x-1) ^ 2), x, 0)
```

ans =

0

We see that the iterated and directional limits coincide. Next we calculate the limit in polar coordinates:

```
>> limit(limit((r ^ 2 * sin(a) ^ 2) * (r * cos(a) - 1) ^ 2 / ((r ^ 2 * sin(a) ^ 2) +
(r * cos(a) - 1) ^ 2), r, 1), a, 0)
```

ans =

0

The limit is zero at the point (1,0). Below we graph the surface, observing the tendency to 0 in a neighborhood of (1,0):

```
>> ezsurf (y ^ 2 *(x-1) ^ 2 / (y ^ 2 +(x-1) ^ 2), [- 2, 2, - 2, 2])
```

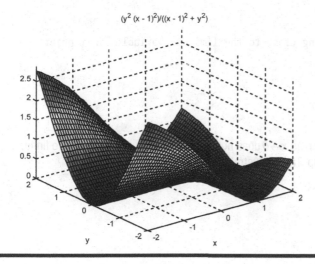

EXERCISE 5-7

Study the continuity of the function of a real variable:

$$f(x)=\frac{1}{1+\sqrt[x]{e}} \; if \; x\neq0 \; and \; f(x)=1 \; if \; x=0$$

The only problematic point is at $x = 0$. Now, the function does exist at $x = 0$ (it has value 1). We will try to find the lateral limits as $x\to0$:

```
>> syms x
>> limit(1 /(1 + exp(x)), x, 0, 'right')

ans =

0

>> limit(1/(1 + exp(x)), x, 0, 'left')

Warning: Could not attach the property of being close to the limit to variable limit point
[limit]

ans =

1
```

As the lateral limits are different, the limit of the function as $x\to0$ does not exist. But as the lateral limits are finite, the discontinuity of the first kind at $x = 0$ is a finite jump. This is illustrated in Figure 5-1:

```
>> fplot ('1 /(1 + exp(x))'[-5, 5])
```

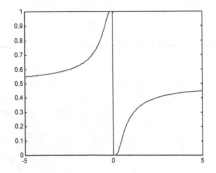

Figure 5-1.

CHAPTER 6

■ ■ ■

Numerical Series and Power Series

Numerical Series of Non-negative Terms

MATLAB enables you to work with numerical series of non-negative terms and with alternating series. In addition, the commands relating to limits allow you to work with different convergence tests for numerical series.

In the case where the sum is convergent, there are various functions available to help you to find the sum. We have the following:

---

symsum(S,v,a,b)   *Sums the series S as the variable v varies from a to b.*

```
syms x;
symsum(x^k/sym('k!'), k, 0, inf)
```

symsum(S,v)   *Sums the series S as the variable v varies from 0 to v-1.*

```
>> symsum(k^2,k)

ans =

k^3/3 - k^2/2 + k/6
```

r = symsum (S)   *Sums the series S as its symbolic variable k (as determined by findsym) ranges from 0 up to k-1.*

```
>> r=symsum(k^2)

r =

k^3/3 - k^2/2 + k/6
```

symsum (S, a, b)   *Sums the series S as its symbolic variable k (determined by findsym) ranges between a and b*

```
>> syms k n
>> symsum(k,0,n-1)

ans =

(n*(n - 1))/2
```

Convergence Criteria: The Ratio Test

There are several criteria for determining whether a series of positive terms is convergent (i.e. has a finite sum). Among the most common are *the ratio test* or *d'Alembert criterion*, which read as follows:

$$\sum_{n=1}^{\infty} a(n) \text{ is convergent if } \lim_{n\to\infty} \frac{a(n+1)}{a(n)} < 1$$

$$\sum_{n=1}^{\infty} a(n) \text{ is divergent if } \lim_{n\to\infty} \frac{a(n+1)}{a(n)} > 1$$

If the limit is 1, we cannot conclude anything about the convergence of the series.

As a first example, we analyze the convergence of the series $\sum_{n=1}^{\infty} \frac{n}{2^n}$.

Using the ratio test we first calculate the limit $\lim_{n\to\infty} \frac{a(n+1)}{a(n)}$.

```
>> syms n
>> f='n/2^n'

f =

n/2^n

>> limit(subs(f,n+1)/subs(f,n),inf)

ans =

1/2
```

As the limit is less than 1, the series is convergent. We can calculate the sum of its first k terms in the following way:

```
>> syms n k
>> symsum(n/2^n,0,k-1)

ans =

2 - (2*(k + 1))/2^k
```

If we want to find the infinite sum of the series we have:

```
>> symsum(n/2^n,0,inf)

ans =

2
```

Therefore we conclude that:

$$\sum_{n=0}^{\infty} \frac{n}{2^n} = 2$$

As a second example, we look at the convergence of the series $\sum_{n=1}^{\infty} \dfrac{n^n}{n!}$.

Using the ratio test we calculate $\lim\limits_{n \to \infty} \dfrac{a(n+1)}{a(n)}$:

```
>> syms n
>> f=n^n/sym('n!')

f =

n^n/factorial(n)

>> limit(subs(f,n+1)/subs(f,n),inf)

ans =

exp(1)
```

As the limit is greater than 1, the series is divergent.

Raabe's Criterion

Raabe's criterion may be used to analyze the convergence of a series if the ratio test, or similar tests, fail. If the ratio test returns a value of 1, one can often use the *criterion of Raabe or Duhamel*, which reads as follows:

$$\sum_{n=1}^{\infty} a(n) \text{ is convergent if } \lim_{n \to \infty}\left[n\left(1 - \frac{a(n+1)}{a(n)} \right) \right] > 1$$

$$\sum_{n=1}^{\infty} a(n) \text{ is divergent if } \lim_{n \to \infty}\left[n\left(1 - \frac{a(n+1)}{a(n)} \right) \right] < 1$$

If the limit is 1, we cannot conclude anything about the convergence of the series.

As an example, we try to determine whether the series $\sum_{n=1}^{\infty} \dfrac{1+n}{n(2+n)(3+n)}$ converges.

Obviously, we initially try to apply the ratio test:

```
>> syms n
>> f='(1+n)/(n*(2+n)*(3+n))'

f =

(1+n)/(n*(2+n)*(3+n))

>> limit(subs(f,n+1)/subs(f,n),inf)

ans =

1
```

As the limit is 1, we cannot conclude anything about the convergence of the series. Instead, we try the Raabe criterion.

```
>> limit(n*(1-subs(f,n+1)/subs(f,n)),inf)
```

```
ans =
```

2

The limit is greater than 1, so we conclude that the series converges. We find its sum in the following way:

```
>> symsum((1+n)/(n*(2+n)*(3+n)),1,inf)
```

```
ans =
```

17/36

The Root Test

The *Cauchy criterion* or *root test* also improves on the ratio test and sometimes the Raabe criterion when analyzing the convergence of a series. The *root test* reads as follows:

$$\sum_{n=1}^{\infty} a(n) \text{ is convergent if } \lim_{n \to \infty} \sqrt[n]{a(n)} < 1$$

$$\sum_{n=1}^{\infty} a(n) \text{ is divergent if } \lim_{n \to \infty} \sqrt[n]{a(n)} > 1$$

If the limit is 1, we cannot say anything about the convergence of the series. As a first example, we try to determine whether the series $\sum_{n=1}^{\infty} \dfrac{5}{2^n}$ converges. We use the root test in the following way:

```
>> syms n
```

```
>> limit((5/2^n)^(1/n),inf)
```

```
ans =
```

1/2

As the limit is less than 1, the series converges.
If we had applied the ratio and Raabe criteria we would have found:

```
>> f='5/2^n'
```

```
f =
```

5/2^n

```
>> limit(subs(f,n+1)/subs(f,n),inf)

ans =

1/2

>> limit(n*(1-subs(f,n+1)/subs(f,n)),inf)

ans =

Inf

>> limit((5/2^n)^(1/n),inf)

ans =

1/2
```

So using either criteria, we would have concluded that the series converges (limit less than 1 for the ratio test and limit greater than 1 for the Raabe criterion).

The sum of the series is calculated by:

```
>> symsum(5/2^n,1,inf)

ans =

5
```

As a further example we analyze whether the following series converges:

$$\sum_{n=1}^{\infty} \tan^n\left(p + \frac{q}{n}\right)$$

according to the values of the parameters p and q.

As its general term is an nth power, it is logical to try to use the root test. We have:

```
>> syms n p q
>> simplify(limit(tan(p+q/n),n,inf))

ans =

tan(p)
```

Then, for values of p (say, in the interval (0, Pi/2)) such that *tan (p) < 1* the series converges. These values of p satisfy *0 < p < Pl/4*. For values of p such that *ran(p) > 1* the series diverges. These values of p satisfy *Pi/4 < p < Pi/2*. MATLAB does not offer the exact value or an approximate value for the sum of this series.

```
>> simplify(symsum(tan(p+q/n),n,1,inf))

ans =

sum(tan(p + q/n), n = 1..Inf)
```

207

Other Convergence Criteria

There are additional criteria one can use to study the convergence of series of positive terms.

The *Gauss majorization criterion* says that if a series of non-negative terms is dominated by a convergent series then it too is convergent (a_n is dominated by b_n if $a_n < b_n$ for all n). In addition, if a series dominates a divergent series, then it is divergent.

The *comparison test of the second kind* ensures that if the limit of the ratio a_n/b_n exists and is positive then the series $\sum a_n$ and $\sum b_n$ are either both convergent or both divergent.

A third approach is given by the result that the two series $\sum_{n=1}^{\infty} a(n)$ and $\sum_{n=1}^{\infty} 2^n a(2^n)$ are either both convergent or both divergent.

As a first example, we consider the following series:

$$\sum_{n=1}^{\infty} \frac{1}{\left(1+\sqrt{n}\right)^2}$$

Initially we try to apply Raabe's criterion and the ratio test:

```
>> f='1/(1+n^(1/2))^2'

f =

1/(1+n^(1/2))^2

>> limit(n*(1-subs(f,n+1)/subs(f,n)),inf)

ans =

1

>> limit(subs(f,n+1)/subs(f,n),inf)

ans =

1
```

In both cases the limit is 1. So at the moment we cannot conclude anything about the convergence of the series.

We now apply the comparison test of the second kind to compare our series with the divergent harmonic series with general term *1/n*:

```
>> limit(subs(f,n)/(1/n),inf)

ans =

1
```

As the limit is greater than zero, we conclude that the initial series is also divergent.

We reach the same conclusion by applying the root test.

```
>> limit(subs(f, n)^1/n, inf)

ans =

0
```

Since the limit is less than 1, the series diverges.

As a second example, consider the following series:

$$\sum_{n=1}^{\infty} \frac{1}{n \, Log(n)}$$

We apply the criterion that ensures that the series $\sum_{n=1}^{\infty} a(n)$ and $\sum_{n=1}^{\infty} \left[2^n a(2^n) \right]$ have the same character of convergence.

```
>> f ='1 / (n * log (n))'

f =

1 / (n * log (n))

>> 2 ^ n * subs(f,2^n)

ans =

1/log(2^n)
```

Thus our series has the same character of convergence as the series with general term $1/(nlog(2))$, and since

$$\frac{1}{n \, Log(2)} > \frac{1}{n}$$

we see that the series with general term $1/(nlog(2))$ diverges. We conclude that the original series also diverges.

Alternating Numerical Series. Dirichlet and Abel's Criteria

So far we have only considered numerical series of positive terms. From now on we will consider numerical series that have alternating positive and negative terms. Usually these series are called *alternating series*.

In the case of alternating series, the concept of absolute convergence is fundamental. A series $\sum a(n)$ is said to be absolutely convergent if the series of moduli $\sum |a(n)|$ is convergent. As the series of moduli is a series of positive terms, we already know how to analyze it. If a series is absolutely convergent then it is convergent, but not conversely.

There are two classical criteria that can be used to analyze the convergence of alternating series, which will allow us to resolve most problems involving alternating series.

Dirichlet's criterion says that if the sequence of partial sums of $\sum a(n)$ is bounded and $\{b(n)\}$ is a decreasing sequence that has limit 0, then the series $\sum a(n)b(n)$ is convergent.

Abel's criterion says that if $\sum a(n)$ is convergent and $\{b(n)\}$ is a monotone convergent sequence, then the series $\sum a(n)b(n)$ is convergent.

As a first example, we consider the alternating series:

$$\sum_{n=1}^{\infty} \frac{(-1)^{1+n}}{1+2n^2}$$

To analyze the convergence of the series, we study whether or not it is absolutely convergent, i.e. if the following series of positive terms is convergent:

$$\sum_{n=1}^{\infty} \left| \frac{(-1)^{1+n}}{1+2n^2} \right|$$

209

We apply to this series of positive terms the comparison test of the second kind, comparing with the convergent series with general term $1/n^2$

```
>> f ='abs((-1)^(1+n)/(1+2*n^2))'

f =

abs((-1)^(1+n)/(1+2*n^2))

>> limit(subs(f,n)/(1/n^2), inf)

ans =

1/2
```

As the limit is greater than zero, the series of positive terms considered is convergent, and so the initial series is absolutely convergent and, therefore, convergent.

As a second example we consider the series:

$$\sum_{n=1}^{\infty} \frac{(-1)^{1+n}}{n}$$

If we put $a(n) = (-1)^{1+n}$ and $b(n) = \dfrac{1}{n}$, we have that $\Sigma a(n)$ has bounded partial sums and $\{b(n)\}$ is monotone decreasing with limit 0.

Using Dirichlet's criterion we conclude that the considered alternating series is convergent.

Power Series

A power series has the following structure:

$$\sum a(n) x^n$$

The main objective is to calculate the range of convergence of the series, i.e., the range of values of x for which the corresponding numerical series is absolutely convergent.

If the variable x is replaced by a numerical value, the power series becomes a numerical series. The criteria used to determine whether the series converges are those already used for numerical series. Since we are considering the absolute convergence of the series, we are considering series of positive terms, so the commonly used criteria are the root and ratio tests.

As a first example, we calculate the interval of convergence for the following power series:

$$\sum_{n=0}^{\infty} \frac{4^{2n}}{n+2}(x-3)^n$$

Via the ratio test we will try to calculate the values of x for which the given series is convergent.

```
>> f ='(4^(2*n)) * ((x-3)^n) / (n + 2)'

f =

(4 ^(2*n)) * ((x-3) ^ n) / (n + 2)
```

```
>> limit(simplify(subs(f,n,n+1)/subs(f,n,n)), n, inf)
```

```
ans =
```

```
16 * x - 48
```

The series will be convergent when $|16x - 48| < 1$. To find the extreme values of the interval of convergence we solve the following equations:

```
>> [solve('16*x-48=1'), solve('16*x-48=-1')]
```

```
ans =
```

```
[49/16, 47/16]
```

Thus, the condition $|16x - 48| < 1$ is equivalent to the following:

```
47/16 < x < 49/16
```

We already know that in this interval the series is convergent. Now we need to analyze the behavior of the series at the end points of the interval. First we consider $x = 49/16$.

```
>> g1=simplify(subs(f,x,49/16))
```

```
G1 =
```

```
1 /(n + 2)
```

We have to analyze the numerical series of positive terms $\displaystyle\sum_{n=1}^{\infty} \frac{1}{n+2}$.

Note that the ratio test and Raabe's criterion return a limit of 1, so we must use an alternative approach.

```
>> limit(simplify(subs(g1,n+1)/subs(g1,n)), n, inf)
```

```
ans =
```

```
1
```

```
>> limit(n*(1-subs(g1,n+1)/subs(g1,n)),inf)
```

```
ans =
```

```
1
```

We will apply the comparison test of the second kind, comparing the series of the problem with the divergent harmonic series with general term $1/n$:

```
>> limit(subs(g1,n)/(1/n),inf)
```

```
ans =
```

```
1
```

As the limit is greater than zero, the series is divergent.
We now analyze the endpoint $x = 47/16$:

```
>> g2=simplify(subs(f,x,47/16))

g2 =

(-1)^n/(n + 2)
```

We have to analyze the alternating series $\sum\limits_{n=1}^{\infty} \dfrac{(-1)^n}{n+2}$.

By Dirichlet's criterion, since the series with general term $(-1)^n$ has bounded partial sums, and the sequence with general term $1/(n+2)$ is decreasing toward 0, the alternating series converges. The interval of convergence of the power series is therefore the half-open interval $[47/16, 49/16)$.

Power Series Expansions

MATLAB includes commands that allow you to address the problem of the local approximation of a real function of a real variable at a point by replacing the initial function by a simple equivalent. The most common way to do this is to replace an arbitrary function $f(x)$ by a power series $P(x)$ so that the values of $f(x)$ and $P(x)$ are close in the neighborhood of the given point. This power series is called a *power series expansion* of the function.

The MATLAB commands used to work with power series are presented in the following table:

taylor (f)	*Returns the MacLaurin series of f up to degree 5.*

	```>> syms x```
	 ```f = exp(x^2);```
	
	 ```>> pretty(taylor(f))```
	
	 ``` 4```
	 ```x 2```
	 ```-- + x + 1```
	 ```2```

taylor (f, n)	*Returns the MacLaurin series of f up to degree n, where n is a natural number.*

	```>> pretty(taylor(f,7))```
	
	 ``` 6 4```
	 ```x x 2```
	 ```-- + -- + x + 1```
	 ```6 2```

(*continued*)

taylor(f, a)	*Returns the Taylor series of f in a neighborhood of the real number a up to degree 5. If a is a natural number it is necessary to use the function taylor(f, 5, a).*

```
>> pretty(simplify(taylor(f,1/2)))

    / 1 \          5          4         3         2
exp| - | (2592 x - 2480 x + 2960 x  + 1800 x  + 250 x + 2969)
    \ 4 /`
-------------------------------------------------------------
3840
```

taylor(f, n, v)	*Finds the MacLaurin series of f up to degree n-1 in the variable v.*

```
>> pretty(taylor(f,3,p))

      2          2      2            2               2
exp(p) + exp(p) (2 p + 1) (p - x)  - 2 p exp(p) (p - x)
```

taylor(f, n, v, a)	*Finds the Taylor series of f in a neighborhood of the real number a up to degree n-1 in the variable v.*

```
>> pretty(taylor(f,3,p,2))

                                            2
exp(4) + 4 exp(4) (x - 2) + 9 exp(4) (x - 2)
```

As a first example we calculate the Taylor polynomial of *sinh(x)* at the point $x = 0$ (the MacLaurin series) up to degree 13.

```
>> syms x

>> f=sinh(x)

f =

sinh(x)

>> taylor(f,13)

ans =

 x^11/39916800 + x^9/362880 + x^7/5040 + x^5/120 + x^3/6 + x
```

As a second example we calculate the Taylor expansion of *1/(1+x)* at the point $x = 2$ up to degree 6.

```
>> syms x
>> f=1/(1+x)

f =

1/(x + 1)
```

```
>> pretty(taylor(f,6,2))
```

```
       2          3          4          5
 (x - 2)     x  (x - 2)   (x - 2)    (x - 2)     5
 --------  - - - --------  + -------- - -------- + -
    27     9     81          243        729       9
```

EXERCISE 6-1

Study the convergence and, if possible, find the sum of the following series:

$$\sum_{n=1}^{\infty} \frac{n^n}{3^n\, n!} \qquad \sum_{n=1}^{\infty} \frac{3+2n}{7^n\, n(1+n)}$$

We apply the ratio test for the first series:

```
>> syms n
>> f=n^n/(sym('n!')*(3^n))
```

```
f =
```

```
n^n/(3^n*factorial(n))
```

```
>> limit(subs(f,n+1)/subs(f,n),inf)
```

```
ans =
```

```
exp(1)/3
```

The limit is less than 1, so the series turns out to be convergent. Therefore, we can try to calculate its sum as follows:

```
>> vpa(simplify(symsum(f,1,inf)))
```

```
ans =
```

```
1.6250941822939141659377675737628
```

Now we apply the ratio test for the second series:

```
>> f=(2*n+3)/(n*(n+1)*(7^n))
```

```
f =
```

```
(2*n + 3)/(7^n*n*(n + 1))
```

```
>> limit(subs(f,n+1)/subs(f,n),inf)

ans =

1/7
```

As the limit is less than 1, the series is convergent. MATLAB will attempt to return the exact sum, but it may be in a complicated form, in terms of special functions. Here we approximate the sum, as before:

```
>> vpa(symsum(f,1,inf))

ans =

0.38339728069090966678282849845975009
```

EXERCISE 6-2

Study the convergence and, if possible, find the sum of the following series:

$$\sum_{n=1}^{\infty} \frac{n}{p^n}, \ \sum_{n=1}^{\infty} \frac{(n+p)!}{p^n n! p!}$$

p = real parameter

We apply the ratio test for the first series:

```
>> syms n;
>> p=sym('p','real');

>> f=n/p^n

f =

n/p^n

>> limit(subs(f,{n},{n+1})/subs(f,{n},{n}),n,inf)

ans =

1/p
```

Thus, if $p > 1$, the series converges, and if $p < 1$, the series diverges. If $p = 1$, we get the series with general term n, which diverges. When p is greater than 1, we find the sum of the series:

```
>> vpa(symsum(f,1,inf))

ans =

piecewise([1.0 < Re(n), n*zeta(n)])
```

We will apply the ratio test to the second series:

```
>> f=sym('(n+p)!')/(sym('p!')*(sym('n!')*(p^n)))
f =

factorial(n + p)/(p^n*factorial(n)*factorial(p))
>> vpa(simplify(limit(subs(f,{n},{n+1})/subs(f,{n},{n}),n,inf)))

ans =

1/p
```

Thus, if $p > 1$, the series converges, and if $p < 1$, the series diverges, and if $p = 1$, we get the series with general term n, which diverges. When p is greater than 1, we try to find the sum of the series:

```
>> vpa(simplify(symsum(f,1,inf)))

ans =

numeric::sum(factorial(n + p)/(p^(1.0*n)*factorial(p)),
p = 1..Inf)/factorial(n)
```

We see that MATLAB has been unable to find the sum.

Thus, if $p > 1$ the two series converge and if $p < 1$ the two series diverge. We have only been able to find the sum of the first series.

EXERCISE 6-3

Study the convergence and, if possible, find the sum of the following series:

$$\sum_{n=1}^{\infty} (1+\frac{1}{n})^{-n^2} \quad \sum_{n=1}^{\infty} \left[\left(\frac{1+n}{n}\right)^{1+n} - \frac{1+n}{n}\right]^{-n}$$

For the first series we apply the ratio test:

```
>> syms n
>> f =(1+1/n)^(-n^2)

f =

1/(1/n + 1)^(n^2)

>> limit(subs(f,n+1)/subs(f, n), inf)

ans =

1/exp (1)
```

As the limit is less than 1, the series converges. MATLAB can sum this series as follows:

```
>> vpa(symsum(f,1,inf))

ans =

0.81741943329783346091309999437311
```

We will apply the ratio test to the second series:

```
>> f = (((n + 1) / n) ^ (n + 1) - a (n + 1) /n) ^(-n)

f =

1 / (((n + 1)/n) ^(n + 1) - (n + 1) / n) ^ n

>> limit (subs(f,n+1) /subs (f, n), inf)

ans =

1 / (exp(1) - 1)
```

As the limit is less than 1, the series converges. The sum can be found with MATLAB as follows:

```
>> vpa(symsum(f,1,inf))

ans =

1.1745855750875866746226188496682
```

EXERCISE 6-4

Study the convergence and, if possible, find the sum of the following series:

$$\sum_{n=1}^{\infty} (\sqrt[n]{n}-1)^n \quad \sum_{n=1}^{\infty} \left(\frac{n^2+2n+1}{n^2+n-1}\right)^{n^2}$$

As the general term of both series is raised to a power of n, the root test may be applicable.

We apply the root test to the first series:

```
>> f = (n ^ (1/n) - 1) ^ n

f =

(n ^ (1/n) - 1) ^ n
```

```
>> limit(subs(f, n)^(1/n), inf)

ans =

0
```

As the limit is less than 1, the series is convergent. The sum is calculated as follows:

```
>> vpa(symsum(f,1,inf))

ans =

0.29759749220552960849982457076294
```

Now we apply the root test to the second series:

```
>> syms n
>> f = ((n^2+2*n+1) /(n^2+n-1))^(n^2)

f =

((n^2 + 2*n + 1) /(n^2 + n-1)) ^(n^2)

>> limit(subs(f,n)^(1/n),inf)

ans =

exp(1)
```

As the limit is greater than 1, the series diverges.

EXERCISE 6-5

Study the convergence and, if possible, find the sum of the following series:

$$\sum_{n=1}^{\infty} \frac{(n+1)(n+2)}{n^5}$$

We try to apply the root, quotient, and Raabe criteria:

```
>> f=(n+1)*(n+2)/n^5

f =

((n + 1)*(n + 2))/n^5

>> limit(subs(f,n)^(1/n),inf)

ans =

1
```

```
>> limit(subs(f,n+1)/subs(f,n),inf)
```

ans =

1

```
>> limit(n*(1-subs(f,n+1)/subs(f,n)),inf)
```

ans =

3

The root and ratio tests tell us nothing, but the Raabe criterion already assures us that the series converges (the limit is greater than 1). We find the sum.

```
>> vpa(symsum(f,1,inf))
```

ans =

6.5228821145797487126104480224049

We can also analyze the series directly by using the comparison test of the second kind, comparing our series with the convergent series with general term *1/n3*:

```
>> limit(f/(1/(n^3)),inf)
```

ans =

1

As the limit is greater than 0, the series is convergent.

EXERCISE 6-6

Study the convergence and, if possible, find the sum of the following series:

$$\sum_{n=1}^{\infty} \frac{1}{n[Log(n)]^p} \qquad p = parameter > 0$$

We apply the criterion that ensures that the series $\sum_{n=1}^{\infty} a(n)$ and $\sum_{n=1}^{\infty} 2^n a(2^n)$ have the same character of convergence.

```
>> f=1/(n*(log(n))^p)
```

f =

1/(n*log(n)^p)

```
>> pretty((2^n)*subs(f,{n},{2^n}))
```

```
      1
    --------
       n p
    log(2 )
```

When $p < 1$, this series dominates the divergent series with general term $n-p = 1/np$. Thus the initial series also diverges.

When $p > 1$, this series is dominated by the convergent series with general term $n-p = 1/np$. Thus the initial series converges.

When $p = 1$, the series reduces to the series:

$$\sum_{n=1}^{\infty} \frac{1}{n \, Log(n)}$$

which can be tested by the same criteria as the previous one.

```
>> f=1/(n*(log(n)))
```

```
f =
```

```
1/(n*log(n))
```

```
>> pretty((2^n)*subs(f,{n},{2^n}))
```

```
      1
    -------
       n
    log(2 )
```

As this series dominates the divergent harmonic series with general term 1/n, it diverges. Therefore the initial series also diverges.

EXERCISE 6-7

Study the convergence of the following series:

$$\sum_{n=1}^{\infty} \frac{(-1)^{1+n} n}{(1+n)^2}$$

If we define $a(n)=(-1)^{1+n}$ and $b(n)=\dfrac{n}{(1+n)^2}$ we have that $a(n)$ has bounded partial sums and $\{b(n)\}$ is monotone decreasing with limit 0.

Using Dirichlet's criterion we conclude that the considered alternating series is convergent.

Alternatively, we could have considered the absolute convergence of the series. In this case we observe that the ratio and root tests, and Raabe's criterion, all give a limit of 1, so we cannot solve the problem.

```
>> f=n/(1+n)^2

f =

n/(n + 1)^2

>> limit(n*(1-subs(f,n+1)/subs(f,n)),inf)

ans =

1

>> limit(subs(f,n+1)/subs(f,n),inf)

ans =

1

>> limit(subs(f,n)^(1/n),inf)

ans =

1
```

Applying the comparison test of the second kind to this series of positive terms, comparing with the convergent series with general term *1/n2*, we find:

```
>> limit(subs(f,n)/(1/n^2),inf)
ans =

Inf
```

As the limit is greater than zero, the series of positive terms considered is convergent, and so the initial series is absolutely convergent and, therefore, convergent. We now calculate its sum.

```
>> f=((-1)^n)*(n/(n + 1)^2)

f =

((-1)^n*n)/(n + 1)^2

>> vpa(symsum(f,1,inf))

ans =

-0.12931985286416790881897546186484
```

EXERCISE 6-8

Study the interval of convergence of the following power series:

$$\sum_{n=0}^{\infty} \frac{1}{(-5)^n} x^{2n+1}$$

We apply the root test:

```
>> syms x n
>> f=x^(2*n+1)/(-5)^n

f =

x^(2*n + 1)/(-5)^n

>> limit(subs(f,{n},{n+1})/subs(f,{n},{n}),n,inf)

ans =

-x^2/5
```

The series is absolutely convergent when $|-x \wedge 2/5| < 1$.

The condition $|-x \wedge 2/5| < 1$ is equivalent to $-sqrt(5) < x < sqrt(5)$. Thus, we have determined the possible intervals of convergence of the power series. We will now analyze the endpoints:

```
>> pretty(simplify(subs(f,{x},{sqrt(5)})))

   1/2
  5
  -----
     n
  (-1)

>> pretty(simplify(subs(f,{x},{-sqrt(5)})))

       n  1/2
  - (-1)   5
```

Both series are obviously divergent alternating series. Therefore, the interval of convergence of the given power series is: $-sqrt(5) < x < sqrt(5)$.

EXERCISE 6-9

Calculate the MacLaurin series of *Ln(x + 1)* up to degree 5. Also find the MacLaurin series up to degree 8.

```
>> syms x
>> f=log(x+1)

f =

log(x + 1)

>> pretty(taylor(f))

  5    4    3    2
 x    x    x    x
 -- - -- + -- - -- + x
 5    4    3    2

>> pretty(taylor(f,8))

  7    6    5    4    3    2
 x    x    x    x    x    x
 -- - -- + -- - -- + -- - -- + x
 7    6    5    4    3    2
```

EXERCISE 6-10

Calculate the Taylor series of 1/(2-*x*) at the point *x* = 1 up to degree 7. Also find the Taylor series of sin(*x*) at the point *x* = 2 up to degree 8.

```
>> syms x

>> f = 1 /(2-x)

f =

-1 /(x-2)

>> pretty(taylor(f,7,1))

                2          3          4          5          6
  x + (x - 1)  + (x - 1)  + (x - 1)  + (x - 1)  + (x - 1)
```

```
>> f=sin(x);
>> pretty(taylor(f,8,pi))
```

$$
\text{pi} - x - \frac{(\text{pi} - x)^3}{6} + \frac{(\text{pi} - x)^5}{120} - \frac{(\text{pi} - x)^7}{5040}
$$

Both series show that the term which would correspond to the greatest degree is void.

■ ■ ■

CHAPTER 7

Derivatives. One and Several Variables

Derivatives

MATLAB implements a special set of commands enabling you to work with derivatives, which is particularly important in the world of computing and its applications. The derivative of a real function at a point measures the instantaneous rate of change of that function in a neighborhood of the point; i.e. how the dependent variable changes as a result of a small change in the independent variable. Geometrically, the derivative of a function at a point is the slope of the tangent to the function at that point. The origin of the idea derived from the attempt to draw the tangent line at a given point on a given curve.

A function $f(x)$ defined in a neighborhood of a point a is said to be differentiable at a if the following limit exists:

$$\lim_{h \to 0} \frac{f(a+h) - f(a)}{h}$$

The value of the limit, if it exists, is denoted by $f'(a)$, and is called the derivative of the function f at the point a. If f is differentiable at all points of its domain, it is simply said to be differentiable. The continuity of a function is a necessary (but not sufficient) condition for differentiability, and any differentiable function is continuous.

The following table shows the basic commands that enable MATLAB to work with derivatives.

diff('f', 'x')	*Finds the derivative of f with respect to x*
	```>> diff('sin(x^2)','x')```
	```ans =```
	```2*x*cos(x^2)```
syms x, diff(f,x)	*Finds the derivative of f with respect to x*
	```>> syms x``` ```>> diff(sin(x^2),x)```
	```ans =```
	```2*x*cos(x^2)```

(*continued*)

diff('f', 'x', n)	*Finds the nth derivative of f with respect to x*

```
>> diff('sin(x^2)','x',2)

ans =

2*cos(x^2) - 4*x^2*sin(x^2)
```

syms x, diff(f, x, n)	*Finds the nth derivative of f with respect to x*

```
>> syms x
>> diff(sin(x^2),x,2)

ans =

2*cos(x^2) - 4*x^2*sin(x^2)
```

R = jacobian(w,v)	*Finds the Jacobian matrix of w with respect to v*

```
>> syms x y z
>> jacobian([x*y*z; y; x+z],[x y z])

ans =

[ y*z, x*z, x*y]
[   0,   1,   0]
[   1,   0,   1]
```

Y = diff(X)	*Calculates differences between adjacent elements of the vector X: [X(2)-X(1), X(3)-X(2), …, X(n)-X(n-1)]. If X is an m×n matrix, diff(X) returns the row difference matrix: [X(2:m,:)-X(1:m-1,:)]*

```
x = [1 2 3 4 5];
y = diff(x)

y =

   1   1   1   1
```

Y = diff(X,*n*)	*Finds differences of order n, for example: diff(X,2)=diff(diff(X))*

```
x = [1 2 3 4 5];
z = diff(x,2)

z =

   0   0   0
```

As a first example, we consider the function $f(x) = x^5-3x^4-11x^3+27x^2+10x-24$ and graph its derivative in the interval [-4,5].

```
>> x=-4:0.1:5;
>> f=x.^5-3*x.^4-11*x.^3+27*x.^2+10*x-24;
>> df=diff(f)./diff(x);
>> plot(x,f)
```

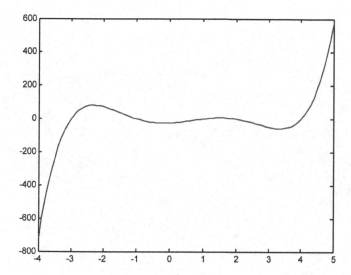

As a second example, we calculate the derivative of the function $log(sin(2x))$ and simplify the result.

```
>> pretty(simplify(diff('log(sin(2*x))','x')))

  2 cot(2 x)
```

As a third example, we calculate the first four derivatives of the following function:

$f(x) = 1/x^2$

```
>> f='1/x^2'

f =
1/x^2

>> [diff(f),diff(f,2),diff(f,3),diff(f,4)]

ans =

[ -2/x^3, 6/x^4, -24/x^5, 120/x^6]
```

Partial Derivatives

The MATLAB commands for differentiation described above can also be used for partial differentiation.

As an example, given the function $f(x,y) = sin(xy)+cos(xy^2)$, we calculate:

$\partial f/\partial x$, $\partial f/\partial y$, $\partial^2 f/\partial x^2$, $\partial^2 f/\partial y^2$, $\partial^2 f/\partial x\partial y$, $\partial^2 f/\partial y\partial x$ and $\partial^4 f/\partial^2 x\partial^2 y$

```
>> syms x y
>> f=sin(x*y)+cos(x*y^2)

f =

sin(x*y)+cos(x*y^2)

>> diff(f,x)

ans =

cos(x*y)*y-sin(x*y^2)*y^2

>> diff(f,y)

ans =

cos(x*y)*x-2*sin(x*y^2)*x*y

>> diff(diff(f,x),x)

ans =

-sin(x*y)*y^2-cos(x*y^2)*y^4

>> diff(diff(f,y),y)

ans =

-sin(x*y)*x^2-4*cos(x*y^2)*x^2*y^2-2*sin(x*y^2)*x

>> diff(diff(f,x),y)

ans =

-sin(x*y)*x*y+cos(x*y)-2*cos(x*y^2)*x*y^3-2*sin(x*y^2)*y

>> diff(diff(f,y),x)

ans =

-sin(x*y)*x*y+cos(x*y)-2*cos(x*y^2)*x*y^3-2*sin(x*y^2)*y
```

```
>> diff(diff(diff(diff(f,x),x),y,y))
```

```
ans =
```

```
sin(x*y)*y^3*x-3*cos(x*y)*y^2+2*cos(x*y^2)*y^7*x+6*sin(x*y^2)*y^5
```

Applications of Differentiation. Tangents, Asymptotes, Extreme Points and Points of Inflection

A direct application of differentiation allows us to find the tangent to a function at a given point, horizontal, vertical and oblique asymptotes of a function, intervals of increase and concavity, maxima and minima and points of inflection.

With this information it is possible to give a complete study of curves and their representation.

If f is a function which is differentiable at x_0, then $f'(x_0)$ is the slope of the tangent line to the curve $y = f(x)$ at the point $(x_0, f(x_0))$. The equation of the tangent will be $y - f(x_0) = f'(x_0)(x - x_0)$.

The horizontal asymptotes of the curve $y = f(x)$ are limit tangents, as $x_0 \to \infty$, which are horizontal. They are defined by the equation $y = \lim_{x_0 \to \infty} f(x_0)$.

The vertical asymptotes of the curve $y = f(x)$ are limit tangents, as $f(x_0) \to \infty$, which are vertical. They are defined by the equation $x = x_0$, where x_0 is a value such that $\lim_{x \to x_0} f(x) = \infty$.

The oblique asymptotes to the curve $y = f(x)$ at the point $x = x_0$ have the equation $y = mx + n$, where $m = \lim_{x \to \infty} \frac{y}{x}$ And $n = \lim_{x \to \infty}(y - mx)$.

If f is a function for which $f'(x_0)$ and $f''(x_0)$ both exist, then, if $f'(x_0) = 0$ and $f''(x_0) < 0$, the function f has a local maximum at the point $(x_0, f(x_0))$.

If f is a function for which $f'(x_0)$ and $f''(x_0)$ both exist, then, if $f'(x_0) = 0$ and $f''(x0) > 0$, the function f has a local minimum at the point $(x0, f(x0))$.

If f is a function for which $f'(x_0), f''(x_0)$ and $f'''(x_0)$ exist, then, if $f'(x_0)$ and $f''(x_0)$ and $f'''(x_0)$ 0, the function f has a turning point at the point $(x_0, f(x_0))$.

If f is differentiable, then the values of x for which the function f is increasing are those for which $f'(x)$ is greater than zero.

If f is differentiable, then the values of x for which the function f is decreasing are those for which $f'(x)$ is less than zero.

If f is twice differentiable, then the values of x for which the function f is concave are those for which $f''(x)$ is greater than zero.

If f is twice differentiable, then the values of x for which the function f is convex are those for which $f''(x)$ is less than zero.

As an example, we perform a comprehensive study of the function:

$$f(x) = \frac{x^3}{x^2 - 1}$$

calculating the asymptotes, maxima, minima, inflexion points, intervals of increase and decrease and intervals of concavity and convexity.

```
>> f='x^3/(x^2-1)'
```

```
f =
```

```
x^3/(x^2-1)
```

```
>> syms x, limit(x^3/(x^2-1),x,inf)

ans =

NaN
```

Therefore, there are no horizontal asymptotes. To see if there are vertical asymptotes, we consider the values of x that make the function infinite:

```
>> solve('x^2-1')

ans =

[ 1]
[-1]
```

The vertical asymptotes are the lines x = 1 and x = -1. Let us see if there are any oblique asymptotes:

```
>> limit(x^3/(x^2-1)/x,x,inf)

ans =

1

>> limit(x^3/(x^2-1)-x,x,inf)

ans =

0
```

The line y = x is an oblique asymptote. Now, the maxima and minima, inflection points and intervals of concavity and growth will be analyzed:

```
>> solve(diff(f))

ans =

[        0]
[        0]
[ 3^(1/2)]
[-3^(1/2)]
```

The first derivative vanishes at the points with abscissa x = 0, x = $\sqrt{3}$ and x = - $\sqrt{3}$. These points are candidates for maxima and minima. To determine whether they are maxima or minima, we find the value of the second derivative at these points:

```
>> [numeric(subs(diff(f,2),0)),numeric(subs(diff(f,2),sqrt(3))),
   numeric(subs(diff(f,2),-sqrt(3)))]

ans =

        0    2.5981   -2.5981
```

230

Therefore, at the point with abscissa x = - √3 there is a maximum and at the point with abscissa x = √ 3 there is a minimum. At x = 0 we know nothing:

```
>> [numeric(subs(f,sqrt(3))),numeric(subs(f,-sqrt(3)))]

ans =

    2.5981    -2.5981
```

Therefore, the maximum point is (- √ 3, -2.5981) and the minimum point is (√ 3, 2.5981).
We will now analyze the inflection points:

```
>> solve(diff(f,2))

ans =

[          0]
[  i*3^(1/2)]
[-i*3^(1/2)]
```

The only possible point of inflection occurs at x = 0, and since f (0) = 0, the possible turning point is (0, 0):

```
>> subs(diff(f,3),0)

ans =

-6
```

As the third derivative at x = 0 does not vanish, the origin is indeed a turning point:

```
>> pretty(simple(diff(f)))

             2   2
         x  (x  - 3)
         ------------
             2    2
          (x  - 1)
```

The curve is increasing when y ' > 0, i.e., in the intervals (- ∞, - √ 3) and (√ 3, ∞).
The curve is decreasing when y ' < 0, that is, in the intervals (-√3,-1), (-1,0), (0,1) and (1, √3).

```
>> pretty(simple(diff(f,2)))

                2
            x (x  + 3)
        2 ------------
              2    3
           (x  - 1)
```

The curve will be concave when y" > 0, that is, in the intervals (-1,0) and (1, ∞).

The curve will be convex when y" < 0, that is, in the intervals (0,1) and (- ∞, -1).

The curve has horizontal tangents at the three points at which the first derivative is zero. The equations of the horizontal tangents are y = 0, y = 2.5981 and y = -2.5981.

The curve has vertical tangents at the points that make the first derivative infinite. These points are x = 1 and x = -1. Therefore, the vertical tangents coincide with the two vertical asymptotes.

Next, we graph the curve together with its asymptotes:

```
>> fplot('[x^3/(x^2-1),x]',[-5,5,-5,5])
```

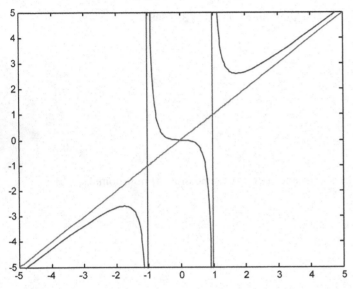

We can also represent the curve, its asymptotes and their horizontal and vertical tangents in the same graph.

```
>> fplot('[x^3/(x^2-1),x,2.5981,-2.5981]',[-5,5,-5,5])
```

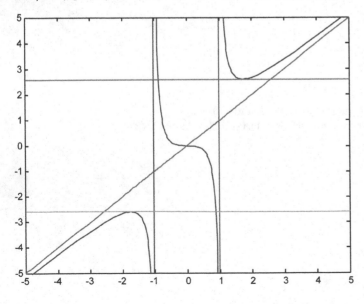

Differentiation in Several Variables

The concept of differentiation for functions of one variable is generalizable to differentiation for functions of several variables. Below we consider partial derivatives for the case of two variable functions.

Given the function $f\colon R^2 \to R$, the **partial derivative of f** with respect to the variable x at the point (a, b) is defined as follows:

$$\frac{\partial f}{\partial x}(a,b) = \lim_{h \to 0} \frac{f(a+h,b)-f(a,b)}{h}$$

In the same way, the partial derivative of f with respect to the variable y at the point (a, b) is defined in the following way:

$$\frac{\partial f}{\partial y}(a,b) = \lim_{h \to 0} \frac{f(a,b+h)-f(a,b)}{h}$$

Generally speaking, we can define the partial derivative with respect to any variable for a function of n variables.

Given the function $f\colon R^n \to R$, the partial derivative of f with respect to the variable x_i ($i = 1,2,...,n$) at the point $(a_1,a_2,...,a_n)$ is defined as follows:

$$\frac{\partial f}{\partial x_i}(a_1,a_2,...,a_n) = \lim_{h \to 0} \frac{f(a_1,a_2,...,a_i+h,...,a_n)-f(a_1,a_2,...,a_n)}{h}$$

The function f is differentiable if all partial derivatives with respect to x_i ($i = 1,2,...,n$) exist and are continuous. Every differentiable function is continuous, and if a function is not continuous it cannot be differentiable.

The *directional derivative of the function f* with respect to the vector $v=(v_1,v_2,...,v_n)$ is defined as the following scalar product:

$$(Df)v = \left(\frac{\partial f}{\partial x_1},\frac{\partial f}{\partial x_2},...,\frac{\partial f}{\partial x_n}\right)\cdot(v_1,v_2,...,v_n)=(\nabla f)\cdot v$$

$\nabla f = \left(\frac{\partial f}{\partial x_1},\frac{\partial f}{\partial x_2},...,\frac{\partial f}{\partial x_n}\right)$ is called the *gradient vector of f*.

The directional derivative of the function f with respect to the vector $v =(dx_1,dx_2,...,dx_n)$ is called the *total differential of f*. Its value is:

$$Df = \left(\frac{\partial f}{\partial x_1}dx_1 + \frac{\partial f}{\partial x_2}dx_2 +...+\frac{\partial f}{\partial x_n}dx_n\right)$$

Partial derivatives can be calculated using the MATLAB commands for differentiation that we already know.

diff(f(x,y,z,...),x)	*Partial derivative of f with respect to x*

```
>> syms x y z
>> diff(x^2+y^2+z^2+x*y-x*z-y*z+1,z)

ans =

2*z - y - x
```

diff (f(x,y,z,...), x, n)	*Nth partial derivative of f with respect to x*

```
>> diff(x^2+y^2+z^2+x*y-x*z-y*z+1,z,2)

ans =

2
```

diff(f(x1,x2,x3,...),xj)	*Partial derivative of f with respect to xj*

```
>> diff(x^2+y^2+z^2+x*y-x*z-y*z+1,y)

ans =

x + 2*y - z
```

diff(f(x1,x2,x3,...),xj,n)	*Nth partial derivative of f with respect to xj*

```
>> diff(x^2+y^2+z^2+x*y-x*z-y*z+1,y,2)

ans =

2
```

diff(diff(f(x,y,z,...),x),y))	*The second partial derivative of f with respect to x and y*

```
>> diff(diff(x^2+y^2+z^2+x*y-x*z-y*z+1,x), y)

ans =

1
```

As a first example, we study the differentiability and continuity of the function:

$$f(x,y) = \frac{2xy}{\sqrt{x^2+y^2}} \text{ if } (x,y) \neq (0,0) \text{ and } f(0,0) = 0.$$

To see if the function is differentiable, it is necessary to check whether it has continuous partial derivatives at every point. We consider any point other than the origin and calculate the partial derivative with respect to the variable *x*:

```
>> syms x y
>> pretty(simplify(diff((2*x*y)/(x^2+y^2)^(1/2),x)))

        3
     2 y
  ----------
          3
          -
          2
     2    2
   (x  + y )
```

Now, let's see if this partial derivative is continuous at the origin. When calculating the iterated limits at the origin, we observe that they do not coincide.

```
>> limit(limit(2*y^3/(x^2+y^2)^(3/2),x,0),y,0)

ans =

NaN

>> limit(limit(2*y^3/(x^2+y^2)^(3/2),y,0),x,0)

ans =

0
```

The limit of the partial derivative does not exist at (0, 0), so we conclude that the function is not differentiable.

However, the function is continuous, since the only problematic point is the origin, and the limit of the function is $0 = f(0, 0)$:

```
>> limit(limit((2*x*y)/(x^2+y^2)^(1/2),x,0),y,0)

ans =

0

>> limit(limit((2*x*y)/(x^2+y^2)^(1/2),y,0),x,0)

ans =

0

>> m = sym('m', 'positive')
>> limit((2*x*(m*x))/(x^2+(m*x)^2)^(1/2),x,0)

ans =

0
```

```
>> a = sym ('a', 'real');
>> f =(2*x*y) /(x^2+y^2) ^(1/2);
>> limit(subs(f,{x,y},{r*cos(a),r*sin(a)}),r,0)

ans =

0
```

The iterated limits and the directional limits are all zero, and by changing the function to polar coordinates, the limit at the origin turns out to be zero, which coincides with the value of the function at the origin. Thus this is an example of a non-differentiable continuous function. A graphical representation helps us to interpret the result.

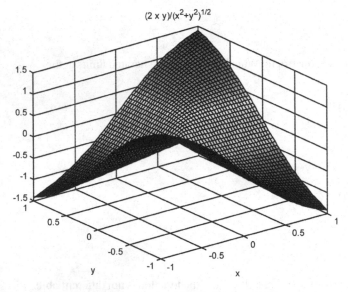

As a second example, we consider the function:

$$f(x,y,z) = \frac{1}{\sqrt{x^2 + y^2 + z^2}}$$

We verify the equation:

$$\frac{\partial^2 f}{\partial x^2} + \frac{\partial^2 f}{\partial y^2} + \frac{\partial^2 f}{\partial z^2} = 0$$

```
>> syms x y z
>> f=1/(x^2+y^2+z^2)^(1/2)

f =

1/(x^2 + y^2 + z^2)^(1/2)
```

```
>> diff(f,x,2)+diff(f,y,2)+diff(f,z,2)

ans =

(3*x^2)/(x^2 + y^2 + z^2)^(5/2) - 3/(x^2 + y^2 + z^2)^(3/2) + (3*y^2)/(x^2 + y^2 + z^2)^(5/2) +
(3*z^2)/(x^2 + y^2 + z^2)^(5/2)

>> simplify(diff(f,x,2)+diff(f,y,2)+diff(f,z,2))

ans =

0
```

As a third example, we calculate the directional derivative of the function:

$$f(x,y,z)=\frac{1}{\sqrt{x^2+y^2+z^2}}$$

at the point $(2,1,1)$ in the direction of the vector $v=(1,1,0)$. We also find the gradient vector of f.

Recall that the *directional derivative of the function f* in the direction of the vector $v=(v_1,v_2,...,v_n)$ is defined as the following dot product:

$$(Df)v=\left(\frac{\partial f}{\partial x_1},\frac{\partial f}{\partial x_2},...,\frac{\partial f}{\partial x_n}\right)\bullet(v_1,v_2,...,v_n)=(\nabla f)\bullet v$$

$\nabla f=\left(\dfrac{\partial f}{\partial x_1},\dfrac{\partial f}{\partial x_2},...,\dfrac{\partial f}{\partial x_n}\right)$ is called the *gradient vector* of f.

First, we calculate the gradient of the function f.

```
>> syms x y z
>> f=1/(x^2+y^2+z^2)^(1/2)

f =

1/(x^2 + y^2 + z^2)^(1/2)

>> Gradient_f=simplify([diff(f,x),diff(f,y),diff(f,z)])

Gradient_f =

[ -x/(x^2 + y^2 + z^2)^(3/2), -y/(x^2 + y^2 + z^2)^(3/2), -z/(x^2 + y^2 + z^2)^(3/2)]
```

We then calculate the gradient vector at the point $(2,1,1)$.

```
>> Gradient_f_p = subs(Gradient_f,{x,y,z},{2,1,1})

Gradient_f_p =

  -0.1361   -0.0680   -0.0680
```

237

Finally, we calculate the directional derivative.

```
>> Directional_derivative_p = dot(Gradient_f_p, [1,1,0])

Directional_derivative_p =

-0.2041
```

Extreme Points in Several Variables

MATLAB allows you to easily calculate maxima and minima of functions of several variables.

A function f: $R^n \to R$, which maps the point $(x_1, x_2,..., x_n) \in R$ to $f(x_1,x_2,...,x_n) \in R$, has an extreme point at $(a_1, a_2, ..., a_n)$ if the gradient vector $\nabla f = \left(\dfrac{\partial f}{\partial x_1}, \dfrac{\partial f}{\partial x_2}, ..., \dfrac{\partial f}{\partial x_n} \right)$ is zero at $(a_1, a_2, ..., a_n)$.

By setting all the first order partial derivatives equal to zero and solving the resulting system, we can find the possible maxima and minima.

To determine the nature of the extreme point, it is necessary to construct the **Hessian matrix**, which is defined as follows:

$$H = \begin{bmatrix} \dfrac{\partial^2 f}{\partial x_1^2} & \dfrac{\partial^2 f}{\partial x_1 \partial x_2} & \cdots\cdots & \dfrac{\partial^2 f}{\partial x_1 \partial x_n} \\ \dfrac{\partial^2 f}{\partial x_1 \partial x_2} & \dfrac{\partial^2 f}{\partial x_2^2} & \cdots\cdots & \dfrac{\partial^2 f}{\partial x_2 \partial x_n} \\ \cdots\cdots & \cdots\cdots & \cdots\cdots & \cdots\cdots \\ \dfrac{\partial^2 f}{\partial x_1 \partial x_n} & \dfrac{\partial^2 f}{\partial x_2 \partial x_n} & \cdots\cdots & \dfrac{\partial^2 f}{\partial x_n^2} \end{bmatrix}$$

First, suppose that the determinant of H is non-zero at the point $(a_1, a_2, ..., a_n)$. In this case, we say that the point is non-degenerate and, in addition, we can determine the nature of the extreme point via the following conditions:

If the Hessian matrix at the point $(a_1, a_2, ..., a_n)$ is positive definite, then the function has a minimum at that point.

If the Hessian matrix at the point $(a_1, a_2, ..., a_n)$ is negative definite, then the function has a maximum at that point.

In any other case, the function has a saddle point at $(a_1, a_2, ..., a_n)$.

If the determinant of H is zero at the point $(a_1, a_2, ..., a_n)$, we say that the point is degenerate.

As an example, we find and classify the extreme points of the function:

$$f(x,y,z) = x^2 + xy + y^2 + z^2$$

We start by finding the possible extreme points. To do so, we set the partial derivatives with respect to all the variables (i.e. the components of the gradient vector of *f*) equal to zero and solve the resulting system in three variables:

```
>> syms x y z
>> f=x^2+y^2+z^2+x*y

f =

x^2 + x*y + y^2 + z^2
```

```
>> [x y z] = solve(diff(f,x), diff(f,y), diff(f,z), x, y, z)

x =

0

y =

0

z =

0
```

The single extreme point is the origin (0,0,0). We will analyze what kind of extreme point it is. To do this, we calculate the Hessian matrix and express it as a function of *x*, *y* and *z*:

```
>> clear all
>> syms x y z
>> f=x^2+y^2+z^2+x*y

f =

x^2 + x*y + y^2 + z^2

>> diff(f,x)

ans =

2*x + y

>> H=simplify([diff(f,x,2),diff(diff(f,x),y),diff(diff(f,x),z);
             diff(diff(f,y),x),diff(f,y,2),diff(diff(f,y),z);
                diff(diff(f,z),x),diff(diff(f,z),y),diff(f,z,2)])

H =

[ 2, 1, 0]
[ 1, 2, 0]
[ 0, 0, 2]

>> det(H)

ans =

6
```

We have seen that the Hessian matrix is constant (i.e. it does not depend on the point at which it is applied), therefore its value at the origin is already found. The determinant is non-zero, so there are no degenerate extreme points.

```
>> eig(H)

ans =

1
2
3
```

We see that the Hessian matrix at the origin is positive definite, because its eigenvalues are all positive. We then conclude that the origin is a minimum of the function.

MATLAB additionally incorporates specific commands for the optimization and search for zeros of functions of several variables. The following table shows the most important ones.

g = inline(expr)	*Constructs an inline function from the string expr*

	```>> g = inline('t^2')```
	
	 ```g =```
	
	 ``` Inline function:```
	 ``` g(t) = t^2```

g = inline(expr,arg1,arg2, …)	*Constructs an inline function from the string expr with the given input arguments*

	```>> g = inline('sin(2*pi*f + theta)', 'f', 'theta')```
	
	 ```g =```
	
	 ``` Inline function:```
	 ``` g(f,theta) = sin(2*pi*f + theta)```

g = inline(expr,n)	*Constructs an inline function from the string expr with n input arguments*

	```>> g = inline('x^P1', 1)```
	
	 ```g =```
	
	 ``` Inline function:```
	 ``` g(x,P1) = x^P1```

(continued)

f = @function	*Enables the function to be evaluated*
	`>> f = @cos`
	`f =`
	`@cos` `>> ezplot(f, [-pi,pi])`
x = fminbnd(fun,x1,x2)	*Returns the minimum of the function in the interval (x1, x2)*
	`>> x = fminbnd(@cos,3,4)`
	`x =`
	`3.1416`
x = fminbnd(fun,x1,x2,options)	*Returns the minimum of the function in the interval (x1, x2) according to the option given by optimset (...). This last command is explained later.*
	`>> x = fminbnd(@cos,3,4,optimset('TolX',1e-12,'Display','off'))`
	`x =`
	`3.1416`
x = fminbnd(fun,x1,x2, options,P1,P2,..)	*Specifies additional parameters P1, P2,... to pass to the target function fun(x,P1,P2,...)*
[x, fval] = fminbnd (...)	*Returns the value x and the value of the function at x at which the objective function has a minimum*
	`>> [x,fval] = fminbnd(@cos,3,4)`
	`x =`
	`3.1416`
	`fval =`
	`-1.0000`

(continued)

[x, fval, f] = fminbnd (...)

In addition returns an indicator of convergence of f ($f > 0$ indicates convergence to the solution, $f < 0$ no convergence and $f = 0$ exceeds the number of steps)

```
>> [x,fval,f] = fminbnd(@cos,3,4)

x =

    3.1416

fval =

   -1.0000

f =

    1
```

[x,fval,f,output] = fminbnd(...)

Gives further information on optimization (output.algorithm gives the algorithm used, output.funcCount gives the number of evaluations of fun and output. iterations gives the number of iterations)

```
>> [x,fval,f,output] = fminbnd(@cos,3,4)

x =

    3.1416

fval =

   -1.0000

f =

    1

output =

    iterations: 7
    funcCount: 8
    algorithm: 'golden section search, parabolic interpolation'
    message: [1x112 char]
```

(continued)

x = fminsearch(fun,x0)

x = fminsearch(fun,x0,options)

x = fminsearch(fun,x0,options, P1,P2,...)

[x,fval] = fminsearch(...)

[x,fval,f] = fminsearch(...)

[x,fval,f,output] = fminsearch(...)

Minimizes a function of several variables with initial values given by x0. The argument x0 can be an interval [a, b] in which a solution is sought. Then, to minimize fun in [a, b], the command x = fminsearch (fun, [a, b]) is used.

```
>> x=fminsearch(inline('(100*(1-x^2)^2+(1-x)^2)'),3)

x =

    1.0000

>> [x,feval]=fminsearch(inline('(100*(1-x^2)^2 +(1-x)^2)'),3)

x =

    1.0000

feval =

    2.3901e-007

>> [x,feval,f]=fminsearch(inline('(100*(1-x^2)^2 +(1-x)^2)'),3)

x =

    1.0000

feval =

    2.3901e-007

f =

    1

>> [x,feval,f,output]=fminsearch(inline('(100*(1-x^2)^2+(1-x)^2)'),3)

x =

    1.0000

feval =

    2.3901e-007

f =

    1

output =

    iterations: 18
    funcCount: 36
    algorithm: 'Nelder-Mead simplex direct search'
    message: [1x196 char]
```

(continued)

x = fzero x0 (fun)

x = fzero(fun,x0,options)

x = fzero(fun,x0,options,P1,P2,...)

[x, fval] = fzero (...)

[x, fval, exitflag] = fzero (...)

[x,fval,exitflag,output] = fzero(...)

Finds zeros of functions. The argument x0 can be an interval [a, b] in which a solution is sought. Then, to find a zero of fun in [a, b] the command x = fzero (fun, [a, b]) is used, where fun has opposite signs at a and b.

```
>> x = fzero(@cos,[1 2])

x =

    1.5708

>> [x,feval] = fzero(@cos,[1 2])

x =

    1.5708

feval =

        6.1232e-017

>> [x,feval,exitflag] = fzero(@cos,[1 2])

x =

    1.5708

feval =

        6.1232e-017

exitflag =

        1

>> [x,feval,exitflag,output] = fzero(@cos,[1 2])

x =

    1.5708

feval =

        6.1232e-017

exitflag =

        1

output =

        interval iterations: 0
        iterations: 5
        funcCount: 7
        algorithm:'bisection, interpolation'message: 'Zero found in
        the interval [1, 2]'
```

(continued)

options = **optimset('p1','v1','p2','v2',...)**	*Creates optimization options parameters p1, p2,... with values v1, v2... The possible parameters are Display (with possible values 'off', 'iter', 'final', 'notify' to hide the output, display the output of each iteration, display only the final output and show a message if there is no convergence); MaxFunEvals, whose value is an integer indicating the maximum number of evaluations; MaxIter whose value is an integer indicating the maximum number of iterations; TolFun, whose value is an integer indicating the tolerance in the value of the function, and TolX, whose value is an integer indicating the tolerance in the value of x*
Val = optimget (options, 'param')	*Returns the value of the parameter specified in the optimization options structure*

As a first example, we minimize the function $cos(x)$ in the interval (3,4).

```
>> x = fminbnd(inline('cos(x)'),3,4)

x =

    3.1416
```

In the following example we conduct the same minimization with a tolerance of 8 decimal places and find both the value of x that minimizes the cosine in the range given and the minimum value of the cosine function in that interval, presenting information relating to all iterations of the process.

```
>> [x, fval, f] = fminbnd (@cos, 3, 4, optimset('TolX',1e-8,...)) (( 'Display', 'iter'));

Func-count     x          f(x)         Procedure
    1       3.38197     -0.971249       initial
    2       3.61803     -0.888633       golden
    3       3.23607     -0.995541       golden
    4       3.13571     -0.999983       parabolic
    5       3.1413      -1              parabolic
    6       3.14159     -1              parabolic
    7       3.14159     -1              parabolic
    8       3.14159     -1              parabolic
    9       3.14159     -1              parabolic

Optimization terminated successfully:
the current x satisfies the termination criteria using OPTIONS.TolX of 1.000000e-008
```

In the following example, taking as initial values (-1.2, 1), we minimize and find the target value of the function of two variables:

$$f(x) = 100(x_2 - x_1^2)^2 + (1 - x_1)^2$$

```
>> [x,fval] = fminsearch(inline('100*(x(2)-x(1)^2)^2+...
   (((1-x (1)) ^ 2'), [- 1.2, 1])

x =

    1.0000 1.0000
```

```
FVal =

   8. 1777e-010
```

The following example computes a zero of the sine function near 3 and a zero of the cosine function between 1 and 2.

```
>> x = fzero(@sin,3)

x =

   3.1416

>> x = fzero(@cos,[1 2])

x =

   1.5708
```

Conditional minima and maxima. The method of "Lagrange multipliers"

Suppose we want to optimize (i.e. maximize or minimize) the function $f(x_1,x_2,...,x_n)$, called the objective function, but subject to certain restrictions given by the equations:

$g_1(x_1,x_2,...,x_n)=0$
$g_2(x_1,x_2,...,x_n)=0$
....
$g_k(x_1,x_2,...,x_n)=0$

This is the setting in which the Lagrangian is introduced. The Lagrangian is a linear combination of the objective function and the constraints, and has the following form:

$$L(X_1,X_2,...Xn,\lambda)=f(X_1,X_2,...X_n)+\sum_{i=1}^{k}\lambda_i g_i(x_1,x_2,...,x_n)$$

The extreme points are found by solving the system obtained by setting the components of the gradient vector of L to zero, that is, $\nabla L(x_1,x_2,...,x_n,\lambda)=(0,0,...,0)$. Which translates into:

$$\nabla L=\left(\frac{\partial L}{\partial x_1},\frac{\partial L}{\partial x_2},...,\frac{\partial L}{\partial x_n},\frac{\partial L}{\partial \lambda_1},\frac{\partial L}{\partial \lambda_2},...,\frac{\partial L}{\partial \lambda_n}\right)=(0,0,...,0)$$

By setting the partial derivatives to zero and solving the resulting system, we obtain the values of $x_1, x_2,..., x_n, \lambda_1, \lambda_2,...,\lambda_k$ corresponding to possible maxima and minima.

To determine the nature of the points $(x_1, x_2,..., x_n)$ found above, the following bordered Hessian matrix is used:

$$\begin{bmatrix} \dfrac{\partial^2 f}{\partial x_1^2} & \dfrac{\partial^2 f}{\partial x_1 \partial x_2} & \cdots & \dfrac{\partial^2 f}{\partial x_1 \partial x_n} & \dfrac{\partial g_i}{\partial x_1} \\ \dfrac{\partial^2 f}{\partial x_1 \partial x_2} & \dfrac{\partial^2 f}{\partial x_2^2} & \cdots & \dfrac{\partial^2 f}{\partial x_2 \partial x_n} & \dfrac{\partial g_i}{\partial x_2} \\ \cdots & \cdots & \cdots & \cdots & \cdots \\ \dfrac{\partial^2 f}{\partial x_1 \partial x_n} & \dfrac{\partial^2 f}{\partial x_2 \partial x_n} & \cdots & \dfrac{\partial^2 f}{\partial x_n^2} & \dfrac{\partial g_i}{\partial x_n} \\ \dfrac{\partial g_i}{\partial x_1} & \dfrac{\partial g_i}{\partial x_2} & \cdots & \dfrac{\partial g_i}{\partial x_n} & 0 \end{bmatrix}$$

The nature of the extreme points can be determined by studying the set of bordered Hessian matrices:

$$H1 = \begin{bmatrix} \dfrac{\partial f}{\partial x_1^2} & \dfrac{\partial g_i}{\partial x_1} \\ \dfrac{\partial g_i}{\partial x_1} & 0 \end{bmatrix} \quad H2 = \begin{bmatrix} \dfrac{\partial^2 f}{\partial x_1^2} & \dfrac{\partial^2 f}{\partial x_1 \partial x_2} & \dfrac{\partial g_i}{\partial x_1} \\ \dfrac{\partial^2 f}{\partial x_1 \partial x_2} & \dfrac{\partial^2 f}{\partial x_2^2} & \dfrac{\partial g_i}{\partial x_2} \\ \dfrac{\partial g_i}{\partial x_1} & \dfrac{\partial g_i}{\partial x_2} & 0 \end{bmatrix} \dots H_n = H$$

For a single restriction g_1, if H1 < 0, H2 < 0, H3 < 0,..., H < 0, then the extreme point is a minimum.

For a single restriction g_1, if H1 > 0, H2 < 0, H3 > 0, H4 < 0, H5 > 0, ... then the extreme point is a maximum.

For a collection of restrictions $g_i(x_1,..., x_n)$ (i = 1, 2,..., k) the lower right 0 will be a block of zeros and the conditions for a minimum will all have sign $(-1)^k$, while the conditions for a maximum will have alternating signs with H1 having sign $(-1)^{k+1}$. When considering several restrictions at the same time, it is easier to determine the nature of the extreme point by simple inspection."

As an example we find and classify the extreme points of the function:

$$f(x,y,z) = x + z$$

subject to the restriction:

$$x^2 + y^2 + z^2 = 1$$

First we find the Lagrangian L, which is a linear combination of the objective function and the constraints:

```
>> syms x y z L p
>> f = x + z

f =

x + z

>> g = x ^ 2 + y ^ 2 + z ^ 2-1

g =

x ^ 2 + y ^ 2 + z ^ 2 - 1
```

247

```
>> L = f + p * g

L =

x + z + p *(x^2 + y^2 + z^2-1)
```

Then, the possible extreme points are obtained by solving the system obtained by setting the components of the gradient vector of *L* equal to zero, that is, $\nabla L(x_1,x_2,...,x_n,\lambda) =(0,0,...,0)$. Which translates into:

```
>> [x, y, z, p] = solve (diff(L,x), diff(L,y), diff(L,z), diff(L,p), x, y, z, p)

x =

 -2^(1/2)/2
  2^(1/2)/2

y =

  2^(1/2)/2
 -2^(1/2)/2

z =

 0
 0

p =

  2^(1/2)/2
 -2^(1/2)/2
```

By matching all the partial derivatives to zero and solving the resulting system, we find the values of x_1, x_2,..., x_n, λ_1, λ_2,...,λ_k corresponding to possible maxima and minima.

We already see that the possible extreme points are:

$$(-\sqrt{2}/2, \sqrt{2}/2, 0) \text{ and } (\sqrt{2}/2, -\sqrt{2}/2, 0)$$

Now, let us determine the nature of these extreme points. To this end, we substitute them into the objective function.

```
>> clear all
>> syms x y z
>> f=x+z

f =

x + z

>> subs(f, {x,y,z},{-sqrt(2)/2,sqrt(2)/2,0})

ans =

  -0.7071
```

```
>> subs(f, {x,y,z},{sqrt(2)/2,-sqrt(2)/2,0})

ans =

    0.7071
```

Thus, at the point $(-\sqrt{2}/2, \sqrt{2}/2, 0)$ the function has a maximum, and at the point $(\sqrt{2}/2, -\sqrt{2}/2, 0)$ the function has a minimum."

Vector Differential Calculus

Here we shall introduce four classical theorems of differential calculus in several variables: the chain rule or composite function theorem, the implicit function theorem, the inverse function theorem and the change of variables theorem.

Consider a function $\bar{F} : R^m \to R^n$:

$$(x_1, x_2,..., x_m) \to [F_1(x_1, x_2,..., x_m),...,F_n(x_1, x_2,..., x_m)]$$

The vector function $\bar{F}$ is said to be differentiable at the point $a = (a_1,...,a_m)$ if each of the component functions F_1, F_2,..., F_n is differentiable.

The Jacobian matrix of the above function is defined as:

$$J = \begin{bmatrix} \dfrac{\partial F_1}{\partial x_1} & \dfrac{\partial F_1}{\partial x_2} & \cdots & \dfrac{\partial F_1}{\partial x_n} \\ \dfrac{\partial F_2}{\partial x_1} & \dfrac{\partial F_2}{\partial x_2} & \cdots & \dfrac{\partial F_2}{\partial x_n} \\ \cdots & \cdots & \cdots & \cdots \\ \dfrac{\partial F_n}{\partial x_1} & \dfrac{\partial F_n}{\partial x_2} & \cdots & \dfrac{\partial F_n}{\partial x_n} \end{bmatrix} = \dfrac{\partial(F_1, F_2,..., F_n)}{\partial(x_1, x_2,..., x_n)}$$

The Jacobian of a vector function is an extension of the concept of a partial derivative for a single-component function. MATLAB has the command *jacobian* which enables you to calculate the Jacobian matrix of a function.

As a first example, we calculate the Jacobian of the vector function mapping (x,y,z) to $(x * y * z, y, x + z)$.

```
>> syms x y z
>> jacobian([x*y*z; y; x+z],[x y z])

ans =

[y * z, x * z, x * y]
[   0,    1,    0]
[   1,    0,    1]
```

As a second example, we calculate the Jacobian of the vector function $f(x,y,z) = (e^x, \cos(y), \sin(z))$ at the point $(0, -\pi/2, 0)$.

```
>> syms x y z

>> J = jacobian ([exp(x), cos(y), sin(z)], [x, y, z])

J =

[exp(x), 0, 0]
[0,-sin(y), 0]
[0, 0, cos(z)]

>> subs(J,{x,y,z},{0,-pi/2,0})

ans =

    1 0 0
    0 1 0
    0 0 1
```

Thus the Jacobian turns out to be the identity matrix.

The Composite Function Theorem

The chain rule or composite function theorem allows you to differentiate compositions of vector functions. The chain rule is one of the most familiar rules of differential calculus. It is often first introduced in the case of single variable real functions, and is then generalized to vector functions. It says the following:

Suppose we have two vector functions

$$\overline{g}:U\subset R^n \to R^m \ and \ \overline{f}:V\subset R^m \to R^p$$

where U and V are open and consider the composite function $\overline{f}\circ\overline{g}:R^n \to R^p$.

If $\overline{g}$ is differentiable at $\overline{x}_0$ and $\overline{f}$ is differentiable at $\overline{y}_0 = \overline{g}(\overline{x}_0)$, then $\overline{f}\circ\overline{g}$ is differentiable at $\overline{x}_0$ and we have the following:

$$D(\overline{f}\circ\overline{g})(\overline{x}_0) = D\overline{f}(\overline{y}_0)D\overline{g}(\overline{x}_0)$$

MATLAB will directly apply the chain rule when instructed to differentiate composite functions.

Let us take for example $f(x,y)=x^2+y$ and $\overline{h}(u)=(\sin(3u),\cos(8u))$. If $g(x,y)=\overline{f}(\overline{h}(u))$ we calculate the Jacobian of g at $(0,0)$ as follows.

```
>> syms x y u
>> f = x ^ 2 + y

f =

x ^ 2 + y

>> h = [sin(3*u), cos(8*u)]

h =

[sin(3*u), cos(8*u)]
```

```
>> g = compose (h, f)

g =

[sin(3*x^2 + 3*y), cos(8*x^2 + 8*y)]

>> J = jacobian(g,[x,y])

J =

[6 * x * cos(3*x^2 + 3*y), 3 * cos(3*x^2 + 3*y)]
[- 16 * x * sin(8*x^2 + 8*y), - 8 * sin(8*x^2 + 8*y)]

>> H = subs(J,{x,y},{0,0})

H =

0   3
0   0
```

The Implicit Function Theorem

Consider the vector function $\bar{F} : A \subset R^{n+m} \to R^m$ where A is an open subset of R^{n+m}

$$(\bar{x},\bar{y}) \xrightarrow{\bar{F}} [F_1(\bar{x},\bar{y}),...,F_m(\bar{x},\bar{y})]$$

If F_i (i = 1, 2,..., m) are differentiable with continuous derivatives up to order r and the Jacobian matrix $J = \partial (F_1,..., F_m) / \partial (y_1,..., y_m)$ has non-zero determinant at a point $(\bar{x}_0,\bar{y}_0)$ such that $\bar{F}(\bar{x}_0,\bar{y}_0) = 0$, then there is an open $U \subset R^n$ containing $\bar{x}_0$ and an open $V \subset R^m$ containing to $\bar{y}_0$ and a single-valued function $\bar{f} : U \to V$ such that $\bar{F}[\bar{x}, \bar{f}(\bar{x})] = \bar{0} \ \forall x \in U$ and $\bar{f}$ is differentiable of order r with continuous derivatives.

This theorem guarantees the existence of certain derivatives of implicit functions. MATLAB allows differentiation of implicit functions and offers the results in those cases where the hypotheses of the theorem are met.

As an example we will show that near the point $(x, y, u, v) = (1,1,1,1)$ the following system has a unique solution:

$$xy + yvu^2 = 2$$
$$xu^3 + y^2v^4 = 2$$

where u and v are functions of x and y ($u = u(x, y)$, $v = v(x, y)$).

First, we check if the hypotheses of the implicit function theorem are met at the point $(1,1,1,1)$.

The functions are differentiable and have continuous derivatives. We need to show that the corresponding Jacobian determinant is non-zero at the point $(1,1,1,1)$.

```
>> clear all
>> syms x y u v
>> f = x * y + y * v * u ^ 2-2

f =

v * y * u ^ 2 + x * y - 2
```

```
>> g = x * u ^ 3 + y ^ 2 * v ^ 4-2

g =

x * u ^ 3 + v ^ 4 * y ^ 2 - 2

>> J = simplify (jacobian([f,g],[u,v]))

J =

[2 * u * v * y, u ^ 2 * y]
[3 * u ^ 2 * x, 4 * v ^ 3 * y ^ 2]

>> D = det (subs(J,{x,y,u,v},{1,1,1,1}))

D =

      5
```

The Inverse Function Theorem

Consider the vector function $\overline{f} : U \subset R^n \to R^n$ where U is an open subset of R^n

$$(x_1, x_2,..., x_n) \to [f_1(x_1, x_2,..., x_n),...,f_n(x_1, x_2,..., x_n)]$$

and assume it is differentiable with continuous derivative.

If there is an $\overline{x}_0$ such that $|J| = |\partial(f_1,...,f_n) / \partial(x_1,...,x_n)| \neq 0$ at x_0, then there is an open set A containing $\overline{x}_0$ and an open set B containing $\overline{f}(\overline{x}_0)$ such that $\overline{f}(A) = B$ and $\overline{f}$ has an inverse function $\overline{f}^{-1} : B \to A$ that is differentiable with continuous derivative. In addition we have:

$D\overline{f}^{-1}(y) = \left[D\overline{f}(\overline{x}) \right]^{-1}$ and if $J = \partial$ (f1,..., fn) / ∂ $(x_1,..., x_n)$ then $|J^{-1}| = 1 / |J|$.

MATLAB automatically performs the calculations related to the inverse function theorem, provided that the assumptions are met.

As an example, we consider the vector function $(u(x, y), v(x, y))$, where:

$$u(x,y) = \frac{x^4 + y^4}{x}, v(x,y) = \sin(x) + \cos(y).$$

We will find the conditions under which the vector function $(x(u,v), y(u,v))$ is invertible, with $x = x(u, v)$ and $y = y(u,v)$, and find the derivative and the Jacobian of the inverse transformation. We will also find its value at the point $(\pi/4, -\pi/4)$.

The conditions that must be met are those described in the hypotheses of the inverse function theorem. The functions are differentiable with continuous derivatives, except perhaps at $x = 0$. Now let us consider the Jacobian of the direct transformation ∂ $(u(x, y), v(x,y)) / \partial(x, y)$:

```
>> syms x y
>> J = simple ((jacobian ([(x^4+y^4)/x, sin(x) + cos(y)], [x, y])))

J =

[3 * x ^ 2-1/x ^ 2 * y ^ 4, 4 * y ^ 3/x]
[cos(x),-sin(y)]
```

```
>> pretty(det(J))
```

$$
- \frac{3 \sin(y)\; x^4 - \sin(y)\; y^4 + 4\; y\; \cos^3(x)\; x}{x^2}
$$

Therefore, at those points where this expression is non-zero, we can solve for *x* and *y* in terms of *u* and *v*. In addition, it must be true that $x \neq 0$.

We calculate the derivative of the inverse function. Its value is the inverse of the initial Jacobian matrix and its determinant is the reciprocal of the determinant of the initial Jacobian matrix:

```
>> I=simple(inv(J));
>> pretty(simple(det(I)))
```

$$
\frac{x^2}{3 \sin(y)\; x^4 - \sin(y)\; y^4 + 4\; y\; \cos^3(x)\; x}
$$

Observe that the determinant of the Jacobian of the inverse vector function is indeed the reciprocal of the determinant of the Jacobian of the original function.

We now find the value of the inverse at the point $(\pi/4, -\pi/4)$:

```
>> numeric(subs(subs(determ(I),pi/4,'x'),-pi/4,'y'))

ans =

   0.38210611216717

>> numeric(subs(subs(symdiv(1,determ(J)),pi/4,'x'),-pi/4,'y'))

ans =

   0.38210611216717
```

Again these results confirm that the determinant of the Jacobian of the inverse function is the reciprocal of the determinant of the Jacobian of the function.

The Change of Variables Theorem

The change of variable theorem is another key tool in multivariable differential analysis. Its applications extend to any problem in which it is necessary to transform variables.

Suppose we have a function *f(x,y)* that depends on the variables *x* and *y*, and that meets all the conditions of differentiation and continuity necessary for the inverse function theorem to hold. We introduce new variables *u* and *v*, relating to the above, regarding them as functions $u = u(x,y)$ and $v = v(x,y)$, so that *u* and *v* also fulfill the necessary conditions of differentiation and continuity (described by the inverse function theorem) to be able to express *x* and *y* as functions of *u* and *v*: *x=x (u,v)* and *y=y(u,v)*.

Under the above conditions, it is possible to express the initial function f as a function of the new variables u and v using the expression:

$f(u,v) = f(x(u,v), y(u,v))|J|$ where J is the Jacobian $\partial\ (x\ (u,\ v),\ y(u,v))\ /\partial(u,\ v)$.

The theorem generalizes to vector functions of n components.

As an example we consider the function $f(x,y) = e^{-(x+y)}$ and the transformation $u = u(x,y) = x + y$, $v = v(x,y) = x$ to finally find $f(u,v)$.

We calculate the inverse transformation and its Jacobian to apply the change of variables theorem:

```
>> syms x y u v
>> [x, y] = solve('u=x+y,v=x','x','y')

x =

v

y =

u-v

>> jacobian([v,u-v],[u,v])

ans =

[0,   1]
[1, - 1]

>> f = exp(x-y);
>> pretty (simple (subs(f,{x,y},{v,u-v}) * abs (det (jacobian ()))
   (((([v, u-v], [u, v])))

                         exp(2 v-u)
```

The requested function is $f(u,v) = e^{\,2v-u}$.

Series Expansions in Several Variables

The familiar concept of a power series representation of a function of one variable can be generalized to several variables. *Taylor's theorem for several variables theorem* reads as follows:

Let $f : R^n \rightarrow R$, $(x_1,...,x_n) \rightarrow f(x_1,...,x_n)$, be differentiable k times with continuous partial derivatives.

The Taylor series expansion of order k of $f(\bar{x})$ at the point $\bar{a} = (a_1,...,a_n)$ is as follows:

$$f(\bar{x}) = f(\bar{a}) + \sum_{i=1}^{n} \frac{\partial f}{\partial x_i}(\bar{a})t_i + \frac{1}{2!}\sum_{i=1}^{n}\sum_{j=1}^{n} \frac{\partial^2 f}{\partial x_i \partial x_j}(\bar{a})t_i t_j +$$

$$\frac{1}{3!}\sum_{i=1}^{n}\sum_{j=1}^{n}\sum_{k=1}^{n} \frac{\partial^3 f}{\partial x_i \partial x_j \partial x_k}(\bar{a})t_i t_j t_k + ... + R(k+1)$$

Here $\bar{x} = (x_1, x_2,...,x_n)$, $\bar{a} = (a_1, a_2,...,a_n)$, $t_i = x_i - a_i$ $(i = 1,2,...,n)$.

R = remainder.

Normally, the series are given up to order 2.

As an example we find the Taylor series up to order 2 of the following function at the point (1,0):

$$f(x,y) = e^{(x-1)^2} \cos(y)$$

```
>> pretty(simplify(subs(f,{x,y},{1,0})+subs(diff(f,x),{x,y},{1,0})*(x-1)
+subs(diff(f,y),{x,y},{1,0})*(y)+1/2*(subs(diff(f,x,2),{x,y},{1,0})* (x-1)^2+subs(diff(f,x,y),{x,y},
{1,0})*(x-1)*(y)+ subs(diff(f,y,2),{x,y},{1,0})* (y)^2)))
```

```
                2
         2     y
  (x - 1)     --- + 1
               2
```

Curl, Divergence and the Laplacian

The most common concepts used in the study of vector fields are directly treatable by MATLAB and are summarized below.

Definition of gradient: If $h = f(x,y,z)$, then the gradient of f, which is denoted by $\Delta f(x, y, z)$, is the vector:

$$Grad(f) = \Delta f(x,y,z) = \frac{\partial f(x,y,z)}{\partial x} i + \frac{\partial f(x,y,z)}{\partial y} j + \frac{\partial f(x,y,z)}{\partial z} k$$

Definition of a scalar potential of a vector field: A vector field $\bar{F}$ is called conservative if there is a differentiable function f such that $\bar{F} = \Delta f$. The function f is known as a scalar potential function for $\bar{F}$.

Definition of the curl of a vector field: The curl of a vector field $F(x,y,z) = Mi + Nj + Pk$ is the following:

$$curl\, F(x,y,z) = \Delta \times F(x,y,z) = \left(\frac{\partial P}{\partial y} - \frac{\partial N}{\partial z}\right) i - \left(\frac{\partial P}{\partial x} - \frac{\partial M}{\partial z}\right) j + \left(\frac{\partial N}{\partial x} - \frac{\partial M}{\partial y}\right) k$$

Definition of a vector potential of a vector field: A vector field F is a vector potential of another vector field G if $F = curl\ (G)$.

Definition of the divergence of a vector field: The divergence of the vector field $F(x,y,z) = Mi + Nj + Pk$ is the following:

$$diverge\, F(x,y,z) = \Delta \Delta F(x,y,z) = \frac{\partial M}{\partial x} + \frac{\partial N}{\partial y} + \frac{\partial P}{\partial z}$$

Definition of the Laplacian: The Laplacian is the differential operator defined by:

$$Laplacian = \Delta^2 = \Delta\Delta\Delta = \frac{\partial^2}{\partial x^2} + \frac{\partial^2}{\partial y^2} + \frac{\partial^2}{\partial z^2}$$

As a first example, we calculate gradient and Laplacian of the function:

$$w = \frac{1}{\sqrt{1 - x^2 - y^2 - z^2}}$$

```
>> gradient=simplify([diff(f,x), diff(f,y), diff(f,z)])

gradient =

[x /(-x^2-y^2-z^2 + 1) ^(3/2), y /(-x^2-y^2-z^2 + 1) ^(3/2), z /(-x^2-y^2-z^2 + 1) ^(3/2)]

>> pretty (gradient)

+-                                                              -+
|              x                    y                    z       |
|    --------------------,  ---------------------,  --------------------- |
|             3                    3                    3        |
|             -                    -                    -        |
|             2                    2                    2        |
|      2    2    2           2    2    2           2    2    2    |
|    (- x  - y  - z  + 1)  (- x  - y  - z  + 1)  (- x  - y  - z  + 1) |
+-                                                              -+

>> Laplacian = simplify ([diff(f,x,2) + diff(f,y,2) + diff(f,z,2)])

Laplacian =

3 /(-x^2-y^2-z^2 + 1) ^(5/2)

>> pretty (Laplacian)

               3
    ---------------------
                5
                -
                2
      2    2    2
    (- x  - y  - z  + 1)
```

As a second example, we calculate the curl and the divergence of the vector field:

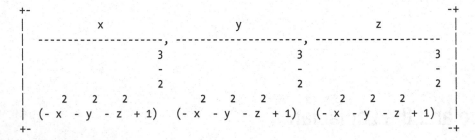

$$\overline{F}(x,y,z) = \tan^{-1}\frac{x}{y}\,\overline{i} + \ln\sqrt{x^2 + y^2}\,\overline{j} + \overline{k}.$$

```
>> M = atan (x/y)

M =

atan (x/y)

>> N = log (sqrt(x^2+y^2))

N =

log ((x^2 + y^2) ^(1/2))
```

```
>> P = 1

P =
     1

>> Curl = simplify ([diff(P,y)-diff(N,z), diff(P,x)-diff(M,z), diff(N,x)-diff(M,y)])

Curl =

[0, 0, (2 * x) /(x^2 + y^2)]

>> pretty (Curl)

   +-               -+
   |           2 x   |
   |  0, 0,  -------  |
   |           2   2  |
   |          x + y   |
   +-               -+

>> Divergence = simplify (diff(M,x) + diff(N,y) + diff(P,z))

Divergence =

(2 * y) /(x^2 + y^2)

>> pretty (divergence)

     2 y
   -------
    2   2
   x + y
```

Rectangular, Spherical and Cylindrical Coordinates

MATLAB allows you to easily convert cylindrical and spherical coordinates to rectangular, cylindrical to spherical coordinates, and their inverse transformations. As the cylindrical and spherical coordinates, we have the following:

In a *cylindrical coordinate* system, a point P in the space is represented by a triplet (r, θ, z), where:

- r is the distance from the origin *(O)* to the projection P' of P in the XY plane
- θ is the angle between the X axis and the segment OP'
- z is the distance PP'

In a *spherical coordinate* system, a point P in the space is represented by a triplet (ρ, θ, φ), where:

- ρ is the distance from P to the origin
- θ is the same angle as the one used in cylindrical coordinates
- φ is the angle between the positive Z axis and the segment OP

The following conversion equations are easily found:

Cylindrical to rectangular:

$$x = r\cos\theta$$
$$y = r\sin\theta$$
$$z = z$$

Rectangular to cylindrical:

$$r = \sqrt{x^2 + y^2}$$

$$\theta = \tan^{-1}\frac{y}{x}$$

$$z = z$$

Spherical to rectangular:

$$x = \rho\sin\phi\cos\theta$$
$$y = \rho\sin\phi\sin\theta$$
$$z = \rho\cos\phi$$

Rectangular to spherical:

$$\rho = \sqrt{x^2 + y^2 + z^2}$$

$$\theta = \tan^{-1}\frac{y}{x}$$

$$\phi = \cos^{-1}\frac{z}{\sqrt{x^2 + y^2 + z^2}}$$

As a first example we express the surfaces with equations given by $xz = 1$ and $x^2 + y^2 + z^2 = 1$ in spherical coordinates.

```
>> clear all
>> syms x y z r t a
>> f = x * z-1

f =

x * z - 1

>> equation = simplify (subs (f, {x, y, z}, {r * sin(a) * cos(t), r * sin(a) * sin(t), r * cos(a)}))

equation =

r ^ 2 * cos(a) * sin(a) * cos(t) - 1
```

```
>> pretty (equation)

  2
 r cos(a) sin(a) cos(t) - 1

g =

x ^ 2 + y ^ 2 + z ^ 2 - 1

>> equation1 = simplify (subs (g, {x, y, z}, {r * sin(a) * cos(t), r * sin(a) * sin(t),
r * cos(a)}))

equation1 =

r ^ 2 - 1

>> pretty (equation1)

  2
 r -1
```

However, MATLAB provides commands that allow you to transform between different coordinate systems. Below are the basic MATLAB commands which can be used for coordinate transformation.

[RHO, THETA, Z] = cart2ctl (X, Y, Z)	*Transforms Cartesian coordinates to cylindrical coordinates*
[RHO, THETA] = cart2pol(X,Y)	*Transforms Cartesian coordinates to polar coordinates*
[THETA, PHI, R] = cart2sph (X, Y, Z)	*Transforms Cartesian coordinates to spherical coordinates*
[X, Y, Z] = pol2cart (RHO, THETA, Z)	*Transforms Cartesian coordinates to cylindrical coordinates*
[X, Y] = pol2cart (RHO, THETA)	*Transforms polar coordinates to Cartesian coordinates*
[x, y, z] = sph2cart (THETA, PHI, R)	*Transforms spherical coordinates to Cartesian coordinates*

The following example transforms the point $(\pi 1, 2)$ in polar coordinates to Cartesian coordinates.

```
>> [X, Y, Z] = pol2cart(pi,1,2)

X =

   -1

Y =

 1. 2246e-016

Z =

   2
```

Next we transform the point $(1,1,1)$ in Cartesian coordinates to spherical and cylindrical coordinates.

```
>> [X, Y, Z] = cart2sph(1,1,1)

X =

   0.7854

Y =

   0.6155

Z =

   1.7321

>> [X, Y, Z] = cart2pol(1,1,1)

X =

   0.7854

Y =

   1,4142


Z =

   1
```

The following example transforms the point $(2,\pi/4)$ in polar coordinates into Cartesian coordinates.

```
>> [X, Y] = pol2cart(2,pi/4)

X =

  -0.3268

Y =

   0.7142
```

EXERCISE 7-1

Study the differentiability of the function:

$$f(x) = x^2 \sin\left(\frac{1}{x}\right) \text{ if } x \neq 0 \text{ and } f(x) = 0 \text{ if } x = 0.$$

We begin by studying the continuity of the function at the point $x = 0$.

```
>> syms x
>> f = x ^ 2 * sin(1/x)

f =

x ^ 2 * sin(1/x)

>> limit(f,x,0, 'right')

ans =

0

>> limit(f,x,0, 'left')

ans =

0

>>
>> limit(f,x,0)

ans =

0
```

We see that the function is continuous at $x = 0$ because the limit of the function as x tends to zero coincides with the value of the function at zero. It may therefore be differentiable at zero.

We now determine whether the function is differentiable at the point $x = 0$:

```
>> syms h, limit((h^2*sin(1/h) - 0)/h,h,0)

ans =

0
```

Thus, we see that:

$$\lim_{h \to 0} \frac{f(0+h) - f(0)}{h} = f'(0) = 0$$

which indicates that the function f is differentiable at the point $x = 0$.

Let us now see what happens at a non-zero point $x = a$:

```
>> pretty(simple(limit((subs(f,{x},{a+h})-subs(f,{x},{a})))/h,h,a)))
```

```
       / 1 \          / 1 \
 4-sin |---| -a sin|  -- |
       \ 2 a /         \ a /
```

Thus, we conclude that:

$$\lim_{h \to 0} \frac{f(a+h)-f(a)}{h} = f'(a) = 4a\sin\left(\frac{1}{2a}\right) - \sin\left(\frac{1}{a}\right)$$

Thus, we have already found the value of the derivative at any non-zero point $x = a$. We represent the function in the figure below.

```
>> fplot ('x ^ 2 * sin (x)', [-1/10,1/10])
```

EXERCISE 7-2

Calculate the derivative with respect to x of the following functions:

$$\log\left(\sin(2x)\right),\ x^{\tan(x)},\ \frac{4}{3}\sqrt{\frac{x^2-1}{x^2+2}},\ \log\left(x+\sqrt{x^2+1}\right).$$

```
>> pretty(simple(diff('log(sin(2*x))','x')))
```

```
2 cot(2 x)
```

```
>> pretty(simple(diff('x^tanx','x')))
```

```
         tanx
        x      tanx
        ------------
             x
```

```
>> pretty(simple(diff('(4/3)*sqrt((x^2-1)/(x^2+2))','x')))
```

$$4 \frac{x}{(x^2 - 1)^{1/2} (x^2 + 2)^{3/2}}$$

```
>> pretty(simple(diff('log(x+(x^2+1)^(1/2))','x')))
```

$$\frac{1}{(x^2 + 1)^{1/2}}$$

EXERCISE 7-3

Calculate the nth derivative of the following functions:

$$\frac{1}{x}, \quad e^{x/2}, \frac{1+x}{1+x}$$

```
>> f='1/x';
>> [diff(f),diff(f,2),diff(f,3),diff(f,4),diff(f,5)]
```

ans =

```
-1/x ^ 2   2/x ^ 3   -6/x ^ 4   24/x ^ 5   -120/x ^ 6
```

We begin to see the pattern emerging, so the nth derivative is given by

$$\frac{(-1)^n n!}{x^{n+1}}.$$

```
>> f='exp(x/2)';
>> [diff(f),diff(f,2),diff(f,3),diff(f,4),diff(f,5)]
```

ans =

```
1/2*exp(1/2*x)   1/4*exp(1/2*x)   1/8*exp(1/2*x)   1/16*exp(1/2*x   1/32*exp(1/2*x)
```

Thus the nth derivative is $\dfrac{e^{x/2}}{2^n}$.

```
>> f='(1+x)/(1-x)';
>> [simple(diff(f)),simple(diff(f,2)),simple(diff(f,3)),simple(diff(f,4))]

ans =

2 /(-1+x) ^ 2-4 /(-1+x) ^ 3 12 /(-1+x) ^ 4-48 /(-1+x) ^ 5
```

Thus, the nth derivative is equal to $\dfrac{2(n!)}{(1-x)^{n+1}}$.

EXERCISE 7-4

Find the equation of the tangent to the curve $f(x) = 2x^3 + 3x^2 - 12x + 7$ at $x = -1$.

Also find the x for which the tangents to the curve are $g(x) = \dfrac{x^2 - x - 4}{x - 1}$ horizontal and vertical. Find the asymptotes.

```
>> f ='2 * x ^ 3 + 3 * x ^ 2-12 * x + 7';
>> g = diff (f)

g =

6*x^2+6*x-12

>> subs(g,-1)

ans =

-12

>> subs(f,-1)

ans =

20
```

We see that the slope of the tangent line at the point $x = -1$ is -12, and the function has value 20 at $x = -1$. Therefore the equation of the tangent to the curve at the point (-1,20) will be:

$$y - 20 = -12\ (x - (-1))$$

We graphically represent the curve and its tangent on the same axes.

```
>> fplot('[2*x^3+3*x^2-12*x+7, 20-12*(x - (-1))]',[-4,4])
```

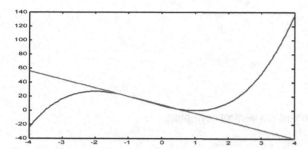

To calculate the horizontal tangent to the curve $y = f(x)$ at $x = x0$, we find the values $x0$ for which the slope of the tangent is zero $(f'(x0) = 0)$. The equation of this tangent will therefore be $y = f(x0)$.

To calculate the vertical tangents to the curve $y = f(x)$ at $x = x0$, we find the values $x0$ which make the slope of the tangent infinite $(f'(x0) = \infty)$. The equation of this tangent will then be $= x0$:

```
>> g ='(x^2-x+4) /(x-1)'
>> solve(diff(g))

ans =

[ 3]
[-1]

>> subs(g,3)

ans =

5

>> subs(g,-1)

ans =

-3
```

The two horizontal tangents have equations:

$$y = g' [-1](x + 1) - 3, \text{ that is, } y = -3.$$

$$y = g'[3](x - 3) + 5, \text{ that is, } y = 5.$$

The horizontal tangents are not asymptotes because the corresponding values of $x0$ are finite (-1 and 3).

We now consider the vertical tangents. To do this, we calculate the values of x that make $g'(x)$ infinite (i.e. values for which the denominator of g' is zero, but do not cancel with the numerator):

```
>> solve('x-1')

ans =

1
```

Therefore, the vertical tangent has equation $x = 1$.

For $x = 1$, the value of $g(x)$ is infinite, so the vertical tangent is a vertical asymptote.

```
subs(g,1)
Error, division by zero
```

Indeed, the line $x = 1$ is a vertical asymptote.

As $\lim_{x \to \infty} g(x) = \infty$, there are no horizontal asymptotes.

Now let's see if there are any oblique asymptotes:

```
>> syms x,limit(((x^2-x+4)/(x-1))/x,x,inf)

ans =

1

>> syms x,limit(((x^2-x+4)/(x-1) - x)/x,x,inf)

ans =

0
```

Thus, there is an oblique asymptote $y = x$.

We now graph the curve with its asymptotes and tangents:

On the same axes (see the figure below) we graph the curve whose equation is $g(x) = (x^2-x + 4)/(x-1)$, the horizontal tangents with equations $a(x) = -3$ and $b(x) = 5$, the oblique asymptote with equation $c(x) = x$ and the horizontal and vertical asymptotes (using the default command *fplot*):

```
>> fplot('[(x^2-x+4)/(x-1),-3,5,x]',[-10,10,-20,20])
```

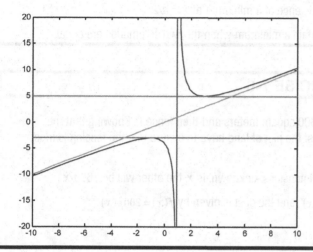

EXERCISE 7-5

Decompose a positive number a as a sum of two summands so that the sum of their cubes is minimal.

Let x be one of the summands. The other will be $a-x$. We need to minimize the sum $x^3+ (a-x)^3$.

```
>> syms x a;
>> f='x^3+(a-x)^3'

f =

x^3+(a-x)^3

>> solve(diff(f,'x'))

ans =

1/2 * a
```

The possible maximum or minimum is at $x = a/2$. We use the second derivative to see that it is indeed a minimum:

```
>> subs(diff(f,'x',2),'a/2')

ans =

3 * a
```

As $a > 0$ (by hypothesis), $4a > 0$, which ensures the existence of a minimum at $x = a/2$.

Therefore $x = a/2$ and $a-x = a-a/2 = a/2$. That is, we obtain a minimum when the two summands are equal.

EXERCISE 7-6

Suppose you want to purchase a rectangular plot of 1600 square meters and then fence it. Knowing that the fence costs 200 cents per meter, what dimensions must the plot of land have to ensure that the fencing is most economical?

If the surface area is 1600 square feet and one of its dimensions, unknown, is x, the other will be 1600/x.

The perimeter of the rectangle is $p(x) = 2x + 2(1600/x)$, and the cost is given by $f(x) = 200p(x)$:

```
>> f ='200 * (2 * x + 2 *(1600/x))'

f =

200 * (2 * x + 2 *(1600/x))
```

This is the function to minimize:

```
>> solve(diff(f))

ans =

[ 40]
[-40]
```

The possible maximum and minimum are presented for $x = 40$ and $x = -40$. We use the second derivative to determine their nature:

```
>> [subs(diff(f,2), 40), subs(diff(f,2), -40)]

ans =

20 - 20
```

$x = 40$ is a minimum, and $x = -40$ is a maximum. Thus, one of the sides of the rectangular field is 40 meters, and the other will measure 1,600/40 = 40 meters. Therefore the optimal rectangle is a square with sides of 40 meters.

EXERCISE 7-7

Given the function of two real variables defined by:

$$f(x,y) = \frac{xy}{x^2 + y^2} \text{ if } x^2 + y^2 \neq 0 \text{ and } f(x,y) = 0 \text{ if } x^2 + y^2 = 0$$

calculate the partial derivatives of f at the origin. Study the differentiability of the function.

To find $\partial f/\partial x$ and $\partial f/\partial y$ at the point (0,0), we directly apply the definition of the partial derivative at a point:

```
>> syms x y h k
>> limit((subs(f,{x,y},{h,0})-0)/h,h,0)

ans =

0

>> limit((subs(f,{x,y},{0,k})-0)/k,k,0)

ans =

0
```

We see that the limits of the two previous expressions when $h \to 0$ and $k \to 0$, respectively, are both zero. That is to say:

$$\lim_{h \to 0} \frac{f(h,0) - f(0,0)}{h} = \frac{\partial f}{\partial x}(0,0) = 0$$
$$\lim_{h \to 0} \frac{f(0,k) - f(0,0)}{h} = \frac{\partial f}{\partial y}(0,0) = 0$$

Thus the two partial derivatives have the same value, namely zero, at the origin.

But the function is not differentiable at the origin, because it is not continuous at (0,0), since it has no limit as $(x,y) \to (0,0)$:

```
>> syms m
>> limit((m*x)^2/(x^2+(m*x)^2),x,0)

ans =

m^2 /(m^2 + 1)
```

The limit does not exist at (0,0), because if we consider the directional limits with respect to the family of straight lines $y = mx$, the result depends on the parameter m.

EXERCISE 7-8

Find and classify the extreme points of the function

$$f(x,y) = -120x^3 - 30x^4 + 18x^5 + 5x^6 + 30xy^2.$$

We begin by finding the possible extreme points. To do so, we equate each of the partial derivatives of the function with respect to each of its variables to zero (i.e. the components of the gradient vector of f) and solve the resulting system in three variables:

```
>> syms x y
>> f = -120 * x ^ 3-30 * x ^ 4 + 18 * x ^ 5 + 5 * x ^ 6 + 30 * x * y ^ 2

f =

5 * x ^ 6 + 18 * x ^ 5-30 * x ^ 4-120 * x ^ 3 + 30 * x * y ^ 2

>> [x y] = solve (diff(f,x), diff(f,y), x, y)

x =

  0
  2
 -2
 -3

y =

  0
  0
  0
  0
```

So the possible extreme points are: (- 2,0), (2,0), (0,0) and (-3,0).

We will analyze what kind of extreme points these are. To do this, we calculate the Hessian matrix and express it as a function of x and y.

```
>> clear all
>> syms x y
>> f=-120*x^3-30*x^4+18*x^5+5*x^6+30*x*y^2

f =

5*x^6 + 18*x^5 - 30*x^4 - 120*x^3 + 30*x*y^2
```

```
>> H=simplify([diff(f,x,2),diff(diff(f,x),y);diff(diff(f,y),x),diff(f,y,2)])

H =

[- 30 * x *(-5*x^3-12*x^2 + 12*x + 24), 60 * y]
[                              60*y, 60*x]
```

Now we calculate the value of the determinant of the Hessian matrix at the possible extreme points.

```
>> det(subs(H,{x,y},{0,0}))

ans =

     0
```

The origin turns out to be a degenerate point, as the determinant of the Hessian matrix is zero at (0,0).

We will now look at the point (- 2,0).

```
>> det(subs(H,{x,y},{-2,0}))

ans =

     57600
```

```
>> eig(subs(H,{x,y},{-2,0}))

ans =

   -480
   -120
```

The Hessian matrix at the point (-2,0) has non-zero determinant, and is also negative definite, because all its eigenvalues are negative. Therefore, the point (-2,0) is a maximum of the function.

We will now analyze the point (2,0).

```
>> det(subs(H,{x,y},{2,0}))

ans =

     288000
```

```
>> eig(subs(H,{x,y},{2,0}))

ans =

     120
    2400
```

The Hessian matrix at the point (2,0) has non-zero determinant, and is furthermore positive definite, because all its eigenvalues are positive. Therefore, the point (2,0) is a minimum of the function.

We will now analyze the point (-3,0).

```
>> det(subs(H,{x,y},{-3,0}))

ans =

    -243000

>> eig(subs(H,{x,y},{-3,0}))

ans =

     -180
     1350
```

The Hessian matrix at the point (-3,0) has non-zero determinant, and, in addition, is neither positive definite nor negative, because it has both positive and negative eigenvalues. Therefore, the point (-3,0) is a saddle point of the function.

EXERCISE 7-9

Find and classify the extreme points of the function:

$$f(x,y,z) = \sqrt{x^2 + y^2} - z$$

subject to the restrictions: $x^2 + y^2 = 16$ and $x + y + z = 10$.

We first find the Lagrangian L, which is a linear combination of the objective function and the constraints:

```
>> clear all
>> syms x y z L p q
>> f =(x^2+y^2) ^(1/2)-z

f =

(x ^ 2 + y ^ 2) ^ (1/2) - z

>> g1 = x ^ 2 + y ^ 2 - 16, g2 = x + y + z - 10

G1 =

x ^ 2 + y ^ 2 - 16

G2 =

x + y + z - 10
```

```
>> L = f + p * g1 + q * g2

L =

(x ^ 2 + y ^ 2) ^ (1/2) - z + q *(x + y + z - 10) + p *(x^2 + y^2 - 16)
```

Then, the possible extreme points are found by solving the system obtained by setting the components of the gradient vector of *L* to zero, that is, $\nabla L(x_1, x_2,...,x_n, \lambda) = (0,0,...,0)$. Which translates into:

```
>> [x, y z, p, q] = solve (diff(L,x), diff(L,y), diff(L,z), diff(L,p), diff(L,q), x, y z, p, q)

x =

-2 ^(1/2)/8 - 1/8

y =

1

z =

2 * 2 ^(1/2)

p =

2 * 2 ^(1/2)

q =

10 - 4 * 2 ^(1/2)
```

Matching all the partial derivatives to zero and solving the resulting system, we find the values of x_1, x_2,..., x_n, λ_1, λ_2,...,λ_k corresponding to possible maxima and minima.

We already have one possible extreme point:

$(-(1+\sqrt{2})/8, 1, 2\sqrt{2})$

We need to determine what kind of extreme point this is. To this end, we substitute it into the objective function.

```
>> syms x y z
>> vpa (subs (f, {x, y, z}, {-2 ^(1/2)/8-1/8,1,2*2^(1/2)}))

ans =

-1.7838845579619739822874 1803905
```

Thus, at the point $(-(1(\quad 2)/8, 1// \quad 2)$, the function has a maximum.

EXERCISE 7-10

Given the function $f(x,y)=10^{-(x+y)}$ and the transformation u = u(x,y) = 2 x + y, v = v(x,y) = x − y, find f(u,v).

We calculate the inverse transformation and its Jacobian in order to apply the change of variables theorem:

```
>> [x, y] = solve('u=2*x+y,v=x-y','x','y')

x =

u + v/3

y =

u - (2 * v) / 3

>> jacobian([u/3 + v/3,u/3-(2*v)/3], [u, v])

ans =

[1/3, 1/3]
[1/3, 2/3]

>> f = 10 ^(x-y);
>> pretty (simple (subs(f,{x,y},{u/3 + v/3,u/3-(2*v)/3}) *))
   abs (det (jacobian([u/3 + v/3,u/3-(2*v)/3], [u, v])))

    v
  10
  ---
   3
```

Thus the requested function is *f(u,v) = 10ᵛ/3.*

EXERCISE 7-11

Find the Taylor series at the origin, up to order 2, of the function:

$$f(x,y) = e^{x+y^2}$$

```
>> f = exp(x+y^2)

f =

>> pretty (simplify (subs(f,{x,y},{0,0}) + subs (diff(f,x), {x, y}, {0,0}) * (x) + subs
(diff(f,y), {x, y}, {0,0}) * (y) + 1/2 * (subs (diff(f,x,2), {x, y}, {0,0}) * (x) ^ 2 + subs
(diff(f,x,y), {x, y}, {0,0}) * (x) * (y) + subs (diff(f,y,2), {x, y}, {0,0}) * (y) ^ 2)))

    2
   x          2
   -- + x + y  + 1
    2
```

EXERCISE 7-12

Express, in Cartesian coordinates, the surface which is given in cylindrical coordinates by $z = r^2 (1 + \sin(t))$.

```
>> syms x y z r t a
>> f = r ^ 2 * (1 + sin(t))

f =

r ^ 2 * (sin(t) + 1)

>> Cartesian = simplify(subs(f, {r, t}, {sqrt(x^2+y^2), bind(y/x)}))

Cartesian =

(x ^ 2 + y ^ 2) * (y / (x *(y^2/x^2 + 1) ^(1/2)) + 1)

>> pretty (Cartesian)

    2    2 /        y             \
  (x  + y ) | --------------- + 1 |
            |    / 2      \1/2     |
            |    | y      |        |
            | x  | -- + 1 |        |
            |    | 2      |        |
            \    \ x      /        /
```

EXERCISE 7-13

Find the unit tangent, the unit normal, and the unit binormal vectors of the twisted cubic: $x = t$, $y = t^2$, $z = t^3$.

We begin by restricting the variable t to the real field:

```
>> x = sym('x','real);
```

We define the symbolic vector *V* as follows:

```
>> syms t, V = [t,t^2,t^3]

V =

[t, t ^ 2, t ^ 3]
```

The tangent vector is calculated by:

```
>> tang = diff(V)

tang =

[1, 2 *, 3 * t ^ 2]
```

The unit tangent vector will be:

```
>> ut = simple (tang/sqrt(dot(tang,tang)))

tu =

[1/(1+4*t^2+9*t^4)^(1/2),2*t/(1+4*t^2+9*t^4)^(1/2),3*t^2/(1+4*t^2+9*t^4)^(1/2)]
```

To find the unit normal vector we calculate $((v' \wedge v'') \wedge v')/(|v' \wedge v''| \, |v'|)$:

```
>> v1 = cross(diff(V),diff(V,2)) ;
>> nu = simple(cross(v1,tang)/(sqrt(dot(v1,v1))*sqrt(dot(tang,tang))))

nu =

[ (-2*t-9*t^3)/(9*t^4+9*t^2+1)^(1/2)/(1+4*t^2+9*t^4)^(1/2),
  (1-9*t^4)/(9*t^4+9*t^2+1)^(1/2)/(1+4*t^2+9*t^4)^(1/2), (6*t^3+3*t)/(9*t^4+9*t^2+1)^(1/2)/
  (1+4*t^2+9*t^4)^(1/2)]
```

The unit binormal vector is the vector product of the tangent vector and the unit normal vector.

```
>> bu = simple(cross(tu,nu))

bu =

[3*t^2/(9*t^4+9*t^2+1)^(1/2),-3*t/(9*t^4+9*t^2+1)^(1/2),1/(9*t^4+9*t^2+1)^(1/2)]
```

The unit binormal vector can also be calculated via $(v' \wedge v \ '') / |v' \wedge v''|$ as follows:

```
>> bu = simple(v1/sqrt(dot(v1,v1)))

bu =
```

```
[3*t^2/(9*t^4+9*t^2+1)^(1/2),-3*t/(9*t^4+9*t^2+1)^(1/2),1/(9*t^4+9*t^2+1)^(1/2)]
```

We have calculated the Frenet frame for a twisted cubic.

CHAPTER 8

∎∎∎

Integration in One and Several Variables. Applications

Integrals

MATLAB includes a specially designed group of commands which allow you to work with integrals in one and several variables. The program will attempt to find primitive functions, provided they are not too algebraically complicated. In cases where the integral cannot be calculated symbolically, MATLAB enables a group of commands that allow you to approximate the integrals using the most common iterative methods.

The following table lists the most common MATLAB commands used for integration in one and several variables.

syms x, int(f(x), x) or int('f(x) ', 'x')	*Computes the indefinite integral* $\int f(x)dx$
	
	 `>> syms x`
	 `>> int((tan(x))^2, x)`
	
	 `ans =`
	
	 `tan(x) - x`
	
	 `>> int('(tan(x))^2', 'x')`
	
	 `ans =`
	
	 `tan(x) - x`

int (int ('f(x,y)', 'x'), 'y'))	*Computes the double integral* $\int \int f(x,y)dxdy$
	
	 `>> simplify(int(int('(tan(x))^2 + (tan(y))^2', 'x'), 'y'))`
	
	 `ans =`
	
	 `atan(tan(x)) * tan(y) - 2 * y * atan(tan(x)) + y * tan(x)`

(continued)

279

syms x y, int (int (f(x,y), x), y)	*Computes the double integral* $\int\int f(x,y)dxdy$
	``>> syms x y
>> simplify(int(int((tan(x))^2 + (tan(y))^2, x), y))

ans =

atan(tan(x)) * tan(y) - 2 * y * atan(tan(x)) + y * tan(x)``` |
| **int (int (int (... int ('f (x, y...z)',**
'x'), 'y')...), 'z') | *Computes the multiple integral* $\int\int\cdots\int f(x,y,\cdots,z)\,dxdy\cdots dz$ |
| | ```>> int(int(int('sin(x+y+z)', 'x'), 'y'), 'z')

ans =

cos(x + y + z)``` |
| **syms x y z,.**
int (int (int
(... int (f (x, y...z), x), y)...), z) | *Computes the multiple integral* $\int\int\cdots\int f(x,y,\cdots,z)\,dxdy\cdots dz$ |
| | ```>> syms x y z
>> int(int(int(sin(x+y+z), x), y), z)

ans =

cos(x + y + z)``` |
| **syms x a b, int(f(x), x, a, b)** | *Computes the definite integral* $\int_a^b f(x)dx$ |
| | ```>> syms x
>> int((cos(x))^2,x,-pi,pi)

ans =

PI``` |
| **int('f(x) ', 'x', 'a', 'b')** | *Computes the definite integral* $\int_a^b f(x)dx$ |
| | ```>> int('(cos(x))^2','x',-pi, pi)

ans =

PI``` |
| **int (int ('f(x,y)', 'x', 'a', 'b'), 'y', ' it, ' to))** | *Computes the integral* $\int_a^b\int_c^d f(x,y)dxdy$ |
| | ```>> int(int('(cos(x+y))^2','x',-pi,pi), 'y',-pi/2,pi/2)

ans =

Pi ^ 2``` |

(*continued*)

syms x y a b c d,
int (int (f(x,y), x, a, b), y, c, d)
	Computes the integral $\int_a^b \int_c^d f(x,y)dxdy$
	
	`>> syms x y`
	`>> int(int((cos(x+y))^2,x,-pi,pi),y,-pi/2, pi/2)`
	
	`ans =`
	
	`pi^2`

int(int(int(....int('f(x,y,...,z)',
'x', 'a', 'b'), 'y', 'c', 'd'),....), 'z', 'e', 'f')
	Computes the multiple definite integral $\int_a^b \int_c^d \cdots \int_e^f f(x,y,\cdots,z)\,dxdy\cdots dz$
	
	`>> int(int(int((cos(x+y+z))^2,x,-pi,pi),`
	`   y,-pi/2,pi/2), z,-2*pi,2*pi)`
	
	`ans =`
	
	`4*pi^3`

syms x y z a b c d e f,
int(int(int(....int(f(x,y,...,z), x, a, b),
y, c, d),...), z, e, f)
	Computes the multiple definite integral $\int_a^b \int_c^d \cdots \int_e^f f(x,y,\cdots,z)\,dxdy\cdots dz$
	
	`>> syms x y z`
	`>> int(int(int((cos(x+y+z))^2,x,-pi,pi),y,-pi/2,pi/2),z,-`
	`   2*pi,2*pi)`
	
	`ans =`
	
	`4*pi^3`

Indefinite Integrals, Change of Variables and Integration by Parts

The integrals whose primitive functions can be calculated symbolically, using changes of variables and integration by parts, can be directly solved using the MATLAB command *int*.

As a first example, we calculate the following indefinite integrals:

$$\int \frac{1}{\sqrt{x^2+1}}\,dx, \quad \int \frac{\ln(x)}{\sqrt{x}}, \quad \int \frac{1}{(2+x)\sqrt{1+x}}\,dx, \quad \int x^3\sqrt{1+x^4}\,dx$$

```
>> pretty(simple(int('1/sqrt(x^2+1)')))

  asinh(x)

>> pretty(simple(int('log(x)/x^(1/2)')))

    1/2
  2 x    (log(x) - 2)

>> pretty(simple(int('1/((2+x)*(1+x)^(1/2))')))

           1/2
  2 atan((x + 1)   )
```

```
>> pretty(simple(int('x^3*sqrt(1+x^4)')))
```

```
          3
          -
          2
     4
  (x  + 1)
  ---------
      6
```

As a second example, we calculate the following integrals by a change of variable:

$$\int \frac{\arctan\left(\dfrac{x}{2}\right)}{x^2+4}\,dx, \int \frac{\cos^3(x)}{\sqrt{\sin(x)}}\,dx$$

```
>> pretty(simple(int(atan(x/2)/(4+x^2),x)))
```

```
      / x \2
  atan| - |
      \ 2 /
  ----------
      4
```

```
>> pretty(simple(int(cos(x)^3 /sin(x)^(1/2), x)))
```

```
         1/2      2
  2 sin (x) (cos (x) + 4)
  -----------------------
             5
```

As a third example, we find the following integrals using integration by parts:

$$\int e^x \cos x\,dx, \int \left(5x^2-3\right)4^{1+3x}\,dx$$

```
>> pretty(simple(int('exp(x) * cos(x) ',' x')))
```

```
  exp(x) (cos(x) + sin(x))
  ------------------------
             2
```

```
>> pretty(simple(int('(5*x^2-3)*4^(3*x+1)','x')))
```

```
   6 x           2  2                        2
  2    (90 log(2)  x  - 30 log(2) x - 54 log(2)  + 5)
  --------------------------------------------------
                       3
                  27 log(2)
```

Integration by Reduction and Cyclic Integration

Integration by reduction is used to integrate functions involving large integer exponents. It reduces the integral to a similar integral where the value of the exponent has been reduced. Repeating this procedure we eventually obtain the value of the original integral.

The usual procedure is to perform integration by parts. This will lead to the sum of an integrated part and an integral of a similar form to the original, but with a reduced exponent.

Cyclic integration is similar except we end up with the same integral that we had at the beginning, except for constants. The resulting equation can be rearranged to give the original integral.

In both cases the problem lies in the proper choice of the function $u(x)$ in the integration by parts.

MATLAB directly calculates the value of this type of integral in the majority of cases. In the worst case, the final value of the integral can be found after one to three applications of integration by parts.

As an example we find the following integral:

$$\int \sin^{13}(x)\cos^{15}(x)dx,$$

```
>> I = int('sin(x)^13 * cos(x)^15', 'x')

I =

cos(x) ^ 18/6006 - (cos(x) ^ 16 * sin(x) ^ 12) / 28 - (3 * cos(x) ^ 16 * sin(x) ^ 10) / 182 -
(5 * cos(x) ^ 16 * sin(x) ^ 8) / 728 - (5 * cos(x) ^ 16 * sin(x) ^ 6) / 2002 - (3 * cos(x) ^ 16 *
sin(x) ^ 4) / 4004 - (3 * cos(x) ^ 16) / 16016
```

Rational and Irrational Integrals. Binomial Integrals

The MATLAB command *int* can also be used to directly calculate the indefinite integrals of rational functions, rational powers of polynomials, binomial expressions and their rational combinations.

As an example, we calculate the following integrals:

$$\int \frac{3x^4 + x^2 + 8}{x^4 - 2x^2 + 1}\,dx, \quad \int \frac{\sqrt{9 - 4x^2}}{x}\,dx, \quad \int x^8 (3 + 5x^3)^{\frac{1}{4}}\,dx$$

The first integral is a typical example of a rational integral.

```
>> I1=int((3*x^4+x^2+8)/(x^4-2*x^2+1),x)

I1 =

3*x - (6*x)/(x^2 - 1) + atan(x*i)*i

>> pretty(simple(I1))

        6 x
  3 x - ------ + atan(x i) i
         2
        x  - 1
```

The second integral is a typical example of an irrational integral.

```
>> I2=int(sqrt(9-4*x^2)/x,x)

I2 =

3*acosh(-(3*(1/x^2)^(1/2))/2) + 2*(9/4 - x^2)^(1/2)

>> pretty(simple(I2))

          /     / 1  \1/2 \
          |   3 | -- |    |
          |     | 2  |    |
          |     \ x  /    |                2 1/2
   3 acosh| - ----------- | + (9  -  4 x )
          \        2      /
```

The third integral is a typical example of a binomial integral.

```
>> I3=int(x^8*(3+5*x^3)^(1/4),x)

I3 =

(5*x^3 + 3)^(1/4)*((4*x^9)/39 + (4*x^6)/585 - (32*x^3)/4875 + 128/8125)

>> pretty(simple(I3))

                  5
                  -
                  4
        3          6          3
  4 (5 x  + 3)  (375 x  - 200 x  + 96)
  -------------------------------------
                73125
```

Definite Integrals and Applications

The definite integral acquires its strength when it comes to applying the techniques of integration to practical problems. Here we present some of the most common applications.

Curve Arc Length

One of the most common applications of integral calculus is to find lengths of arcs of curve.

For a planar curve with equation $y = f(x)$, the arc length of the curve between the points with x coordinates $x = a$ and $x = b$ is given by the expression:

$$L = \int_a^b \sqrt{1 + f'(x)^2}\, dx$$

For a planar curve with parametric coordinates $x = x(t)$, $y = y(t)$, the arc length of the curve between the points corresponding to the parameter values $t = t_0$ and $t = t_1$ is given by the expression:

$$L = \int_{t_0}^{t_1} \sqrt{x'(t)^2 + y'(t)^2}\, dt$$

For a curve given in polar coordinates by the equation r = f(a), the arc length of the curve between the points corresponding to the parameter values $a = a_0$ and $a = a_1$ is given by the expression:

$$L = \int_{a_0}^{a_1} \sqrt{r^2 + r'(a)^2}\, dr$$

For a space curve with parametric coordinates x = x(t), y = y(t), z = z(t), the arc length of the curve between the points corresponding to the parameter values t = t_0 and t = t_1 is given by the expression:

$$L = \int_{t_0}^{t_1} \sqrt{x'(t)^2 + y'(t)^2 + z'(t)^2}\, dt$$

For a space curve in cylindrical coordinates given by the equations x = r·cos, y = r·sin (a), z = z, the arc length of the curve between the points corresponding to parameter values a = a_0 and a = a_1 is given by the expression:

$$L = \int_{a_0}^{a_1} \sqrt{r^2 + r'^2 + z'^2}\, dr$$

For a space curve in spherical coordinates given by the equations x = r·sin (a)·cos (b), y = r·sin (a)·sin (b), z = r·cos(a), the arc length of the curve between the points corresponding to the parameter values a = a_0 and a = a_1 is given by the expression:

$$L = \int_{a_0}^{a_1} \sqrt{dr^2 + r^2 da^2 + r^2 \sin^2(a) db^2}\, dr^2$$

As a first example we consider a power cord that hangs between two towers which are 80 meters apart. The cable adopts the catenary curve whose equation is:

$$y = 100 \cosh \frac{x}{100}$$

We calculate the arc length of the cable between the two towers.
We begin by graphing the catenary in the interval [– 40,40].

```
>> syms x
>> ezplot(100*cosh(x/100), [-40,40])
```

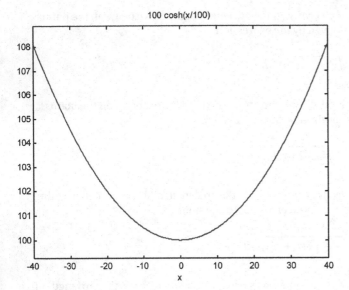

The length of the catenary is calculated as follows:

```
>> f=100*cosh(x/100)

f =

100*cosh(x/100)

>> pretty(simple(int((1+diff(f,x)^2)^(1/2),x,-40,40)))

            / 2 \
  200 sinh | - |
            \ 5 /
```

If we want to approximate the result we do the following:

```
>> vpa(int((1+diff(f,x)^2)^(1/2),x,-40,40))

ans =

82.150465160563101708042002766894
```

As a second example, we find the length of the cardoid defined for values from $a = 0$ to $a = 2pi$ by the polar equation $r = 3-3cos(a)$.

We graph the curve to get an idea of the length we are trying to find.

```
>> ezpolar('3-3*cos(a)',[0,2*pi])
```

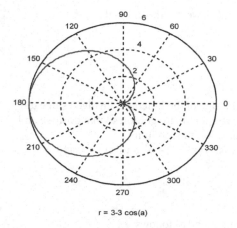

r = 3-3 cos(a)

Now we calculate the requested length.

```
>> r='3-3*cos(a)';
>> diff(r,'a')

ans =

3*sin(a)

>> R=simple(int('((3-3*cos(a))^2+(3*sin(a))^2)^(1/2)','a','0','2*pi'))

R =

24
```

The Area between Two Curves

Another common application of integral calculus is the calculation of the area bounded between curves.

The area between a curve with equation $y = f(x)$ and the x-axis is given, in general, by the integral:

$$S = \left| \int_a^b f(x)\,dx \right|$$

where $x = a$ and $x = b$ are the abscissas of the end points of the curve.

If the curve is given in parametric coordinates by $x = x(t), y = y(t)$, then the area is given by the integral:

$$S = \left| \int_a^b y(t)\,x'(t)\,dt \right|$$

for the parameter values $t = a$ and $t = b$ corresponding to the end points of the curve.

If the curve is given in polar coordinates by $r = f(a)$, then the area is given by the integral:

$$S = \frac{1}{2} \int_{a_0}^{a_1} f(a)^2\,da$$

for the parameter values $a = a_0$ and $a = a_1$ corresponding to the end points of the curve.

287

To calculate the area between two curves with equations y = f(x) and y = g(x), we use the integral:

$$S = \int_a^b |f(x) - g(x)| \, dx$$

where $x = a$ and $x = b$ are the abscissas of the end points of the two curves.

When calculating these areas it is very important to take into account the sign of the functions involved since the integral of a negative portion of a curve will be negative. One must divide the region of integration so that positive and negative values are not computed simultaneously. For the negative parts one takes the modulus.

As a first example, we calculate the area bounded between the two curves: $f(x) = 2 - x^2$ and $g(x) = x$

We begin by plotting the two curves.

```
>> fplot('[2-x^2,x]',[-2*pi,2*pi])
```

We need to find the points of intersection of the two curves. They are calculated as follows:

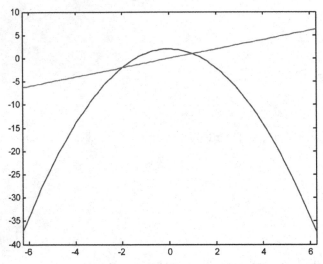

```
>> solve('2-x^2=x')

ans =

 -2
  1
```

We are now able to calculate the requested area.

```
>> int('2-x^2-x','x',-2,1)

ans =

9/2
```

As a second example, we calculate the length of, and the area enclosed by, the parameterized curves:

$$x(t) = \frac{\cos(t)[2-\cos(2t)]}{4} \quad y(t) = \frac{\sin(t)[2+\cos(2t)]}{4}$$

We begin by producing a graphical representation of the enclosed area.

```
>> x=(0:.1:2*pi);
>> t=(0:.1:2*pi);
>> x=cos(t).*(2-cos(2*t))./4;
>> y=sin(t).*(2+cos(2*t))./4;
>> plot(x,y)
```

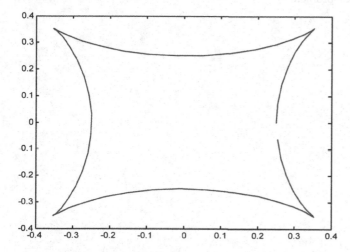

This is the figure generated as the parameter varies between 0 and 2π. We must calculate its length and the area it encloses. To avoid cancelling positive areas with negative areas, we will only work with the first half quadrant and multiply the result by 8.

For the length we have:

```
>> A=simple(diff('cos(t)*(2-cos(2*t))/4'))

A =

-(3*sin(t)*(2*sin(t)^2 - 1))/4

>> B=simple(diff('sin(t)*(2+cos(2*t))/4'))

B =

(3*cos(t)^3)/2 - (3*cos(t))/4

>> L=8*int('sqrt((-(3*sin(t)*(2*sin(t)^2 - 1))/4)^2+((3*cos(t)^3)/2 - (3*cos(t))/4)^2)','t',0,pi/4)

L =

3
```

For the area we have:

```
>> S=8*simple(int('(sin(t)*(2+cos(2*t))/4)*(-3/8*sin(t)+3/8*sin(3*t))', 't',0,pi/4))

S =

-(3*pi - 16)/32
```

As a third example, we calculate the length and the area enclosed by the curve given in polar coordinates by:

$$r = \sqrt{\cos(2a)}$$

We begin by graphing the curve to get an idea of the problem.

```
>> a=0:.1:2*pi;
>> r=sqrt(cos(2*a));
>> polar(a,r)
```

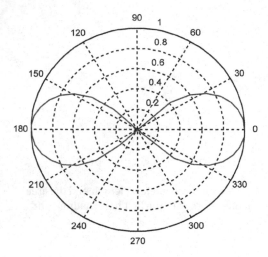

We observe that the curve repeats its structure four times as a varies between 0 and $\pi/4$. We calculate the area S enclosed by it in the following way:

```
>> clear all
>> syms a
>> S=4*(1/2)*int((sqrt(cos(2*a)))^2,a,0,pi/4)

S =

1
```

Surfaces of Revolution

The surface area generated by rotating the curve with equation y = f(x) around the x-axis is given by the integral:

$$S = 2\pi \int_a^b f(x)\sqrt{1 + f'(x)^2}\, dx$$

in Cartesian coordinates, where x=a and x=b are the x-coordinates of the end points of the rotating curve, or

$$S = 2\pi \int_{t_0}^{t_1} y(t)\sqrt{x'(t)^2 + y'(t)^2}\, dt$$

in parametric coordinates, where t_0 and t_1 are the values of the parameter corresponding to the end points of the curve. The area generated by rotating the curve with equation $x = f(y)$ around the y-axis is given by the integral:

$$S = 2\pi \int_a^b f(y)\sqrt{1 + f'(y)^2}\, dy$$

where y = a and y = b are the y-coordinates of the end points of the rotating curve.

As a first example, we calculate the surface area generated by rotating the cubic curve $12x - 9x^2 + 2x^3$ around the x-axis, between x = 0 and x = 5/2.

```
>> I=2*pi*vpa(int('(2*x^3-9*x^2+12*x)*sqrt(1+(6*x^2-18*x+12)^2)','x',0,5/2))

Warning: Explicit integral could not be found.

I =

50.366979807381457286723333012298*pi
```

As a second example, we calculate the surface area generated by rotating the parametric curve given by $x(t) = t - sin(t)$, $y(t) = 1-cos(t)$ around the x-axis, between t = 0 and t = 2π.

```
>> clear all
>> syms t
>> x=t-sin(t)

x =

t - sin(t)

>> y= 1-cos(t)

y =

1 - cos(t)

>> V=2*pi*int(y*(sqrt(diff(x,t)^2+diff(y,t)^2)),t,0,2*pi)

V =

(64*pi)/3
```

The approximate area is found as follows:

```
>> V=vpa(2*pi*int(y*(sqrt(diff(x,t)^2+diff(y,t)^2)),t,0,2*pi))

V =

67.020643276582255753869725509963
```

Volumes of Revolution

The volume generated by rotating the curve with equation $y = f(x)$ around the x-axis is given by the integral:

$$V = \pi \int_a^b f(x)^2\, dx$$

where $x = a$ and $x = b$ are the x-coordinates of the end points of the rotating curve.

The volume generated by rotating the curve with equation $x = f(y)$ around the y-axis is given by the integral:

$$V = \pi \int_a^b f(y)^2\, dy$$

where $y = a$ and $y = b$ are the y-coordinates of the end points of the rotating curve.

If one cuts a volume by planes parallel to one of the three coordinate planes (for example, the plane $z = 0$) and if the equation $S(z)$ of the curve given by the cross section is given in terms of the distance of the plane from the origin (in this case, z) then the volume is given by:

$$V = \int_{z_1}^{z_2} S(z)\, dz$$

As a first example, we calculate the volumes generated by rotating the ellipse

$$\frac{x^2}{4} + \frac{y^2}{9} = 1$$

around the x-axis and around the y-axis.

The given volumes are found by calculating the following integrals:

```
>> V1=int('pi*9*(1-x^2/4)','x',-2,2)

V1 =

24*pi

>> V2=int('pi*4*(1-y^2/9)','y',-3,3)

V2 =

16*pi
```

As a second example, we calculate the volume generated by rotating the curve given in polar coordinates by $r = 1 + cos(a)$ around the x-axis.

The curve is given in polar coordinates, but there is no difficulty in calculating the values of $x(a)$ and $y(a)$ needed to implement the volume formula in Cartesian coordinates. We have:

$$x(a) = r(a)\cos(a) = (1 + \cos(a))\cos(a)$$

$$y(a) = r(a)\sin(a) = (1 + \cos(a))\sin(a)$$

The requested volume is then calculated in the following way:

```
>> x='(1+cos(a))*cos(a)';

>> y='(1+cos(a))*sin(a)';

>> A=simple(diff(x))

A =

- sin(2*a) - sin(a)

>> V=pi*abs(int('((1+cos(a))*sin(a))^2*(-sin(2*a)-sin(a))','a',0,pi))

V =

(8*pi)/3
```

Curvilinear Integrals

Let $\bar{F}$ be a continuous vector field in R^3 and c: [a, b] → R^3 be a continuous differentiable curve in R^3. We define the line integral of $\bar{F}$ along the curve c as follows:

$$\int_c \bar{F} \cdot ds = \int_a^b \bar{F}[c(t)] \cdot c'(t)dt$$

As a first example, we consider the curve $c(t)=[\sin(t),\cos(t),t]$ with $0 < t < 2\pi$, and the vector field $F(x,y,z) = x\bar{i} + y\bar{j} + z\bar{k}$. We calculate the curvilinear integral:

$$\int_c \bar{F} \cdot ds$$

```
>> syms t
>> pretty(int(dot([sin(t),cos(t),t],[cos(t),-sin(t),1]),t,0,2*pi))

        2
   2 pi
```

As a second example, we calculate the integral:

$$\int_c \sin(z)dx + \cos(z)dy - \sqrt[3]{xy}\,dz$$

where the curve c is given by the parametric equations:

$$x = \cos^3(a),\ y = \sin^3(a),\ z = a,\ 0 < a < \frac{7\pi}{2}$$

```
>> syms a
>> [diff(cos(a)^3),diff(sin(a)^3),diff(a)]

ans =

[ -3*cos(a)^2*sin(a), 3*cos(a)*sin(a)^2, 1]

>> int((dot([sin(a),cos(a),-sin(a)^3*cos(a)^3],[-3*cos(a)^2*sin(a), 3*sin(a)^2*cos(a),1]))^(1/3),
a,0,7*pi/2)

ans =

2*(-1)^(1/3) + 3/2

>> pretty(int((dot([sin(a), cos(a) -sin(a)^3 * cos(a)^3], [- 3 * cos(a)^2 * sin(a), 3 * sin(a)^2 *
cos(a), 1]))^(1/3), 0, 7 * pi/2))

         1
         -
     3   3
  2 (-1)  + -
         2

>> vpa(int((dot([sin(a), cos(a) -sin(a)^3 * cos(a)^3], [-3 * cos(a)^2 * sin(a), 3 * sin(a)^2 *
cos(a), 1])) ^ (1/3), 0, 7 * pi/2))

ans =

1.7320508075688772935274463415059*i + 2.5
```

As a third example, we calculate the integral:

$$\int_c x^3 dy - y^3 dx$$

where c is the circle $x^2 + y^2 = a^2$.

```
>> pretty(int('a*cos(t)^3*diff(a*sin(t),t)-a*sin(t)^3 *diff(a*cos(t),t)','t',0,2*pi))
```

$$
\frac{3\ pi\ a^2}{2}
$$

Improper Integrals

MATLAB works with improper integrals in the same way as it works with any other type of definite integral. We will not discuss theoretical issues concerning the convergence of improper integrals here, but within the class of improper integrals we will distinguish two types:

1. ***Integrals with infinite limits***: the domain of definition of the integrand is a half-line [(a,∞) or (-∞, a)] or the entire line (-∞,∞).

2. ***Integrals of discontinuous functions***: the given function is continuous in an interval [a, b] except at finitely many so-called isolated singularities.

Complicated combinations of these two cases may also occur. One can also generalize this to the more general setting of Stieltjes integrals, but to discuss this would require a course in mathematical analysis.

As an example, we calculate the values of the following integrals:

$$
\int_0^b \frac{dx}{\sqrt{x'}} \qquad \int_0^\infty \frac{e^{-x}\sin(x)}{x}dx
$$

```
>> syms x a b
>> pretty(limit(int(1/sqrt(x),x,a,b),a,0))
```

$$
2\ b^{1/2}
$$

```
>> pretty(simple(int(exp(-x)*sin(x)/x,x,0,inf)))
```

$$
\frac{PI}{4}
$$

Parameter Dependent Integrals

Consider the function of the variable $y: \int_a^b f(x,y)dx = F(y)$ defined in the range $c \le y \le e$, where the function $f(x, y)$ is continuous on the rectangle $[a, b] \times [c, e]$ and the partial derivative of f with respect to y is continuous in the same rectangle, then for *all* y in the range $c \le y \le e$:

$$
\frac{d}{dy}\left[\int_a^b f(x,y)dx\right] = \int_a^b \frac{d}{dy}f(x,y)dx
$$

This result is very important, because it allows us to differentiate an integral by differentiating under the integral sign.

Integrals dependent on a parameter can also be improper, and in addition the limits of integration may also depend on a parameter.

If the limits of integration depend on a parameter, we have the following:

$$\frac{d}{dy}\left[\int_{a(y)}^{b(y)} f(x,y)\,dx\right] = \int_{a(y)}^{b(y)} \frac{d\,f(x,y)}{dy}\,dx + b'(y)\cdot f[b(y),y] - a'(y)\cdot f[a(y),y]$$

provided that $a(y)$ and $b(y)$ are defined in the interval $[c, e]$ and have continuous derivatives $a'(y)$ and $b'(y)$, and the curves $a(y)$ and $b(y)$ are contained in the box $[a, b] \times [c, e]$.

Furthermore, if the function $\int_a^b f(x,y)\,dx = F(y)$ is defined on the interval $[c, e]$ and $f(x, y)$ is continuous on the rectangle $[a, b] \times [c, d]$, then the following holds:

$$\int_c^e \int_a^b f(x,y)\,dx\,dy = \int_a^b \int_c^e f(x,y)\,dy\,dx$$

i.e., integration under the integral sign is allowed and the order of integration over the variables is irrelevant.

As an example, we solve by differentiation with respect to the parameter a > 0 the following integrals:

$$\int_0^\infty \frac{\arctan(ax)}{x(1+x^2)}\,dx, \quad \int_0^\infty \frac{1-e^{-x^2}}{x^2}\,dx$$

For the first integral, we will start by integrating the derivative of the integrand with respect to the parameter a, which will be easier to integrate. Once this integral is found, we integrate with respect to a to find the original integral.

```
>> a = sym('a', 'positive')

a =

a

>> pretty(simple(sym((int(diff(atan(a*x)/(x*(1+x^2)),a),x,0,inf)))))

    pi
  -------
  2 a + 2
```

Now, we integrate this function with respect to the variable a:

```
>> pretty(simple(sym(int(pi/(2*a+2),a))))

  pi log(a + 1)
  -------------
        2
```

To solve the second integral, we define:

$$f(a) = \int_0^\infty \frac{1 - e^{-ax^2}}{x^2} \, dx$$

As in the first integral, we differentiate the integrand with respect to the parameter a, find the integral, and then integrate with respect to a. The desired integral is then given by setting $a = 1$.

```
>> Ia=simple(sym(int(diff((1-exp(-a*x^2))/x^2,a),x,0,inf)))

Ia =

(pi/a)^(1/2)/2

>> s=simple(sym(int(Ia,a)))

s =

(pi*a)^(1/2)
```

By putting $a = 1$, we have $(1) = I(a) = \sqrt{\pi}$

Approximate Numerical Integration

MATLAB contains functions for performing numerical integration using Simpson's method and Lobatto's method. The syntax of these functions is as follows:

q = quad(f,a,b)	Finds the integral of f between a and b by Simpson's method with a tolerance of 10^{-6}

	```>> F = @(x)1./(x.^3-2*x-5);```
	```Q = quad(F,0,2)```
	```Q =```
	```-0.4605```

q = quad(f,a,b,tol)	Finds the integral of f between a and b by Simpson's method with a tolerance given by tol

	```>> Q = quad(F,0,2,1.0e-20)```
	```Q =```
	```-0.4607```

q = quad(f,a,b,tol,trace)	Finds the integral of f between a and b by Simpson's method with tolerance tol, presenting a trace of the iteration
q = quad(f,a,b,tol,trace,p1,p2,...)	Includes extra arguments p1, p2, ... for the function f, f (x, p1, p2, ...)

(continued)

q = quadl(f,a,b)	Finds the integral of f between a and b by Lobatto's method with a tolerance of 10^{-6}

```
>> clear all
>> syms x
>> f=inline(1/sqrt(x^3+x^2+1))
f =
Inline function:
f(x) = 1.0./sqrt(x.^2+x.^3+1.0)
>> Q = quadl(f,0,2)
Q =
1.2326
```

q = quadl(f,a,b,tol)	Finds the integral of f between a and b by Lobatto's method with tolerance tol

```
>> Q = quadl(f,0,2,1.0e-25)
Q =
1.2344
```

q = quadl(f,a,b,tol,trace)	Finds the integral of f between a and b by Lobatto's method with tolerance tol, presenting a trace of the iteration
q = quad(f,a,b,tol,trace,p1,p2,...)	Includes extra arguments p1, p2, ... for the function f, f (x, p1, p2, ...)
[q,fcnt] = quadl(f,a,b,...)	Returns the number of function evaluations
q = dblquad(f,xmin,xmax, ymin, ymax)	Finds the double integral of f (x, y) over the specified domain with a tolerance of 10^{-6}

```
>> clear all
>> syms xy
>> z = inline(y*sin(x)+x*cos(y))
z =
Inline function:
z(x,y) = x.*cos(y)+y.*sin(x)
>> D=dblquad(z,-1,1,-1,1)
D =
1.0637e-016
```

q = dblquad(f,xmin,xmax, ymin, ymax, tol)	Finds the double integral of f (x, y) over the specified domain with tolerance tol
q = dblquad(f,xmin,xmax, ymin, ymax, tol, @ quadl)	Finds the double integral of f (x, y) over the specified domain with tolerance tol using the quadl method
q = dblquad(f,xmin,xmax, ymin, ymax, tol, method, p1, p2, ...)	Includes extra arguments p1, p2, ... for the function f, f (x, p1, p2, ...)

As a first example, we calculate the following integral using Simpson's method:

$$\int_0^2 \frac{1}{x^3 - 2x - 5}\,dx$$

```
>> F = inline('1./(x.^3-2*x-5)');
>> Q = quad(F,0,2)
Q =
-0.4605
```

Here we see that the value of the integral remains unchanged even we increase the tolerance to 10^{-18}.

```
>> Q = quad(F,0,2,1.0e-18)
Q =
-0.4605
```

Next we evaluate the integral using Lobatto's method.

```
>> Q = quadl(F,0,2)
Q =
-0.4605
```

Now we evaluate the double integral

$$\int_\pi^{2\pi} \int_0^\pi y\sin(x) + \cos(y)\,dx\,dy$$

```
>> Q = dblquad(inline('y*sin(x)+x*cos(y)'), pi, 2*pi, 0, pi)

Q =
-9.8696
```

Special Integrals

MATLAB provides in its basic module a comprehensive collection of special functions which help to facilitate the computation of integrals. The following table sets out the most important examples.

gamma(a)	Gamma function: $\Gamma(a)=\int_0^\infty e^{-t}t^{a-1}dt$
gammainc(x,a)	Incomplete Gamma function $\Gamma(x,a)=\dfrac{1}{\Gamma(a)}\int_0^x e^{-t}t^{a-1}dt$
gammaln(a)	Logarithm of the gamma function $Log\ \Gamma(a)$
beta(z,w)	Beta function $\beta(z,w)=\int_0^1 (1-t)^{w-1}t^{z-1}dt=\dfrac{\Gamma(z)\Gamma(w)}{\Gamma(z+w)}$
betainc(x,z,w)	Incomplete Beta function $\beta(z,w)=\int_0^1 (1-t)^{w-1}t^{z-1}dt=\dfrac{\Gamma(z)\Gamma(w)}{\Gamma(z+w)}$
betaln (x,z,w)	Logarithm of the Beta function Log β(z, w)
[SN,CN,DN] = ellipj(u,m)	The Jacobi elliptic functions $u=\int_0^\Phi \dfrac{1}{\sqrt{1-m\sin^2(\Phi)}}d\Phi$
	SN (u) = sin (ϕ),
	CN (u) = cos (ϕ),
	DN (u) = $\sqrt{1-m\sin^2(\Phi)}$
	Complete elliptic functions of the 1st (k) and 2nd (e) kind
k = ellipke(m)	$k(m)=\int_0^1 \sqrt{\dfrac{1-t^2}{1-mt^2}}dt=\int_0^{\pi/2}\dfrac{1}{\sqrt{1-m\sin^2(\theta)}}d\theta=F(\pi/2,m)$
[k,e] = ellipke(m)	$e(m)=\int_0^1 \sqrt{\dfrac{1-mt^2}{1-t^2}}dt=\int_0^{\pi/2}\sqrt{1-m\sin^2(\theta)}d\theta=E(\pi/2,m)$
erf (X) = error function	F = $erf(x)=\dfrac{2}{\sqrt{\pi}}\int_0^x e^{-t^2}dt=2F_{N(0,1/2)}(x)$ (normal distribution)
erfc(X) = complementary error function	$erfc(x)=\dfrac{2}{\sqrt{\pi}}\int_x^\infty e^{-t^2}dt=1-erf(x)$
erfcx(X) = complementary scaled error function	$erfcx(x)=e^{x^2}erfc(x)\cong\dfrac{1}{\sqrt{\pi}}\dfrac{1}{x}$
erfinv (X) = error inverse	$x=erfinv(y)\Leftrightarrow y=erf(x)$
expint (x)	Exponential integral

As a first example, we calculate the normal distribution (0,1/2) for values between 0 and 1 spaced ¼ apart.

```
>> erf(0:1/4:1)

ans =
0 0.28 0.52 0.71 0.84
```

Next we calculate the values of the Gamma function at the first four even numbers.

```
>> gamma([2 4 6 8])

ans =
1.00 6.00 120.00 5040.00
```

Bearing in mind the above result we see that $\Gamma(a) = (a-1)!$ for the first four even numbers.

```
>> [factorial(1),factorial(3),factorial(5),factorial(7)]

ans =
1.00 6.00 120.00 5040.00
```

Then, for $z = 3$ and $w = 5$, we find that:

$$beta(z,w) = exp(gammaln(z)+gammaln(w)-gammaln(z+w))$$

$$betaln(z,w) = gammaln(z)+gammaln(w)-gammaln(z+w)$$

```
>> beta(3,5)

ans =
0.01
```

```
>> exp(gammaln(3)+gammaln(5)-gammaln(3+5))

ans =
0.01
```

```
>> betaln(3,5)

ans =
-4.65
```

```
>> gammaln(3)+gammaln(5)-gammaln(3+5)

ans =
-4.65
```

Also, for $z = 3$ and $w = 5$ we check that:

$$beta(z,w) = \Gamma(z)\Gamma(w) / \Gamma(z+w)$$

```
>> gamma(3)*gamma(5)/gamma(3+5)

ans =
0.01
```

```
>> beta(3,5)

ans =
0.01
```

As another example, suppose we want to calculate the length of a full period of the sinusoid $y = 3\sin(2x)$. The length of this curve is given by the formula:

$$4\int_0^{\frac{1}{4}\pi} \sqrt{1 - \left(\frac{\partial}{\partial x} y(x)\right)^2}\, dt = \int_0^{\pi/2} \sqrt{1 + 36 \cdot \cos^2(2x)}\, dx = 2\int_0^{\pi/2} \sqrt{37 - 36 \cdot \sin^2(t)}\, dt$$

In the last step we have made the change of variable $t = 2x$, in addition to using $cos^2(t) = 1\text{-}sin^2(t)$. The integral can now be calculated by:

```
>> [K,E]=ellipke(36/37)

K =
3.20677433446297
E =
1.03666851510702

>> 2*sqrt(37)*E

ans =
12.61161680006573
```

Definite Integrals and Applications. Several Variables

The applications of integrals of functions of several variables occupy a very important place in the integral calculus and in mathematical analysis in general. In the following sections we will see how MATLAB can be used to calculate areas of planar regions, surface areas, and volumes, via multiple integration.

Planar Areas and Double Integration

If we consider a planar region S, we can find its area through the use of double integrals. If the boundary of the region S is determined by curves whose equations are given in Cartesian coordinates, its area A is found by means of the formula:

$$A = \iint_S dx\, dy$$

If, for example, S is determined by $a < x < b$ and $f(x) < y < g(x)$ then the area will be given by:

$$A = \int_a^b dx \int_{f(x)}^{g(x)} dy$$

If S is determined by $h(a) < x < k(b)$ and $c < y < d$, the area will be given by:

$$A = \int_c^d dy \int_{h(a)}^{h(b)} dx$$

If the region S is determined by curves whose equations are given in polar coordinates with radius vector r and angle a, its area A is given by the formula:

$$A = \iint_S r \, da \, dr$$

If, for example, S is determined by $s < a < t$ and $f(a) < r < g(a)$, then the area is given by:

$$A = \int_s^t da \int_{f(a)}^{g(a)} r \, dr$$

As a first example, we calculate the area of the region bounded by the x-axis, the parabola $y^2 = 4x$ and the straight line $x + y = 3$.

It is convenient to begin with a graphical representation.

We see that the region can be limited to y between 0 and 2 $(0 < y < 2)$ and for x between the curves $x = y^\wedge 2/4$ and $x = 3 - y$. Then, we can calculate the requested area as follows:

```
>> A=int(int('1','x','y^2/4','3-y'),'y',0,2)

A =

10/3
```

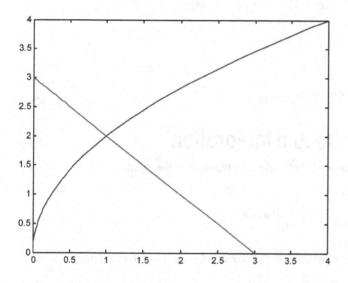

As a second example, we calculate the area outside the circle with polar equation $r = 2$, and inside the cardioid with polar equation $r = 2 (1 + \cos(a))$.

First of all, we graph the area of integration.

```
>> a=0:0.1:2*pi;
>> r=2*(1+cos(a));
>> polar(a,r)
>> hold on;
>> r=2*ones(size(a));
>> polar(a,r)
```

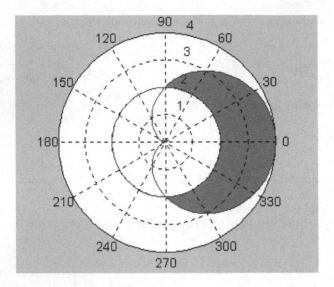

Looking at the graph, we see that, by symmetry, we can calculate half of the area by varying a between 0 and *Pi/2* $(0 < a$ Pi/2) and r between the curves $r = 2$ and $r = 2\ (1 + cos(a))$:

```
>> pretty(int(int('r','r',2,'2*(1+cos(a))'),'a',0,pi/2))
```

```
 pi
 -- + 4
 2
```

The requested area is therefore $2\ (\pi/2 + 4) = \pi + 8$ square units.

Calculation of Surface Area by Double Integration

The area S of a curved surface expressed as $z = f(x, y)$, which is defined over a region R in the xy-plane, is:

$$S = \iint_R \sqrt{1 + \left(\frac{\partial z}{\partial x}\right)^2 + \left(\frac{\partial z}{\partial y}\right)^2}\ dx\,dy$$

The area S of a curved surface expressed as $x = f(y, z)$, which is defined over a region R in the yz-plane, is:

$$S = \iint_R \sqrt{1 + \left(\frac{\partial x}{\partial y}\right)^2 + \left(\frac{\partial x}{\partial z}\right)^2}\ dy\,dz$$

The area S of a curved surface expressed as $y = f(x, z)$, which is defined over a region R in the xz-plane, is:

$$S = \iint_R \sqrt{1 + \left(\frac{\partial y}{\partial x}\right)^2 + \left(\frac{\partial y}{\partial z}\right)^2}\ dx\,dz$$

As an example, we calculate the area of the surface of the cone with equation $x^2 + y^2 = z^2$, limited above the xy-plane and cut by the cylinder $x^2 + y^2 = b\,y$.

The projection of the surface onto the xy-plane is the region bounded by the circle with equation $x^2 + y^2 = by$, so, with MATLAB the calculation is as follows:

```
>> clear all
>> syms x y z a b
>> z = sqrt((x^2+y^2)/a)

z =
 ((x^2 + y^2)/a)^(1/2)

>> pretty(int(int((1 + diff(z,x)^2 + diff(z,y)^2)^(1/2), x,-(b*y-y^2)^(1/2), (b * y - y^2)^(1/2)),
y, 0, b))

        2 / 1    \1/2
  pi b  | - + 1 |
        \ a     /
  ------------------
          4
```

Calculation of Volumes by Double Integration

The volume V of a cylindroid with upper boundary the surface with equation z = f(x,y), lower boundary the xy-plane and laterally bounded by the cylindrical surface meeting the xy-plane orthogonally at the border of a region R, is:

$$V = \iint_R f(x,y)\,dx\,dy = \iint_R z\,dx\,dy$$

The volume V of a cylindroid with upper boundary the surface with equation x = f(y,z), lower boundary the yz-plane and laterally bounded by the cylindrical surface meeting the yz-plane at the border of a region R, is:

$$V = \iint_R f(y,z)\,dy\,dz = \iint_R x\,dy\,dz$$

The volume V of a cylindroid with upper boundary the surface with equation y = f(x,z), lower boundary the xz-plane and laterally bounded by the cylindrical surface meeting the xz-plane at the border of a region R, is:

$$V = \iint_R f(x,z)\,dx\,dz = \iint_R y\,dx\,dz$$

As a first example, we calculate the volume in the first octant bounded between the xy-plane, the plane $z = x + y + 2$ and the cylinder $x^2 + y^2 = 16$.

The requested volume is found by means of the integral:

```
>> pretty(simple(int(int('x+y+2', 'y', 0, 'sqrt(16-x^2)'), 'x', 0, 4)))

          128
    8 pi + ---
           3
```

As a second example, we calculate the volume bounded by the paraboloid $x^2 + 4y^2 = z$ and by the cylinders with equations $y^2 = x$ and $x^2 = y$.

The volume is calculated using the following integral:

```
>> pretty(int(int('x^2 + 4 * y^2', 'y','x^2', 'sqrt(x)'), 'x', 0, 1))
```

```
    3
    -
    7
```

Calculation of Volumes and Triple Integrals

The volume of a three-dimensional body R, whose equations are expressed in Cartesian coordinates, is given by the triple integral:

$$\iiint_R dx\,dy\,dz$$

The volume of a three-dimensional body R, whose equations are expressed in cylindrical coordinates, is given by the triple integral:

$$\iiint_R r\,dz\,dr\,da$$

The volume of a three-dimensional body R, whose equations are expressed in spherical coordinates, is given by the triple integral:

$$\iiint_R r^2 \sin(b)\,dr\,db\,da$$

As a first example, we calculate the volume bounded by the paraboloid $ax^2 + y^2 = z$, and the cylinder with equation $z = a^2 - y^2$ for $a > 0$.

The volume will be four times the following integral:

```
>> a = sym('a', 'positive')

a =

a

>> pretty(simple(vpa(int(int(int('1','z','a*x^2+y^2','a^2-y^2'),'y',0,
'sqrt((a^2-a*x^2)/2)'),'x',0,'sqrt(a)'))))
```

```
                          7
                          -
                          2
    0.27768018363489789043849256187879 a
```

or, what is the same:

```
>> V=4*(simple(int(int(int('1','z','a*x^2+y^2','a^2-y^2'),'y',0, 'sqrt((a^2-
a*x^2)/2)')'),'x',0,'sqrt(a)')))

V =

(pi*(2*a^7)^(1/2))/4
```

As a second example, we calculate the volume bounded by the cylinders with equations $z = x^2$ and $4 - y^2 = z$. If we solve the system formed by the equations of the two surfaces we get an idea of the boundary points:

```
>> [x,y]=solve('x^2+0*y','4-y^2+0*x')

x =

 0
 0


y =

  2
 -2
```

Now we graphically represent the volume we need to calculate.

```
>> ezsurf('4-y^2+0*x',[-2,2],[-2,2])
>> hold on;
>> ezsurf('x^2+0*y',[-2,2],[-2,2])
```

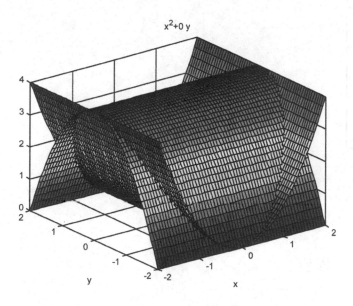

Finally, we calculate the volume as follows.

```
>> V=4*int(int(int('1','z','x^2','4-y^2'),'y',0,'sqrt(4-x^2)'),  'x',0,2)

V =

8 * pi
```

Green's Theorem

Let C be a closed piecewise smooth simple planar curve and R the region consisting of C and its interior. If f and g are continuous functions with continuous first partial derivatives in an open region D containing R, then Green's theorem tells us that:

$$\int_C m(x,y)\,dx + n(x,y)\,dy = \iint_R \left(\frac{\partial n}{\partial x} - \frac{\partial m}{\partial y} \right) dA$$

As an example, using Green's theorem, we calculate the integral:

$$\int_c \left(x + e^{\sqrt{y}} \right) dx + (2y + \cos(x))\,dy$$

where C is the boundary of the region enclosed by the parabolas $y = x^2$ and $x = y^2$.
The two parabolas intersect at the points (0,0) and (1,1). This gives us the limits of integration.

```
>> clear all
>> fplot('[x^2,sqrt(x)]',[0,1.2])
```

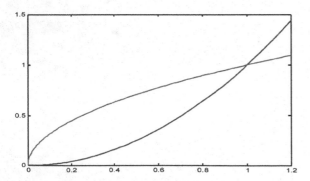

We can now calculate the integral:

```
>> syms x y
>> m = x + exp(sqrt(y))

m =

x + exp(y^(1/2))

>> n = 2 * y + cos(x)
```

```
n =

2*y + cos(x)

>> I = vpa(int(int(diff(n,x)-diff(m,y), y, x^2, sqrt(x)), x, 0, 1))

I =

-0.67644120041679251512532326651204
```

The Divergence Theorem

Suppose Q is a domain with the property that each straight line passing through a point inside the domain cuts its border at exactly two points. In addition, suppose the boundary S of the domain Q is a closed piecewise smooth oriented surface with outward pointing unit normal n on the boundary. If f is a vector field that has continuous partial derivatives on Q, then the Divergence Theorem tells us that:

$$\iint_S f \bullet n\, dS = \iiint_Q Div(f)\, dV$$

The left-hand side of the former equality is called the outflow of the vector field f through the surface S.

As an example, we use the divergence theorem to find the outflow of the vector field $f = (xy + x^2y\,z, yz + xy^2\,z, xz + xyz^2)$ through the surface of the cube defined in the first octant by the planes $x = 2$, $y = 2$ and $z = 2$.

```
>> clear all
>> syms x y z
>> M = x * y + x ^ 2 * z * y

M =
y * z * x ^ 2 + y * x

>> N = y * z + x * y ^ 2 * z

N =
 x * z * y ^ 2 + z * y

>> P = x * z + x * y * z ^ 2

P =
x * y * z ^ 2 + x * z

>> simple Div = (diff(M,x) + diff(N,y) + diff(P,z))

Div =

x + y + z + 6 * x * y * z

>> I = int(int(int(Div,x,0,2), y, 0, 2), z, 0, 2)

I =

72
```

Stokes' Theorem

Suppose S is an oriented surface of finite area defined by a function $f(x,y)$, with boundary C having unit normal n. If F is a continuous vector field defined on S, such that the function components of F have continuous partial derivatives at each non-boundary point of S, then Stokes' Theorem tells us:

$$\int_C F \bullet dr = \iint_S (rot\,F) \bullet n\,ds$$

As an example, we use Stokes' theorem to evaluate the line integral:

$$\int_C -y^3 dx + x^3 dy - z^3 dz$$

where C is the intersection of the cylinder $x^2 + y^2 = 1$ and the plane $x + y + z = 1$, and the orientation of C is counterclockwise in the xy-plane.

The curve C bounds the surface S defined by $z = 1 - x - y = f(x,y)$ for (x, y) in the domain $D = \{(x,y) / x^2 + y^2 = 1\}$. We put $F = -y^3\,i + x^3\,j - z^3\,k$.

Now we calculate $rot(F)$ and find the above integral over the surface S.

```
>> F = [- y ^ 3, x ^ 3, z ^ 3]

F =

[- y ^ 3, x ^ 3, z ^ 3]

>> clear all
>> syms x y z
>> M = - y ^ 3

M =

- y ^ 3

>> N = x ^ 3

N =

x ^ 3

>> P = z ^ 3

P =

z ^ 3
```

```
>> rotF=simple([diff(P,y)-diff(N,z),diff(P,x)-diff(M,z),diff(N,x)-diff(M,y)])

rotF =

[0, 0, 3 * x ^ 2 + 3 * y ^ 2]
```

Therefore, we have to calculate the integral $\int_D (3x^2 + 3y^2)\, dx\, dy$. Changing to polar coordinates, this integral is calculated as:

```
>> pretty (simple (int (int('3*r^3', 'a',0,2*pi), 'r', 0, 1)))

  3 pi
  ----
   2
```

EXERCISE 8-1

Calculate the following integrals:

$$\int \sec(x)\csc(x)dx, \ \int x\cos(x)dx, \ \int a\cos(2x)dx$$

```
>> pretty(simple(int('sec(x)*csc(x)')))

  log(tan(x))
```

```
>> pretty(simple(int('x*cos(x)')))

  cos(x) + x sin(x)
```

```
>> pretty(simple(int('acos(2*x)')))

                       2 1/2
                (1 - 4 x )
  x acos(2 x) - -------------
                      2
```

EXERCISE 8-2

Find the following integrals:

$$\int \frac{\sqrt{9-4x^2}}{x}\, dx, \quad \int x^8 \left(3+5x^3\right)^{\frac{1}{4}} dx$$

```
>> pretty(simple(int('(9-4*x^2)^(1/2)/x')))

          /      / 1  \1/2 \
          |   3 | -- |    |
          |     | 2 |     |
          |     \ x /     |              2 1/2
   3 acosh| - ----------- | + (9 - 4 x )
          \        2      /
```

```
>> pretty(simple(int('x^8*(3+5*x^3)^(1/4)')))
```

$$
\frac{4\,(5 x^3 + 3)^{\frac{5}{4}}\,(375 x^6 - 200 x^3 + 96)}{73125}
$$

EXERCISE 8-3

Find the following integrals: $a = \int_0^\infty x^3 e^{-x} dx$ *and* $b = \int_0^\infty x^2 e^{-x^3} dx$

We have $a = \Gamma(4)$.

Making the change of variable $x^3 = t$ we see that $b = \int_0^\infty \frac{1}{3} e^{-t} dt = \Gamma(1)/3$.

Therefore, for the calculation of *a* and *b* we will use the following MATLAB syntax:

```
>> a = gamma(4)

a =

     6

>> b = (1/3) * gamma(1)

b =

    0.3333
```

EXERCISE 8-4

Solve the following integrals:

$$\int_0^\infty \frac{x^3}{e^x}dx, \quad \int_0^5 \frac{x^3}{e^x}dx$$

As $\Gamma(p)=\int_0^\infty x^{p-1}e^{-x}dx$, the first integral is solved as:

```
>> gamma (4)

ans =

    6
```

As $\Gamma(x,p)=\frac{1}{\Gamma(p)}\int_0^x t^{p-1}e^{-t}dt = gammainc(x,p)$, the second integral is solved as follows:

```
>> gamma(4) * gammainc(5.4)

ans =

    4.4098
```

EXERCISE 8-5

Solve the following integrals:

$$\int_0^5 \frac{x^4}{(1-x)^{-3}}dx, \quad \int_0^8 \frac{\sqrt[4]{2-\sqrt[3]{x}}}{\sqrt{x}}dx$$

$\beta(p,q)=\int_0^1 x^{p-1}(1-x)^{q-1}dx$ and $betainc(z,w)=\frac{1}{\beta(p,q)}\int_0^1 t^{z-1}(1-t)^{w-1}dt$, which means the first integral is solved as:

```
>> beta (5,4) * betainc(1/2,5,4)

ans =

    0.0013
```

For the second integral, we make the change of variable $x^{1/3} = 2t$, so the integral becomes the following:

$$6 \cdot \int_0^1 \frac{\sqrt{t}\,(1-t)^{\frac{1}{4}}\,dt}{2^{4/3}}$$

whose value is calculated using the MATLAB expression:

```
>> 6 * 2 ^(3/4) * beta(3/2,5/4)

ans =

    5.0397
```

EXERCISE 8-6

Find the value of the following integrals:

$$\int_3^\infty \frac{1}{\sqrt{6x^3 - 37x^2 + 72x - 45}}\,dx \quad \text{and} \quad \int_0^1 \frac{x^2+1}{\sqrt{x^4 - 5x^2 + 4}}\,dx$$

Via a change of variable one can convert such integrals to standard elliptic integrals. MATLAB enables symbolic functions that calculate the values of elliptic integrals of the first, second and third kind.

$$k(m) = \int_0^1 \sqrt{\frac{1-t^2}{1-mt^2}}\,dt = \int_0^{\pi/2} \frac{1}{\sqrt{1-m\sin^2(\theta)}}\,d\theta = F(\pi/2, m)$$

$$e(m) = \int_0^1 \sqrt{\frac{1-mt^2}{1-t^2}}\,dt = \int_0^{\pi/2} \sqrt{1-m\sin^2(\theta)}\,d\theta = E(\pi/2, m)$$

The function $[k, e] = ellipke(m)$ estimates the two previous integrals.

For the first integral of the problem, as the subradical polynomial is of degree 3, we make the change of variable $x = a + t^2$, a being one of the roots of the subradical polynomial. We take the root $x = 3$ and make the change $x = 3 + t^2$, with which we obtain the integral:

$$\frac{1}{3}\sqrt{6} \cdot \int_0^\infty \frac{1}{\left(t^2 + 4/3\right)\left(t^2 + 3/2\right)}\,dt$$

Now we make the change of variable $t = (2/\sqrt{3})$ *tan(u)*, so the integral transforms into the full elliptic integral of the first kind:

$$2\int_0^{\pi/2}\frac{1}{\sqrt{9-\sin^2(u)}}du=\frac{2}{3}\int_0^{\pi/2}\frac{1}{\sqrt{1-\frac{1}{9}\sin^2(u)}}du$$

whose value is calculated using the expression:

```
>> (2/3) * ellipke(1/9)
```

ans =

    1.07825782374982

For the second integral we put $x = sin\ t$ and we get:

$$5\int_0^2\frac{1}{\sqrt{4-\sin^2(t)}}dt-\int_0^2\sqrt{4-\sin^2(t)}dt=\frac{5}{2}\int_0^2\frac{1}{\sqrt{1-\frac{1}{4}\sin^2(t)}}dt-2\int_0^2\sqrt{1-\frac{1}{4}\sin^2(t)}dt$$

We have reduced the problem to two elliptic integrals, the first of the first kind and the second of the second kind, whose values can be calculated using the expression:

```
>> [K, E] = ellipke (1/4)
```

K =

    1.68575035481260

E =

    1.46746220933943

```
>> I = (5/2) * K-2 * E
```

I =

    1.27945146835264

EXERCISE 8-7

Calculate the length of a full period of the sinusoid y = 3sin(2x).

The length of this curve is given by the formula:

$$4\int_0^{\pi/4} \sqrt{1-\left(\frac{\partial}{\partial x}y(x)\right)^2}\,dt = \int_0^{\pi/2}\sqrt{1+36\cos^2(2x)}dx = 2\int_0^{\pi/2}\sqrt{37-36\sin^2(t)}dt$$

In the last step, we have made the change of variable *2x = t*, using in addition *cos²(t) = 1 - sin²(t)*. The value of the integral can be calculated now by:

```
>> [K, E] = ellipke (36/37)

K =

   3.20677433446297

E =

   1.03666851510702

>> 2 * sqrt (37) * E

ans =

   12.61161680006573
```

EXERCISE 8-8

Calculate the integral

$$\int_{-2}^{\infty} 3\frac{e^{-2t}}{t}t\,dt$$

This is an exponential type integral. We make the change of variable *v = 2t* and obtain the equivalent integral:

$$3\int_{-4}^{\infty} \frac{e^{-t}}{t}dt$$

which is calculated via the MATLAB expression:

```
>> 3 * expint(-4)

ans =

-58.89262341016866 - 9.42477796076938i
```

The solution would normally be taken to be the real part of the previous result.

EXERCISE 8-9

Calculate the area bounded by the curve $y = x^3 - 6x^2 + 8x$ *and the x-axis.*

We begin by graphing the area.

```
>> fplot('[x^3-6*x^2+8*x,0]',[-1,5])
```

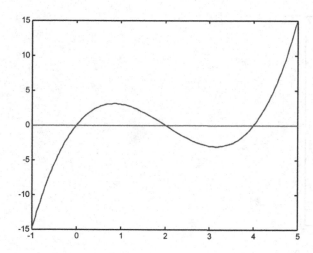

The points where the curve cuts the x-axis are (0,0), (0,2) and (0,4), as we see by solving the following equation:

```
>> solve('x^3-6*x^2+8*x')

ans =

  0
  2
  4
```

As there is both a positive region and a negative region, the area is calculated as follows:

```
>> A = abs(int(x^3-6*x^2+8*x,0,2)) + abs(int(x^3-6*x^2+8*x,2,4))

A =

8
```

EXERCISE 8-10

Calculate the area bounded between the parabolas $y = 6x - x^2$ *and* $y = x^2 - 2x$.

We begin by plotting the area.

```
>> fplot('[6*x-x^2,x^2-2*x]',[-1,7])
```

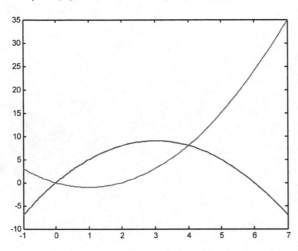

We find the points of intersection of the two curves:

```
>> [x, y] = solve('y=6*x-x^2,y=x^2-2*x')

x =

  0
  4

y =

  0
  8
```

The points of intersection are (0,0) and (4,8).

The area is then calculated as follows:

```
>> A = abs(int('(6*x-x^2)-(x^2-2*x)',0,4))

A =

64/3
```

EXERCISE 8-11

Calculate the area enclosed by the three rose petals defined in polar coordinates by $r = 5\cos(3a)$.

We begin by graphing the curve.

```
>> ezpolar('5*cos(3*a)')
```

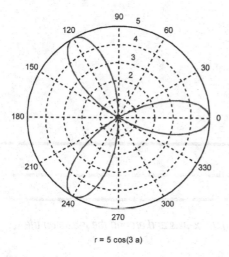

r = 5 cos(3 a)

The total area can be calculated by multiplying by 6 the area as *a* ranges between 0 and $\pi/6$ (the upper half of the horizontal petal). We will then have:

```
>> A=6*int((1/2)*5^2*cos(3*a)^2,0,pi/6)

A =

(25*pi)/4
```

EXERCISE 8-12

Calculate the area between the x-axis and the full arc of the cycloid with parametric equations:

$$x = 5(t - \sin(t))$$
$$y = 5(1 - \cos(t))$$

where t ranges between 0 and 2π.

The requested area is given by the integral:

```
>> A=int(5*(1-cos(t))*diff(5*(t-sin(t))),0,2*pi)

A =

75*pi
```

EXERCISE 8-13

Calculate the volumes generated by rotating the curve y = sin(x) around the x-axis and around the y-axis on the interval [0,π]

```
>> Vox=pi*int('sin(x)^2',0,pi)

Vox =

pi^2/2

>> Voy=2*pi*int('x*sin(x)',0,pi)

Voy =

2*pi^2
```

EXERCISE 8-14

Calculate the volume generated by rotating around the y-axis the arc of the cycloid with parametric equations:

$$x = (t - \sin(t))$$
$$y = (1 - \cos(t))$$

where *t* varies between 0 and 2π.

The requested volume is given by the integral:

```
>> V=2*pi*int('(t-sin(t))*(1-cos(t))*(1-cos(t))',0,2*pi)
```

```
V =
```

```
6*pi^3
```

EXERCISE 8-15

Calculate the volume generated by rotating the polar curve

$$r = 2 * \sin(a)$$

around the x-axis. We first plot the curve:

```
>> ezpolar('2*sin(a)')
```

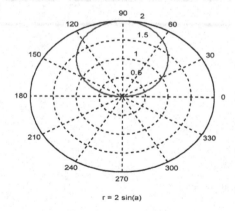

r = 2 sin(a)

We note that the integral will be given by varying the angle between 0 and π. By symmetry, we can calculate the result by doubling the corresponding volume generated for the angle between 0 and $\pi/2$.

The volume is then calculated by the following integral:

```
>> V=2*2*pi/3*int((2*sin(a))^3*sin(a),0,pi/2)

V =

2*pi^2
```

EXERCISE 8-16

Calculate the length of the curve:

$$y = 2x\sqrt{x}$$

as x varies between 0 and 2.

The length is calculated directly by the following integral:

```
>> L=int((1+(diff('2*x*sqrt(x)'))^2),0,2)

L =

20
```

EXERCISE 8-17

Calculate the length of the astroid:

$$x^{2/3} + y^{2/3} = 2^{2/3}$$

The curve can be expressed parametrically as follows:

$$x = 2\cos(t)^3$$
$$y = 2\sin(t)^3$$

We now represent the astroid to find the limits of variation of the integral.

```
>> ezplot('2*cos(t)^3','2*sin(t)^3')
```

Looking at the graph we can see that the integral can be found by multiplying by 4 the length obtained as the parameter varies between 0 and $\pi/2$.

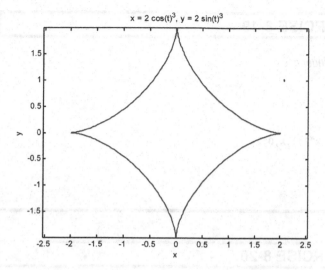

The length of the astroid is calculated by the following integral:

```
>> L=4*int(((diff('2*cos(t)^3'))^2+(diff('2*sin(t)^3'))^2)^(1/2),0,pi/2)

L =

12
```

EXERCISE 8-18

Calculate the integral:

$$\iint_S xe^{\frac{-x^2}{y}}\,dxdy$$

where S is the planar region bounded by x = 0, y = x²+1 and y = 2.

The region S is determined by $1 < y < 2$ and $0 < x < y^{1/2}$.

The integral is calculated as follows:

```
>> int(int('x*exp(-x^2/y)','x',0,'sqrt(y)'),'y',1,2)

ans =

3/4 - 3/(4*exp(1))
```

EXERCISE 8-19

Calculate the volume enclosed between the two cylinders:

$z = x^2$ and $z = 4 - y^2$.

The problem is solved by calculating the integral:

```
>> 4*int(int(int(1,z,x^2,4-y^2),y,0,sqrt(4-x^2)),x,0,2)

ans =

8*pi
```

EXERCISE 8-20

Calculate the integral:

$$\iiint_V \frac{1}{(x+y+z+1)^3}\,dxdydz$$

where V is the volume enclosed between the three coordinate planes and the plane $x + y + z = 1$.

The body V is determined by:

$0 < x < 1, 0 < y < 1 - x, 0 < z < x - y$

The integral that solves the problem is the following:

```
>> x=sym('x','positive')

x =

x
>> vpa(int(int(int(1/(x+y+z+1)^3,z,0,1-x-y),y,0,1-x),x,0,1))
Warning: Explicit integral could not be found.

ans =

0.034073590279972654708616060729088
```

CHAPTER 9

■ ■ ■

Differential Equations

First Order Differential Equations

Although it implements only a relatively small number of commands related to this topic, MATLAB's treatment of differential equations is nevertheless very efficient. We shall see how we can use these commands to solve each type of differential equation algebraically. Numerical methods for the approximate solution of equations and systems of equations are also implemented.

The basic command used to solve differential equations is **dsolve**. This command finds symbolic solutions of ordinary differential equations and systems of ordinary differential equations. The equations are specified by symbolic expressions where the letter D is used to denote differentiation, or D2, D3, etc., to denote differentiation of order 2,3,..., etc. The letter preceded by D (or D2, etc.) is the dependent variable (which is usually y), and any letter that is not preceded by D (or D2, etc.) is a candidate for the independent variable. If the independent variable is not specified, it is taken to be x by default. If x is specified as the dependent variable, then the independent variable is t. That is, x is the independent variable by default, unless it is declared as the dependent variable, in which case the independent variable is understood to be t.

You can specify initial conditions using additional equations, which take the form $y(a) = b$ or $Dy(a) = b$,..., etc. If the initial conditions are not specified, the solutions of the differential equations will contain constants of integration, C1, C2,..., etc. The most important MATLAB commands that solve differential equations are the following:

> **dsolve('equation', 'v'):** This solves the given differential equation, where v is the independent variable (if 'v' is not specified, the independent variable is x by default). This returns only explicit solutions.

> **dsolve('equation', 'initial_condition',..., 'v'):** This solves the given differential equation subject to the specified initial condition.

> **dsolve('equation', 'cond1', 'cond2',..., 'condn', 'v'):** This solves the given differential equation subject to the specified initial conditions.

> **dsolve('equation', 'cond1, cond2,..., condn', 'v'):** This solves the given differential equation subject to the specified initial conditions.

> **dsolve('eq1', 'eq2',..., 'cqn', 'cond1', 'cond2',..., 'condn' , 'v'):** This solves the given system of differential equations subject to the specified initial conditions.

> **dsolve('eq1, eq2,..., eqn', 'cond1, cond2,..., condn' , 'v'):** This solves the given system of differential equations subject to the specified initial conditions.

> **maple('dsolve(equation, func(var))'):** This solves the given differential equation, where var is the independent variable and func is the dependent variable (returns implicit solutions).

maple('dsolve({equation, cond1, cond2,... condn}, func(var))'): This solves the given differential equation subject to the specified initial conditions.

maple('dsolve({eq1, eq2,..., eqn}, {func1(var), func2(var),... funcn(var)})'): This solves the given system of differential equations (returns implicit solutions).

maple('dsolve(equation, func(var), 'explicit')'): This solves the given differential equation, offering the solution in explicit form, if possible.

Examples are given below.

First, we solve differential equations of first order and first degree, both with and without initial values.

```
>> pretty(dsolve('Dy = a*y'))
```

```
 C2 exp(a t)
```

```
>> pretty(dsolve('Df = f + sin(t)'))
```

```
            sin(t)   cos(t)
  C6 exp(t) - ------ - ------
               2        2
```

The previous two equations can also be solved in the following way:

```
>> pretty(sym(maple('dsolve(diff(y(x), x) = a * y, y(x))')))
```

```
y(x) = exp(a x) _C1
```

```
>> pretty(maple('dsolve(diff(f(t),t)=f+sin(t),f(t))'))
```

```
f(t) = - 1/2 cos(t) - 1/2 sin(t) + exp(t) _C1
```

```
>> pretty(dsolve('Dy = a*y', 'y(0) = b'))
```

```
exp(a x) b
```

```
>> pretty(dsolve('Df = f + sin(t)', 'f(pi/2) = 0'))
```

```
    /  pi \
  exp| - -- | exp(t)
    \  2 /            sin(t)   cos(t)
  ------------------ - ------ - ------
         2              2        2
```

Now we solve an equation of second degree and first order.

```
>> y = dsolve('(Dy) ^ 2 + y ^ 2 = 1', ' y(0) = 0', 's')
```

```
y =

 cosh((pi*i)/2 + s*i)
 cosh((pi*i)/2 - s*i)
```

We can also solve this in the following way:

```
>> pretty(maple('dsolve({diff(y(s),s)^2 + y(s)^2 = 1, y(0) = 0}, y(s))'))
```

$y(s) = sin(s)$, $y(s) = - sin(s)$

Now we solve an equation of second order and first degree.

```
>> pretty(dsolve('D2y = - a ^ 2 * y ', 'y(0) = 1, Dy(pi/a) = 0'))
```

$$\frac{exp(-a\ t\ i)}{2} + \frac{exp(a\ t\ i)}{2}$$

Next we solve a couple of systems, both with and without initial values.

```
>> dsolve('Dx = y', 'Dy = -x')
```

ans =

```
    y: [1x1 sym]
    x: [1x1 sym]
```

```
>> y
```

y =

```
    cosh((pi*i)/2 + s*i)
    cosh((pi*i)/2 - s*i)
```

```
>> x
```

x =

x

```
>> y=dsolve('Df = 3*f+4*g', 'Dg = -4*f+3*g')
```

y =

```
    g: [1x1 sym]
    f: [1x1 sym]
```

```
>> y.g
```

ans =

```
    C27*cos(4*t)*exp(3*t) - C28*sin(4*t)*exp(3*t)
```

```
>> y.f
```

ans =

```
      C28*cos(4*t)*exp(3*t) + C27*sin(4*t)*exp(3*t)
```

```
>> y=dsolve('Df = 3*f+4*g, Dg = -4*f+3*g', 'f(0)=0, g(0)=1')
```

y =

```
      g: [1x1 sym]
      f: [1x1 sym]
```

```
>> y.g
```

ans =

```
      cos(4*t)*exp(3*t)
```

```
>> y.f
```

ans =

```
      sin(4*t)*exp(3*t)
```

Numerical Solutions of Differential Equations

MATLAB provides commands in its Basic module allowing for the numerical solution of ordinary differential equations (ODEs), differential algebraic equations (DAEs) and boundary value problems. It is also possible to solve systems of differential equations with boundary values and parabolic and elliptic partial differential equations.

Ordinary Differential Equations with Initial Values

An ordinary differential equation contains one or more derivatives of the dependent variable y with respect to the independent variable t. A first order ordinary differential equation with an initial value for the independent variable can be represented as:

$$y' = f(t, y)$$
$$y(t_0) = y_0$$

The previous problem can be generalized to the case where y is a vector, $y = (y_1, y_2, ..., y_n)$.

MATLAB's Basic module commands relating to ordinary differential equations and differential algebraic equations with initial values are presented in the following table:

Command	Class of problem solving, numerical method and syntax
ode45	*Ordinary differential equations by the Runge–Kutta method*
ode23	*Ordinary differential equations by the Runge–Kutta method*
ode113	*Ordinary differential equations by Adams' method*
ode15s	*Differential algebraic equations and ordinary differential equations using NDFs (BDFs)*
ode23s	*Ordinary differential equations by the Rosenbrock method*
ode23t	*Ordinary differential and differential algebraic equations by the trapezoidal rule*
ode23tb	*Ordinary differential equations using TR-BDF2*

The common syntax for the previous seven commands is the following:

```
[T, y] = solver(odefun,tspan,y0)
[T, y] = solver(odefun,tspan,y0,options)
[T, y] = solver(odefun,tspan,y0,options,p1,p2...)
[T, y, TE, YE, IE] = solver(odefun,tspan,y0,options)
```

In the above, *solver* can be any of the commands *ode45, ode23, ode113, ode15s, ode23s, ode23t,* or *ode23tb*.

The argument *odefun* evaluates the right-hand side of the differential equation or system written in the form $y' = f(t, y)$ or $M(t, y)y' = f(t, y)$, where $M(t, y)$ is called a *mass matrix*. The command *ode23s* can only solve equations with constant mass matrix. The commands *ode15s* and *ode23t* can solve algebraic differential equations and systems of ordinary differential equations with a singular mass matrix. The argument *tspan* is a vector that specifies the range of integration $[t_0, t_f]$ (*tspan*= $[t_0, t_1,...,t_f]$, which must be either an increasing or decreasing list, is used to obtain solutions for specific values of t).The argument y_0 specifies a vector of initial conditions. The arguments $p1$, $p2$,... are optional parameters that are passed to *odefun*. The argument *options* specifies additional integration options using the command options *odeset* which can be found in the program manual. The vectors T and y present the numerical values of the independent and dependent variables for the solutions found.

As a first example we find solutions in the interval [0,12] of the following system of ordinary differential equations:

$$
\begin{aligned}
y_1' &= y_2 y_3 & y_1(0) &= 0 \\
y_2' &= y_1 y_3 & y_2(0) &= 1 \\
y_3' &= -0.51 y_1 y_2 & y_3(0) &= 1
\end{aligned}
$$

For this, we define a function named *system1* in an M-file, which will store the equations of the system. The function begins by defining a column vector with three rows which are subsequently assigned components that make up the syntax of the three equations (Figure 9-1).

```
function dy = system1(t,y)
dy = zeros(3,1);      %column vector
dy(1) = y(2) * y(3);
dy(2) = -y(1) * y(3);
dy(3) = -0.51 * y(1) * y(2);
```

Figure 9-1.

We then solve the system by typing the following in the Command Window:

>> **[T, Y] = ode45(@system1,[0 12],[0 1 1])**

T =

```
     0
0.0001
0.0001
0.0002
0.0002
0.0005
  .
  .
  .
11.6136
11.7424
11.8712
12.0000
```

Y =

```
0 1.0000 1.0000
0.0001 1.0000 1.0000
0.0001 1.0000 1.0000
0.0002 1.0000 1.0000
0.0002 1.0000 1.0000
0.0005 1.0000 1.0000
0.0007 1.0000 1.0000
0.0010 1.0000 1.0000
0.0012 1.0000 1.0000
0.0025 1.0000 1.0000
0.0037 1.0000 1.0000
0.0050 1.0000 1.0000
0.0062 1.0000 1.0000
0.0125 0.9999 1.0000
0.0188 0.9998 0.9999
0.0251 0.9997 0.9998
0.0313 0.9995 0.9997
0.0627 0.9980 0.9990
  .
  .
```

```
0.8594-0.5105 0.7894
0.7257-0.6876 0.8552
0.5228-0.8524 0.9281
0.2695-0.9631 0.9815
-0.0118-0.9990 0.9992
-0.2936-0.9540 0.9763
-0.4098-0.9102 0.9548
-0.5169-0.8539 0.9279
-0.6135-0.7874 0.8974
-0.6987-0.7128 0.8650
```

To better interpret the results, the above numerical solution can be graphed (Figure 9-2) by using the following syntax:

```
>> plot(T, Y(:,1), '-', T, Y(:,2),'-', T, Y(:,3),'. ')
```

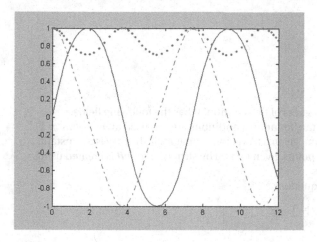

Figure 9-2.

Ordinary Differential Equations with Boundary Values

MATLAB also allows you to solve ordinary differential equations with boundary conditions. The boundary conditions specify a relationship that must hold between the values of the solution function at the end points of the interval on which it is defined. The simplest problem of this type is the system of equations

$$y' = f(x,y)$$

where x is the independent variable, y is the dependent variable and y' is the derivative *with respect to* x (i.e., $y' = dy/dx$). In addition, the solution on the interval $[a, b]$ has to meet the following boundary condition:

$$g(y(a),y(b)) = 0$$

More generally this type of differential equations can be expressed as follows:

$$y' = f(x,y,p)$$
$$g(y(a),y(b),p) = 0$$

where the vector p consists of parameters which have to be determined simultaneously with the solution via the boundary conditions.

The command that solves these problems is *bvp4c*, whose syntax is as follows:

```
Sol = bvp4c(odefun, bcfun, solinit)
Sol = bvp4c(odefun, bcfun, solinit, options)
Sol = bvp4c(odefun, bcfun, solinit, options, p1,p2...)
```

In the syntax above *odefun* is a function that evaluates $f(x, y)$. It may take one of the following forms:

```
dydx = odefun(x,y)
dydx = odefun(x,y,p1,p2,...)
dydx = odefun(x,y,parameters)
dydx = odefun(x,y,parameters,p1,p2,...)
```

The argument *bcfun* in *bvp4c* is a function that computes the residual in the boundary conditions. Its form is as follows:

```
Res = bcfun(ya, yb)
Res = bcfun(ya,yb,p1,p2,...)
Res = bcfun(ya, yb,parameters)
Res = bcfun(ya,yb,parameters,p1,p2,...)
```

The argument *solinit* is a structure containing an initial guess of the solution. It has the following fields: x (which gives the ordered nodes of the initial mesh so that the boundary conditions are imposed at $a =$ solinit.x(1) and $b =$ solinit.x(end)); and y (the initial guess for the solution, given as a vector, so that the i-th entry is a constant guess for the i-th component of the solution at all the mesh points given by x). The structure *solinit* is created using the command *bvpinit*. The syntax is solinit = bvpinit(x,y).

As an example we solve the second order differential equation:

$$y'' + |y| = 0$$

whose solutions must satisfy the boundary conditions:

$$y(0) = 0$$
$$y(4) = -2$$

The previous problem is equivalent to the following:

$$y_1' = y_2$$
$$y_2' = -|y_1|$$

We consider a mesh of five equally spaced points in the interval [0,4] and our initial guess for the solution is $y_1 = 1$ and $y_2 = 0$. These assumptions are included in the following syntax:

```
>> solinit = bvpinit (linspace (0,4,5), [1 0]);
```

The M-files depicted in Figures 9-3 and 9-4 show how to enter the equation and its boundary conditions.

```
function dydx = twoode(x,y)
  dydx = [ y(2)
          -abs(y(1))];
```

Figure 9-3.

```
function res = twobc(ya,yb)
  res = [ ya(1)
          yb(1) + 2];
```

Figure 9-4.

The following syntax is used to find the solution of the equation:

```
>> Sun = bvp4c(@twoode, @twobc, solinit);
```

The solution can be graphed (Figure 9-5) using the command *bvpval* as follows:

```
>> y = bvpval(Sun, linspace(0.4));
>> plot(x, y(1,:));
```

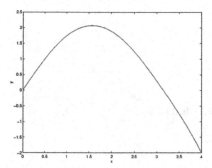

Figure 9-5.

Partial Differential Equations

MATLAB's Basic module has features that enable you to solve partial differential equations and systems of partial differential equations with initial boundary conditions. The basic function used to calculate the solutions is *pdepe*, and the basic function used to evaluate these solutions is *pdeval*.

The syntax of the function *pdepe* is as follows:

```
Sol = pdepe(m, pdefun, icfun, bcfun, xmesh, tspan)
Sol = pdepe(m, pdefun, icfun, bcfun, xmesh, tspan, options)
Sun = pdepe(m,pdefun,icfun,bcfun,xmesh,tspan,options,p1,p2...)
```

The parameter *m* takes the value 0, 1 or 2 according to the nature of the symmetry of the problem (block, cylindrical or spherical, respectively). The argument *pdefun* defines the components of the differential equation, *icfun* defines the initial conditions, *bcfun* defines the boundary conditions, *xmesh* and *tspan* are vectors $[x_0, x_1,...,x_n]$ and $[t_0, t_1,...,t_f]$ that specify the points at which a numerical solution is requested ($n, f \geq 3$), *options* specifies some calculation options of the underlying solver (RelTol, AbsTol,NormControl, InitialStep and MaxStep to specify relative tolerance, absolute tolerance, norm tolerance, initial step and max step, respectively) and *p*1, *p*2,... are parameters to pass to the functions *pdefun*, *icfun* and *bcfun*.

pdepe solves partial differential equations of the form:

$$c\left(x,t,u,\frac{\partial u}{\partial t}\right)\frac{\partial u}{\partial t} = x^{-m}\frac{\partial}{\partial x}\left(x^m f\left(x,t,u,\frac{\partial u}{\partial x}\right)\right) + s\left(x,t,u,\frac{\partial u}{\partial x}\right)$$

where $a \leq x \leq b$ and $t_0 \leq t \leq t_f$. Moreover, for $t = t_0$ and for all *x* the solution components meet the initial conditions:

$$u(x,t_0) = u_0(x)$$

and for all *t* and each *x* = *a* or *x* = *b*, the solution components satisfy the boundary conditions of the form:

$$p(x,t,u) + q(x,t)f\left(x,t,u,\frac{\partial u}{\partial x}\right) = 0$$

In addition, we have that *a* = xmesh (1), b = xmesh (end), tspan (1) = t_0 and tspan (end) = t_f. Moreover *pdefun* finds the terms *c, f* and *s* of the partial differential equation, so that:

   [f, s] = pdefun(x, t, u, dudx)

Similarly *icfun* evaluates the initial conditions

   u = icfun(x)

Finally, *bcfun* evaluates the terms *p* and *q* of the boundary conditions:

   [pl, ql, pr, qr] = bcfun(xl, ul, xr, ur, t)

As a first example, we solve the following partial differential equation ($x \in [0,1]$ and $t \geq 0$):

$$\pi^2\frac{\partial u}{\partial t} = \frac{\partial}{\partial x}\left(\frac{\partial u}{\partial x}\right)$$

satisfying the initial condition:

$$u(x,0) = \sin \pi x$$

and the boundary conditions:

$$u(0,t) \equiv 0$$

$$\pi e^{-t} + \frac{\partial u}{\partial x}(1,t) = 0$$

We begin by defining functions in M-files as shown in Figures 9-6 to 9-8.

```
function [c,f,s] = pdex1pde(x,t,u,DuDx)
c = pi^2;
f = DuDx;
s = 0;
```

Figure 9-6.

```
function u0 = pdex1ic(x)
u0 = sin(pi*x);
```

Figure 9-7.

```
function [pl,ql,pr,qr] = pdex1bc(xl,ul,xr,ur,t)
pl = ul;
ql = 0;
pr = pi * exp(-t);
qr = 1;
```

Figure 9-8.

Once the support functions have been defined, we define the function that solves the equation (see the M-file in Figure 9-9).

```
function pdex1

m = 0;
x = linspace(0,1,20);
t = linspace(0,2,5);

sol = pdepe(m,@pdex1pde,@pdex1ic,@pdex1bc,x,t);
%Extracts the first component of the solution as u
u = sol(:,:,1);

%The solution is represented graphically as a surface
figure(1)
surf(x,t,u)
title('Numerical solution with 20 grid points.')
xlabel('Distance x')
ylabel('Time t')

%Profile of the solution
figure(2)
plot(x,u(end,:))
title('Solution in t=2')
xlabel('Distance x')
ylabel('u(x,2)')
```

Figure 9-9.

To view the solution (Figures 9-10 and 9-11), we enter the following into the MATLAB Command Window:

```
>> pdex1
```

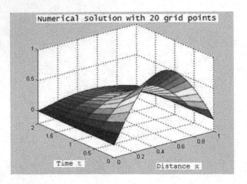

Figure 9-10.

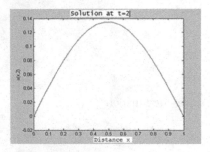

Figure 9-11.

As a second example, we solve the following system of partial differential equations ($x \in [0,1]$ and $t \geq 0$):

$$\frac{\partial u_1}{\partial t} = 0.024 \frac{\partial^2 u_1}{\partial x^2} - F(u_1 - u_2)$$

$$\frac{\partial u_2}{\partial t} = 0.170 \frac{\partial^2 u_2}{\partial x^2} + F(u_1 - u_2)$$

$$F(y) = \exp(5.73y) - \exp(-11.46y)$$

satisfying the initial conditions:

$$u_1(x,0) \equiv 1$$
$$u_2(x,0) \equiv 0$$

and the boundary conditions:

$$\frac{\partial u_1}{\partial x}(0,t) \equiv 0$$

$$u_2(0,t) \equiv 0$$

$$u_1(1,t) \equiv 1$$

$$\frac{\partial u_2}{\partial x}(1,t) \equiv 0$$

To conveniently use the function *pdepe*, the system can be written as:

$$\begin{bmatrix}1\\1\end{bmatrix} .* \frac{\partial}{\partial t}\begin{bmatrix}u_1\\u_2\end{bmatrix} = \frac{\partial}{\partial x}\begin{bmatrix}0.024(\partial u_1/\partial x)\\0.170(\partial u_2/\partial x)\end{bmatrix} + \begin{bmatrix}-F(u_1-u_2)\\F(u_1-u_2)\end{bmatrix}$$

The left boundary condition can be written as:

$$\begin{bmatrix}0\\u_2\end{bmatrix} + \begin{bmatrix}1\\0\end{bmatrix} .* \begin{bmatrix}0.024(\partial u_1/\partial x)\\0.170(\partial u_2/\partial x)\end{bmatrix} + \begin{bmatrix}0\\0\end{bmatrix}$$

and the right boundary condition can be written as:

$$\begin{bmatrix}u_1-1\\0\end{bmatrix} + \begin{bmatrix}0\\1\end{bmatrix} .* \begin{bmatrix}0.024(\partial u_1/\partial x)\\0.170(\partial u_2/\partial x)\end{bmatrix} = \begin{bmatrix}0\\0\end{bmatrix}$$

We start by defining the functions in M-files as shown in Figures 9-12 to 9-14.

```
function [c,f,s] = pdex4pde(x,t,u,DuDx)
c = [1; 1];
f = [0.024; 0.17] .* DuDx;
y = u(1) - u(2);
F = exp(5.73*y)-exp(-11.47*y);
s = [-F; F];
```

Figure 9-12.

```
function [pl,ql,pr,qr] = pdex4bc(xl,ul,xr,ur,t)
pl = [0; ul(2)];
ql = [1; 0];
pr = [ur(1)-1; 0];
qr = [0; 1];
```

Figure 9-13.

```
function u0 = pdex4ic(x);
u0 = [1; 0];
```

Figure 9-14.

Once the support functions are defined, the function that solves the system of equations is given by the M-file shown in Figure 9-15.

```
function pdex4
m = 0;
x = [0 0.005 0.01 0.05 0.1 0.2 0.5 0.7 0.9 0.95 0.99 0.995 1];
t = [0 0.005 0.01 0.05 0.1 0.5 1 1.5 2];

sol = pdepe(m,@pdex4pde,@pdex4ic,@pdex4bc,x,t);
u1 = sol(:,:,1);
u2 = sol(:,:,2);

figure
surf(x,t,u1)
title('u1(x,t)')
xlabel('Distance x')
ylabel('Time t')

figure
surf(x,t,u2)
title('u2(x,t)')
xlabel('Distancia x')
ylabel('Tiempo t')
```

Figure 9-15.

To view the solution (Figures 9-16 and 9-17), we enter the following in the MATLAB Command Window:

>> pdex4

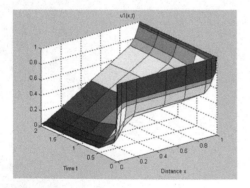

Figure 9-16.

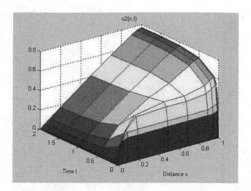

Figure 9-17.

<hr>

EXERCISE 9-1

Solve the following Van der Pol system of equations:

$$y_1' = y_2 \qquad\qquad y_1(0) = 0$$
$$y_2' = 1000(1 - y_1^2)y_2 - y_1 \quad y_2(0) = 1$$

We begin by defining a function named *vdp100* in an M-file, where we will store the equations of the system. This function begins by defining a column vector with two empty rows which are subsequently assigned the components which make up the equation (Figure 9-18).

```
function dy = vdp1000(t,y)
dy = zeros(2,1);    % Column vector
dy(1) = y(2);
dy(2) = 1000*(1 - y(1)^2)*y(2) - y(1);
```

Figure 9-18.

We then solve the system and plot the solution $y_1 = y_1(t)$ given by the first column (Figure 9-19) by typing the following into the Command Window:

```
>> [T, Y] = ode15s(@vdp1000,[0 3000],[2 0]);
>> plot(T, Y(:,1),'-')
```

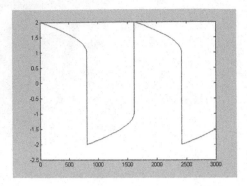

Figure 9-19.

Similarly we plot the solution $y_2 = y_2(t)$ (Figure 9-20) by using the syntax:

```
>> plot(T, Y(:,2),'-')
```

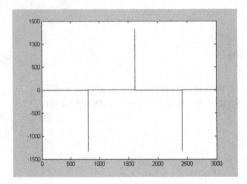

Figure 9-20.

EXERCISE 9-2

Given the following differential equation:

$$y'' + (\lambda - 2q\cos(2x))y = 0$$

subject to the boundary conditions $y(0) = 1$, $y'(0) = 0$, $y'(\pi) = 0$, find a solution for $q = 5$ and $\lambda = 15$ based on an initial solution defined on 10 equally spaced points in the interval $[0, \pi]$ and graph the first component of the solution on 100 equally spaced points in the interval $[0, \pi]$.

The given equation is equivalent to the following system of first order differential equations:

$$y_1' = y_2$$
$$y_2' = -(\lambda - 2q\cos 2x)y_1$$

with the following boundary conditions:

$$y_1(0) - 1 = 0$$
$$y_2(0) = 0$$
$$y_2(\pi) = 0$$

The system of equations is introduced in the M-file shown in Figure 9-21, the boundary conditions are given in the M-file shown in Figure 9-22, and the M-file in Figure 9-23 sets up the initial solution.

```
function dydx = mat4ode(x,y,lambda)
q = 5;
dydx = [    y(2)
         -(lambda - 2*q*cos(2*x))*y(1) ];
```

Figure 9-21.

```
function res = mat4bc(ya,yb,lambda)
res = [   ya(2)
          yb(2)
          ya(1)-1 ];
```

Figure 9-22.

```
function yinit = mat4init(x)
yinit = [   cos(4*x)
            -4*sin(4*x) ];
```

Figure 9-23.

The initial solution for $\lambda = 15$ and 10 equally spaced points in $[0,\pi]$ is calculated using the following MATLAB syntax:

```
>> lambda = 15;
solinit = bvpinit(linspace(0,pi,10), @mat4init, lambda);
```

The numerical solution of the system is calculated using the following syntax:

```
>> sol = bvp4c(@mat4ode,@mat4bc,solinit);
```

To graph the first component on 100 equally spaced points in the interval $[0, \pi]$ we use the following syntax:

```
>> xint = linspace(0,pi);
Sxint = bvpval(ground, xint);
plot(xint, Sxint(1,:)))
axis([0 pi-1 1.1])
xlabel('x')
ylabel('solution y')
```

341

The result is presented in Figure 9-24.

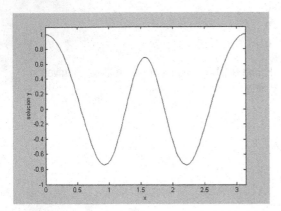

Figure 9-24.

EXERCISE 9-3

Solve the following differential equation:

$$y'' + (1 - y^2)y' + y = 0$$

in the interval [0,20], taking as initial solution $y = 2$, $y' = 0$. Solve the more general equation

$$y'' + \mu(1 - y^2)y' + y = 0 \quad \mu > 0$$

The general equation above is equivalent to the following system of first-order linear equations

$$y_1' = y_2$$
$$y_2' = \mu(1 - y_1^2)y_2 - y_1$$

which is defined for $\mu = 1$ in the M-file shown in Figure 9-25.

```
function dydt = vdp1(t,y)
dydt = [y(2); (1-y(1)^2)*y(2)-y(1)];
```

Figure 9-25.

Taking the initial solution $y_1 = 2$ and $y_2 = 0$ in the interval [0,20], we can solve the system using the following MATLAB syntax:

```
>> [t, y] = ode45(@vdp1,[0 20],[2; 0])
```

t =

    0
    0.0000
    0.0001
    0.0001
    0.0001
    0.0002
    0.0004
    0.0005
    0.0006
    0.0012
      .
      .
    19.9559
    19.9780
    20,0000

y =

    2.0000 0
    2.0000 - 0.0001
    2.0000 - 0.0001
    2.0000 - 0.0002
    2.0000 - 0.0002
    2.0000 - 0.0005
      .
      .
    1.8729 1.0366
    1.9358 0.7357
    1.9787 0.4746
    2.0046 0.2562
    2.0096 0.1969
    2.0133 0.1413
    2.0158 0.0892
    2.0172 0.0404

We can graph the solutions (Figure 9-26) by using the syntax:

```
>> plot(t, y(:,1),'-', t, y(:,2),'-')
>> xlabel('time t')
>> ylabel('solution y')
>> legend('y_1', 'y_2')
```

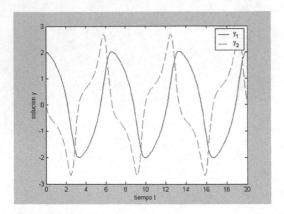

Figure 9-26.

To solve the general system with the parameter μ, we define the system in the M-file shown in Figure 9-27.

```
function dydt = vdp2(t,y,mu)
dydt = [y(2); mu*(1-y(1)^2)*y(2)-y(1)];
```

Figure 9-27.

Now we can graph the first solution $y_1 = 2$ and $y_2 = 0$ corresponding to $\mu = 1000$ in the interval [0,1500] using the following syntax (see Figure 9-28):

```
>> [t, y] = ode15s(@vdp2,[0 1500],[2; 0],[],1000);
>> xlabel('time t')
>> ylabel('solution y_1')
```

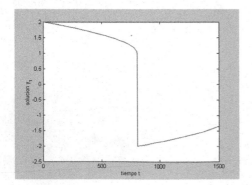

Figure 9-28.

To graph the first solution $y_1 = 2$ and $y_2 = 0$ for another value of the parameter, for example $\mu = 100$, in the interval [0,1500], we use the following syntax (see Figure 9-29):

```
>> [t, y] = ode15s(@vdp2,[0 1500],[2; 0],[],100);
>> plot(t, y(:,1),'-');
```

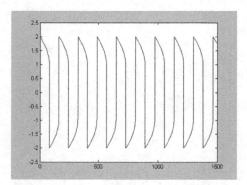

Figure 9-29.

Get the eBook for only $10!

Now you can take the weightless companion with you anywhere, anytime. Your purchase of this book entitles you to 3 electronic versions for only $10.

This Apress title will prove so indispensible that you'll want to carry it with you everywhere, which is why we are offering the eBook in **3 formats** for only $10 if you have already purchased the print book.

Convenient and fully searchable, the PDF version enables you to easily find and copy code—or perform examples by quickly toggling between instructions and applications. The MOBI format is ideal for your Kindle, while the ePUB can be utilized on a variety of mobile devices.

Go to www.apress.com/promo/tendollars to purchase your companion eBook.